ENERGY MAGICK
OF THE
VAMPYRE

"*Energy Magick of the Vampyre* is both a personal book about the dark mysteries as well as an excellent instructive description of the eroto-mysticism of Vampyric magic. It goes beyond what you've read before and puts Vampyric magic in its proper context. The book is written by one of the most experienced teachers of the Left-Hand Path and is a book that raises the pulse and brings to life what is hidden in the shadows.

THOMAS KARLSSON, PH.D., AUTHOR OF
NIGHTSIDE OF THE RUNES

"*Energy Magick of the Vampyre* is an entertaining introduction to the most fascinating and compelling aspects of antinomianism: the achievement of immortality. Complete with a side trip into the minds of Anton LaVey, Michael Aquino, William Burroughs, and others, this book details the most important influences and methods of the modern Left-Hand Path of Western magic and what they can do for you. It is as if the techniques of occultism, mass manipulation, and self-help were thrown together into a strangely appealing stew for those wishing to create their own egregore."

MARK STAVISH, AUTHOR OF *EGREGORES*

"Don Webb's latest work, *Energy Magick of the Vampyre*, expresses the masterful understanding that energy and Vampyrism are directly connected. The methodology of Vampyre magic within this book is centered in the practical, focused on consistent application and practice in the real world. I suggest this book to the beginner and adept alike as it balances the perspectives of the mindscape of a Vampyre in daily life. This is a must-have!"

MICHAEL W. FORD, AUTHOR OF
SEKHEM APEP: TYPHONIAN VAMPYRE MAGICK

"There's a reason why Don Webb is one of my favorite contemporary occult authors: everything he writes is enlightening in one way or another. A born storyteller if I've ever met one, he takes us on a barnstorming journey across the world of magic both archetypal and modern, pursuing the path of the Vampyre without all the biting and the garlic. An inventive, highly instructive, entertaining, and easy-to-follow manual of the Left-Hand Path for the 21st century like no other."

FRATER U∴D∴, COAUTHOR OF *LIVING MAGIC*

"*Energy Magick of the Vampyre* is all about that energy—and obtaining, keeping, and using it for one's own best purposes. If the word 'vampyre' frightens you then this book is probably not for you—unless it scares you, you know, in a *good* way. Aha—I just conjured up some energy there, now didn't I? Webb's guide is an encyclopedic how-to that blasts most other 'occult' tomes out of the water. What this book can do for you is multifarious. It can help you define what a 'Vampyre' is, in case you know a few; it can help you see where this form of magick can be possible and beneficial in your life; and it can begin your journey on a path. It is not the end-all, be-all of attaining the rank of energy Vampyre, but it is, I believe, one's best starting place. Read the book."

RT. REV. DENISE DUMARS, M.A.,
HEIROPHANT OF THE LYCEUM OF AUSET HAUHET

ENERGY MAGICK
OF THE
VAMPYRE

SECRET TECHNIQUES FOR
PERSONAL POWER AND MANIFESTATION

DON WEBB

Inner Traditions
Rochester, Vermont

Inner Traditions
One Park Street
Rochester, Vermont 05767
www.InnerTraditions.com

Text stock is SFI certified

Cataloging-in-Publication Data for this title is available from the Library of Congress

ISBN 978-1-64411-132-1 (print)
ISBN 978-1-64411-133-8 (ebook)

Printed and bound in the United States by Lake Book Manufacturing, Inc.
The text stock is SFI certified. The Sustainable Forestry Initiative® program
promotes sustainable forest management.

10 9 8 7 6 5 4 3 2

Text design and layout by Debbie Glogover
This book was typeset in Garamond Premier Pro with Golden Whiskey Aged,
Acherus Grotesque, Gill Sans MT Pro, and ITC Legacy Sans Std used as display
typefaces

To send correspondence to the author of this book, mail a first-class letter to the
author c/o Inner Traditions • Bear & Company, One Park Street, Rochester, VT
05767, and we will forward the communication.

To Lilith Aquino,
who invited me into the Order of the Vampyre
and Gifted the world with APKTH

Warnings to the Reader

This is a book for adult humans in good physical and mental health. If you are not grounded in mind and body, you should not tamper with the Vampyric Current.

This book is not about blood fetishism—blood magic is NOT part of Vampirism.

This book does not condone any illegal activities.

None of the operations described in this book are enhanced or amplified in any way by using drugs or herbs, legal or illegal.

This book does not confer upon you the powers and experiences that come through the mentorship and fellowship in the Order of the Vampyre.

CONTENTS

BOOK THE FIRST

VAMPYRE THEORY AND PRACTICE

BOOK THE SECOND
THE VAMPYRIC INITIATION

BOOK THE THIRD
ADVANCED PRACTICES

BOOK THE FOURTH
A VAMPYRIC MISCELLANY

My Encounter with the Order of the Vampyre

Growing up in the sixties, I encountered the vampire archetype in the form of Barnabas Collins in the series *Dark Shadows*. Villain turned hero, stylish dresser, overpowering with women, possessed of ritual skill, he captured my imagination. My early magical experiments were based on the scripts—and put aside long before high school. In my abortive first attempt at college I discovered the wonderworld of drugs and the novels of Carlos Castaneda. This led to failing out of school and returning in shame to my little hometown.

Losing my source of drugs, I worked at re-creating the energy effect I had seen (or convinced myself I had seen). I also tried to figure out what my life would be without college; I had considered myself "better" than my friends who simply joined the work force. I had access to beautiful wild spaces, including Palo Duro Canyon. I had a great public library, and I had no social life. I developed my own neo-shamanic practices. I reached a point where I had gone as far as I could by myself. The groups/practitioners I discovered around me were druggies, sexual predators, or schizophrenics. Maybe I was one of these as well.

I decided to give magic one last try. I went to a stead of power and I addressed it. If I were to learn magic, send me a teacher. It was a hot day and out of nowhere a cooling breeze came up, and I hiked home. Nothing else happened for three months, and then a change in life's circumstances required me to move to Austin, Texas. By then, I had given up magical practice in any form. I was trying to make it as a freelance writer.

When I arrived in Austin, I decided to sublimate my magical interests into role-playing games. I joined a group. In 1988, I watched a Geraldo Rivera special on Satanism in America. At the time, I was engaged in a research project on the Salem witch trials, and as I watched the special, I noted how all the forms of mass hysteria of the 1690s were alive and well. An odd-looking man, Michael Aquino of the Temple of Set, mocked the proceedings, and Geraldo cut to commercial.

The next night at my role-playing game, I mentioned how much I would like to send Mr. Aquino fan mail. One of my fellow gamers asked me to drive her home after the game. When I did so, she said, "Do you really want to send Dr. Aquino a fan letter? I'm seeing him next week." I noticed the title "Dr." and I thought, "Oh, great, a self-titled occultist." But I also thought (as I drove up to the nice two-story home), "She doesn't look like an occultist"—meaning she isn't wearing crappy jewelry and living in a crappy apartment. I wrote my letter, and also verified that Aquino had a real Ph.D.

I joined the Temple of Set in 1989. It had six degrees: Setian, Adept, Priest/Priestess, Magister/Magistra, Magus/Maga, and Ipsissimus/Ipsissima. In the second degree you could join an order; this was compared to an area of study at a university. During the first degree one learned the basics of Setian philosophy and demonstrated competence in magic. Setians meet once a year at the International Conclave.

My first encounter with Vampyric magic was within my local group, the Bull of Ombos Pylon. The sentinel was a member of the Order of the Vampyre. She taught us how to exchange energy. She initiated us with a nip on the neck, not drawing blood; I've never seen blood in any form in thirty-one years of Setian ritual. It is symbolic. Then, by use of the Gaze, she took and returned energy to us.

My next encounter was in a long phone call with a Setian that lived in Ohio. He had been a member longer than me, and he was going to explain it all to me. If you were smart and straight you joined the Order of the Trapezoid. If you were a male homosexual you joined . . . , and so on. Finally "If you were really good looking but not necessarily smart you joined the OV." I bought into this hook, line, and sinker.

That fall I went to my first conclave. I spotted an OV member, and in my cynical (but also aroused) thinking thought she had probably posed for *Playboy*. My cynical observation was incorrect—she had posed for *Penthouse*. However, as far as the not-so-smart part goes, she was getting a degree in biophysics from a well-respected university. At the time I was a college dropout.

I met other members of the Order of the Vampyre. They came in two groups. The first group were Adepts of two to three years of experience. They were all of much better than average appearance, arrogant and annoying on the outside, deeply insecure on the inside. Those in the second group were third- and fourth-degree initiates. Some of these were of average appearance, but all of them were deeply charismatic and filled with a deeply playful spontaneity, sort of like sexy Zen masters. They gave out more energy than anyone around—when they wanted to. In the ritual chamber these folk were like lightbulbs: when they turned it ON their presence filled the chamber, and when they turned it OFF they were hard to spot (even in a room that just had about eighty people). The first group looked like average occultniks, except better looking and with more women in the mix. How did folks go from group one to group two? I was mystified, but also 100 percent sure this was not the group for me. Oh, I had some of the characteristics: I was arrogant and annoying on the outside, deeply insecure on the inside. I was also fifty pounds overweight, wore flip-flops 90 percent of the time, and thought of Goodwill as a great place to shop. Whatever these guys were, I wasn't.

A year passed. I entered the Order of the Trapezoid at the invitation of Grandmaster Stephen Flowers. I learned his method of magical research: hard scholarship plus magical re-creation. He had made a road to the runes, so I turned my view toward Egypt—we were the Temple of Set, after all. That year the International Conclave of the Temple of Set was in San Francisco. One evening I was walking along with Mr. Aquino in a group headed toward a restaurant. He had a wolf-headed walking stick: it looked *just like* the cane of Barnabas Collins.

I discovered later that Mr. Aquino was a *Dark Shadows* fan, and fans with deep pockets can obtain original props.

The leadership of the Pylon passed to me, along with the turmoil of the third degree. I lost fifty pounds and learned to dress by asking salesmen at JC Penney. As a Master, I released my creation into the world in the form of a new order within the temple and with my book *The Seven Faces of Darkness: Practical Typhonian Magic*. Egypt had her hooks in me. I focused on the Egyptian Utterance that had transformed Michael Aquino into a Magus: Xepera Xeper Xeperu. I studied it linguistically, which meant going back to college. I studied it historically. I studied it culturally. And I studied its effect on the hundreds who had passed through the Temple of Set's doors. Then I saw it as a form, and I was transformed thereby. I became a Magus, the only degree in the Temple of Set that requires nine different Initiators to say yes. At the request of Michael Aquino, I took over the reins as High Priest of the Temple of Set.

As High Priest, I added two things to the temple's repertoire: some authentically re-created Egyptian and Greco-Egyptian magic and the energy techniques I had taught myself. I embraced 98 percent of the temple's philosophy—it held human consciousness to be on a much higher level than animal consciousness. I saw some philosophical strengths in this and some weaknesses as well.

A year or so later I was scanning the roster, looking for an address. I noted that not only was I listed as a member of the Order of the Vampyre, but I was also listed as a "Master" of this order. I contacted Magistra Lilith Aquino at once. Clearly there was an error. No, she told me, I was a Master of energy work. Initiation can come as a blinding flash or a long, agonizing process. It can come as bliss or pain or a wordless feeling. Lilith's short message to me came as a wordless flash.

I had never understood the true nature of the order. Blinded by their glamour and contemptuous of the pop-culture myth that guided their aesthetic, I had never paid much attention to their practice. In that flash, I saw that they were the masters of three things: working from the outside to the inside, dealing with wordless/silent states, and dealing with the body as a medium for Truth. I realized that I had indeed been working in their school since my earliest youth.

Since I felt that I "owed" Lilith something (see chapter 24, "Debt and Gifts," in the advanced practices section of this book), I took my current task of teaching the Word of Xeper and related it to the Order of the Vampyre, creating the "Manual of Vampyric Alchemy." I also sought to correct the view of animal and human consciousness by designing a working called "The Way of the Sacred Animals" for another conclave. Here I dealt with the animals that the Egyptians had included in their vision of the divine. I orchestrated the work to build up energy and turn it over to Mr. and Mrs. Aquino. It built and built— Stephen Flowers had been my controller of energy—the best and brightest Setians of all degrees had refined and raised the energy. Mr. Aquino rose and spoke in his strongest, best form (in the temple we do not write scripts for the two highest degrees). He spoke of the Egyptian watching the dog run in the night and making him Anubis. It was beautiful and poetic. It was powerful. And it caused a huge interest in the coming years in shape-shifting and neo-shamanism.

However, amid all the bliss in the chamber, I noticed that Lilith Aquino did not look like she was having a good time. She looked overwhelmed. Had the energy level been too much? In the next few months she had the spiritual crisis that we in the Temple of Set call the fifth degree. She became obsessed with animal consciousness, animal rights, shape-shifting, and above all, wolves. With some linguistic help from Stephen and me, she uttered her Word of ARKTE. I took her through her process from the fourth to the fifth degree; she who had been my teacher became also my student. Her ultimate power—the great Vampyric power of Transformation through Reception—had led her into an utterance. All of the Western high magic nonsense of Magi being guys in their early thirties who founded and led an organization based on their masculine charisma was demolished.

Then 2019 came around. A major change happened in my family— it was a loss—unexpected, devastating, bleak. It also had a hefty economic price tag. I quickly sold a book of short stories to a distinguished small press, but its owner passed away. So no help there. One night largely on a whim I pitched this book to Inner Traditions. It would be fun and quick to write, I assumed. I would focus on the fun/sexy stuff such as the Gaze and the energy inventory. I would talk about beginnings—after all, 99 percent of all books on magic are beginnings.

Then as I wrote the book, three friends died. Others began a struggle with cancer. I couldn't write only the fun side, I knew that I had to deal with loss and gain and the effect of decades. My usual practice—of writing as far away from the subject as possible—wasn't an option in dealing with a magical field that has its roots in emotion and its branches in Life, Death, and Life-in-Death. (By the way, the short fiction collection came into being in 2020 as *Building Strange Temples,* and I got my my first *Washington Post* review.) The fact that the words herein were born in woe does not mean they are tinged with woe. Instead these words were a medicine for me, and I trust they will help you find certain subtle medicines within you. Let's get started.

BOOK THE FIRST

VAMPYRE THEORY AND PRACTICE

OR

The Scholomance

1

Maps and Bills

Images of vampires dominate media, role-playing, cosplaying, video games—the "vampire" seems to have a major appeal to the privileged class seeking some form of glamorous deviance in a permissive society with little power on a dying planet. This book is neither about the "reality" of badly costumed bloodsuckers, nor the standard psychological interpretations of a pop-culture phenomenon. It is about something much older, much more liberating, and much more subtle. It is not about a return to a prerational state but instead about integrating some very old modes of human (and more-than-human) moods and gifts into the lives of a new elect. This elect won't be marked by gender, race, or even economic class—but may be recognized by a certain glint in their gaze.

When they *want* to be seen.

This book presents an alternative spiritual path and magical technology called the Vampyric Way. It is a sneaky way to avoid a lifetime of sleep and an eternity of deep slumber. It's a path for a very patient, strong-willed traveler who has placed four tools in her pack—Desire, Strangeness, Love, and Fear. She must begin the path alone and unsure, her traveling will summon her guides, and before she comes to the end of her path she will have to serve as a guide. Much of her myth is reflected in popular fiction and film, but at a crucial juncture she will find something older, darker, and more real.

Modern humans have many maps of themselves. To bolster our self-importance, we create models to explain our hidden greatness, our excuses for our shortcomings—we read/google/watch endless narratives to let us either think it's going to get better *or* it's not our fault. To augment this, we share our thoughts on social media, our image in countless selfies, and seek out formal and informal groups to recite the Mad Libs of our lives placed into the blanks of spells to keep us Asleep. This is the way of the world—perhaps not as alarming as garbage islands in the Pacific or areas of the Middle East that have been the host to warfare for three thousand years, but it has an equally deadly train-track aspect. We keep charging along to our doom.

This book offers an antinomian path, a path to freedom and even immortality. But since it runs contrariwise to the world it may be seen as demanding or silly or implausible. It will require its awakened readers to challenge basic cultural assumptions (both those assumptions that you are heir to by being an English speaker in the twenty-first century and those assumptions you have absorbed by being part of the "enlightened" esoteric subculture). Some of the items that you will be invited to question (because this is a book of questions, not answers) and experiment with cover areas as basic as life and death, gender and sex, reason and belief, control and free will, high and low culture, and even your own role in your enslavement. But not to worry, if you stay away from the four dozen or so experiments suggested formally and informally in the book, you can remain Asleep.

I'm going to begin with a terrible curse, something that all world-changing artifacts have, then move on to a teaching tale and brief introduction to the myth of the Vampyre as a myth of personal salvation. The rest of the book will be a how-to book of self-initiation that will consist of ideas, methods to test the ideas, and methods to store the vast energies these ideas can unlock. I will tread some familiar territory (like *Dracula*), some unfamiliar territory (like medieval Tibetan tantra or the works of Jean Gebser, Marshall, or McLuhan), and some truly esoteric territory (like teachings from the Temple of Set's Order of the Vampyre and other lesser-known Left-Hand Path groups). You'll get some homework, too, from visiting graveyards and nightclubs to contacting some Neolithic spirits.

The Terrible Curse

My Intent is hidden in the Sign of Ink that conceals all Mysteries. By the virtue of my Steganography I send to my readers the Vampyric Current. Those who study and seek Absolute Liberty I Bless, that they shall be given the correct Teacher at the correct time and later shall spread their black wings and teach others. Hail Vampyres! But to those who would cheat me by stealing this book, or by ignoring the warnings above, or by misleading others with my words, the Vampyric Current shall seize their throats and pull from them the two fires as they stumble faster toward the Doom that would have been theirs regardless. Hail Victims! The Curse is even now upon you.

Now that the formalities are done, let's begin with three notions about maps and meet the four Bills and his Master.

Smart humans generally understand Alfred Korzybski's dictum, "The map is not the territory." We sleep and forget this but awaken to remember that subjective models are not the same thing as what they objectively model. Maps simplify, maps organize, maps may often mislead. Due to a flaw in most GPS systems, people driving to my home are misled to a spot about an eighth of a mile away. I tell people before they come to see me and explain the color of my home's bricks. Yet I still have people stop several yards away and bang their fists on their read-out rather than look around. Humans who invented words are blinded by their invention. Okay, so far so good—you wouldn't have found this book without grasping this. The next two ideas are a tad harder.

One map does not equal another map (even when it shows the same territory). When I'm dealing with terrain, people get it. A map showing population density is different from one showing elevation. Sure there may be some correlation—not many people live on the top of Pike's Peak, for example—but humans have no trouble understanding that these are not interchangeable maps. However, humans totally lose this distinction in reading maps of the self. They can see a map of human chakras (derived from Hindu teachings) and the diagram of the

Sephiroth (derived from the Kabbalah) and immediately start explaining how Tiphareth equals the heart chakra. They took two ideas with centuries of nuance behind them and use them to explain each other. Thus, they avoid the hard work of understanding (in both theory and practice) these difficult ideas. They then congratulate themselves in their actions. They remove difficulty from learning and thereby replace learning with data. Data can be purchased (by the honest) or found in unofficial PDF form (by the thief) but does not change the self. I tell my readers this because their occult-industry training would tell them that rather than learning the ideas in this book, they should work out correspondences with other ideas they likewise do not know. Thus, we will see someone writing, "Webb's Vampyric self = Crowley's Holy Guardian Angel." This mind-set leads to the exotic form of Sleep called the Right-Hand Path; it may bring a drowsy joy but not the chilling thrill of freedom. So as you learn the terms in chapter 2 and then discover them through the exercises, keep in mind that you are learning a new map; don't rush to write old names on it.

The third idea is hinted at by the first. In subjective matters the map changes the territory. This substance we call "mind" or "imagination" is fluid. It takes the shape that it is told it has. For decades it was observed that if one underwent Freudian psychoanalysis, one would dream of hot dogs and doughnuts, tunnels and bullet trains, and killing off dad-substitute to screw mom-substitute—BUT, if one had a Jungian analyst one dreamed of circular cities with four gates, caves with wise old men and alchemical motifs. The mind can become anything—it can change politics, gender, age, ideas of afterlife, and so on. It "thinks" it's choosing to do so. Honest self-observation will tell you that you—like all the idiots around you—"think" to file experiences and insights according to a randomly assembled matrix. It contains the issues and strengths of your family of origin, folk physics, politics chosen by a variety of means. It may have some good stuff like Picasso's views on art or a decent understanding of relativity—or it may have bad stuff like Uncle John's racism or ethical glosses you picked up in third-year Sunday school. But everything you experience goes into two piles—the "known," meaning your brain does its job and files it away in the cabinet (even if a rough fit), and the "unknown," meaning your brain will either return to processing it through a truth process (see chapter 4), dreaming, forgetting, or developing an unquestioning belief. If you can learn a new map you can assimilate new things. If you learn a new map you have new sources of energy and new potentials.

I'm telling you about maps now, because in the next few chapters I'll be giving you one. It will be hard to assimilate if you are in a comfortable life position. When we are comfortable, we seldom need new maps. But that's okay: you bought (or checked out) a book, the invention that humans use to store new maps until needed.

We will begin our discussion by looking at Bill. We're going to give Bill some very comfortable and common maps. Then we are going to introduce Bill to the Vampyre. Bill does not know this, but he is on the edge of a cliff; that is to say, he's like all of us when we are comfortable. Here is Bill's cliff: In the next few weeks Bill's branch office is closing. Two people from Bill's pay grade will get nice promotions and move to a more interesting city, the other two will get a month's pay and be stuck in a downturn that's about to happen because the company president is involved in tricky negotiations. Bill's longtime secret crush, Angela, is about to find out that her boyfriend is cheating on her, and she's going to be on the rebound. Bill's mom is about to get a diagnosis of pancreatic cancer, and Bill's short story that he wrote in college is about to be purchased by a major magazine. In other words, Bill's known life is about to change. Let's look at four Bills on the day of his birthday. We'll call them Bill Normal, Bill the Beast, Bill the Superbill, and Bill the Wizard.

At 3:15, Mr. Brann called Bill Normal into the break room. "Happy Birthday!" Brann had assembled Angela, Norma, Carlos, and Tom. There was a red velvet cake (Bill's favorite), lemonade, and coffee. Angela looked happy. Norma, the slightly punk girl, was staring at Angela (and for sure not at the cake). Carlos was pouring himself coffee, not waiting on anyone. Tom, who had long hair, bothered Bill Normal because sometimes Bill N. "felt" something around him—it must be Tom's gayness. After everyone had cake, Elizabeth Levenda, the BIG boss came in. She smiled at Bill N. and went to talk with Mr. Brann. Bill N. went back to work at 4:08—secure that his job was safe. The Big Boss had smiled RIGHT at him. Norma was cleaning up the break room. Norma was super nice; she had talked him into submitting that short story. But he never "got" her—he only "understood" women whom he was interested in, or who were stand-ins for his mom. The next week Bill N. was fired along with Tom and Angela.

At 3:14, Bill the Beast could smell Mr. Brann coming down the hall. He had been smelling fear on him for days. But today he smelled just like Bill's dad smelled the day he left his family. That was that. Bill the Beast sucker punched Brann and went to the break room. He grabbed a handful of icing and stuffed it in his mouth, then he tried to grab Angela. She broke free, so he went for Tom. Carlos cracked a chair over his head. Now Bill is doing twenty hard in state prison.

Bill the Superbill knew that Brann would be throwing a birthday party. He underpaid his staff and fed stories of their incompetence to Ms. Levenda—a bad long-term strategy. Bill S. had already realized the branch would be closed, so he had emailed Ms. Levenda and asked for a meeting today. He had a proposal to create a three-county superagency headed up by himself and Norma. Norma, whose blog showed that she was shy, asexual, and hardworking, would be perfect. She would never challenge his place in the hierarchy. Carlos was a threat—he was Bill's equal and more desirable because of his ancestry. Bill had tried to counter that by taking business Spanish at the community college. Angela and Tom were distractions for his current orbit. Sure enough, Ms. Levenda showed up at three. At the party she announced that Bill S. would be running the new branch. Layoffs would be announced later.

Bill the Wizard was all smiles. By a rune casting he knew that financial resources were in chaos. He had performed a working whereby he enchanted Ms. Levenda. He would compel her to be at his party. When Mr. Brann called him into the break room, he knew that his favorite cake was there as a tribute to his Will. He offered a small bite to Hermes. Just before Ms. Levenda arrived, Angela mentioned the James Bond movies, and, to impress her, Bill began to explain how Aleister Crowley had told Ian Fleming about John Dee's use of "007." Ms. Levenda smiled at

Bill W. and tried to get his attention, but he was clearly just interested in the attractive woman. So, she went on to have a meeting with Mr. Brann. The next week Bill W. was fired along with Tom and Angela.

Now, it might seem that Bill the Superbill is the "best" of the lot. But you notice he has no pleasure, just calculations. It's clear that Bill the Wizard has some aspects that give him the potential for a mysterious and powerful life, but self-importance dooms him to be no more than Emperor of his Apartment. Normal Bill at least has the seeming advantage of his anxieties not being from worrying about the "real world." Bill the Beast probably had the best early-warning system, but early trauma rules him (instead of him ruling the world).

Now let's look at the Vampyre. Now, there isn't Bill the Vampyre; when Bill Awakened the Vampyre, he needed another name. He had chosen "Ishmael" for his Vampyric self, but we'll get to the powers and problems of Vampyre naming later. Let's just look at Ishmael's version of events, how they were possible, and begin to see how the Vampyre way is grounded in, but transcends, "real" life. Then we will devote the rest of the book to the Vampyre.

Ishmael has eight servants. Each is in thrall to him, meaning they provide him more energy than he provides them. You've met four of them—Normal Bill, Bill the Beast, Bill the Superbill, and Bill the Wizard. You've learned about two more, Norma and Mr. Brann. Finally, we'll talk about two you haven't met: his familiar—a rescue cat named Ink—and his mother. Let's consider what each of these servants does.

Normal Bill is a caretaker, but Ishmael retreats from the world much of the time, not unlike the popular vampire myth of avoiding sunlight. Contrary to the myth, Ishmael loves seeing the dawn (occasionally), and sunlight in the forest is an actual source of strength. Ishmael cannot withstand the continual onslaught of socialized humans. His perception of actual motives and intents of other humans who are nevertheless caught in the nets of social interactions both drains his energy and drives him to rage. Normal Bill is fed a dose of energy—we'll explain energy later—in the form of a romantic narrative. He is empowered by having a "secret identity" and works hard for his master. Normal Bill, who is an enthralled form of the "social self" (see chapter 2), is relaxed and, when the need arises, he is happy to be stupid. Normal Bill can be blind to the motivations of the humans around him. He can talk about phone apps and current HBO shows. Recently Ishmael was visiting an abandoned private graveyard—behind a No Trespassing sign—when the landowner showed up. Normal Bill gave a perfect bumbling story of having not seen the sign and left the area looking embarrassed. At the birthday party Normal Bill acted as a watchman for certain cues.

Bill the Beast is (in some ways) most like Ishmael. He has access to the life force in a direct way. His senses have not been blunted by social convention. Bill the Beast knows when women are menstruating, when humans have cancer, when humans have extraordinary stress. He had told Ishmael of Mr. Brann's increasing stress levels for weeks, so he knew that big changes were happening. He had told Ishmael that Angela was faking happiness and was horny to boot. Bill the Beast knew Carlos fancied himself Bill's rival by watching his body language, and he knew Tom was straight and shy and enamored of Norma—but still wanted him. Bill the Beast enjoyed each bite of cake and sip of coffee with a level of pleasure that would have shocked everyone in the room. Bill the Beast blocked Carlos from even speaking to Ms. Levenda by exerting primate dominance cues. Ishmael controlled Bill the Beast by altering the energy expressed in heart rate and breath. Bill the Beast was a totally faithful dog that got to play at being a wolf.

Bill the Superbill was in many ways Ishmael's best creation. He prevented Ishmael from sinking into old (i.e., Neolithic) moods and remaining focused on the modern world. A weaponized version of the social self, Bill the Superbill presented a danger to Ishmael—the danger of disbelief. Bill the Superbill had been created to take pleasure in the world of humans. Like Ishmael he could draw energy directly from the world—primarily by dominating the world through logic. His tendency would be to let Ishmael Sleep by telling himself that the "Vampyre" myth was a transitional state needed to process some unprocessed adolescent tendencies. Ishamel kept him in check by periodically overwhelming him with bliss (described in the third book). Bill the Superbill had investigated the source of Mr. Brann's stress and provided a strategy to let Ishmael move to a place of security and power. He was 100 percent in charge in dealing with Ms. Levenda, and, after the meeting with her, he retreated to an inner world of logic while Bill the Beast and Ishmael enjoyed the party.

Bill the Wizard was Ishmael's ace in the hole. He was assembled from self-importance, the desire to be the ruler of the situation. Magic is the art of producing a change in the subjective universe to create a change in the objective universe. Bill the Wizard didn't take no as an answer from the universe. Ms. Levenda didn't have an interest in Bill? No problem: he took a discarded letter from her to Mr. Brann and wrote "Sigil" on it. Now she was interested in Bill though she couldn't say why. No one was sure when the business crisis would come? No problem: with magical means Bill the Wizard determined when *he* should act in it. But Bill the Wizard had problems. He was lazy and he had a fairly good track record. Bill the Wizard had aced tests he hadn't studied for, gotten laid by women out of his league, had landlords excuse him from paying rent, and kept jobs where he did next to nothing. Sounds pretty dang cush, doesn't it? Except that Bill the Wizard feeds on denial and has lost jobs (always someone else's fault), failed tests (the subtle forces of the universe needed him to fail to preserve him for his "true" destiny), lost girlfriends (his sexual magic was being drawn to another shakti), or even been kicked out (the earth spirits were being dominated by a rival sorcerer). Ishmael must keep Bill the Wizard enthralled by sharing wonder with him and using self-examination to destroy the current of denial. Both Bill the Superbill and Bill the Wizard have extensive maps of the world, but Ishmael has no maps, just a scroll of where he has been.

The other servants are outside of Ishmael's body, so it might seem that they're in a different class. But like most human complexes they are consciousness not yoked to the Source and so are that blend of mechanical toys and free-willed beings that all the Bills are. Norma is an asexual romantic. Sometimes she imagines herself lesbian, sometimes bisexual. Ishmael discovered Norma's inner nature by listening patiently (indeed Ishmael may be the truest friend she has) and by cyber-snooping until he found her blog. The former activity would rank Ishmael as a "good" person, the latter as "evil"—but Ishmael is beyond conventional good and evil. Conventional thinking would suggest that Norma needs a "cure" to be more in the "real" world, but Ishmael takes people as they are and doesn't seek to reform them. He controls Norma, acting "as if" she were the great caregiver she imagines herself to be. Simply by remembering her birthday—as she remembers other people's—giving her cards, and sharing poetry, Ishmael feeds her hidden self. Norma, of course, knew his favorite cake and made sure that Mr. Brann threw the party. Norma makes sure that his office always has paper and markers. Norma lets him know any office gossip, and Norma feeds him healing, magical energy when he is ill. Ishmael knows that Norma would put him up if he needed a place to stay and that he must come up with some demand of her soon or she will escape his clutches.

Mr. Brann would be startled to know that he is a servant. His mannerisms—from the false paternal airs to the occasional real concern—reminded Ishmael of Bill's father. So, he got all of the Bills to send him that signal. Eventually he released all his father's projections onto Mr. Brann. Mr. Brann seemed to act more and more paternal. Ishmael knew these were sleepwalker commands and probably wouldn't save him if the commands ran counter to Mr. Brann's survival programs, but for most day-to-day concerns Mr. Brann acted like his father and gave Bill/Ishmael someone with whom to work out some personal baggage. Also Mr. Brann would occasionally gift Ishmael with used items connected with masculinity, like his old bowling ball. This attitude meant that he always spoke of Bill's talents with pride to Ms. Levenda and therefore subtly made folks in the office see Bill as his successor.

Conventional morality might be offended by the next set of servants, but the Vampyre is beyond conventional morality. Some might be surprised that Ishmael does not have a sexual servant. He had kept one for a while but desired a partner to have in this life and the next—which means he desired another Vampyre. So, he freed his servants and instructed them to seek serenity. As is usually the case, they tried to fulfill their commands but sadly fell back into the life pattern they had before.

His familiar, the cat Ink, had showed up at his house on the night of a full moon. The poor scraggly girl had "as many parasites as I've ever seen," according to the vet. Ishmael willed her to have life force while taking care of her needs in conventional ways as well. He gave her two tasks: to sense if the house was safe and—the most important task for an animal servant—to remind him to play. Vampyres, because of their direct perception of the predatory nature of the universe, have a tendency to be morbid—and morbidity weakens the Vampyric being. Politically correct folks would say they are equals. The Vampyre understands that no relationship is equal but, unlike bullies and thugs, knows that no relationship is without exchange. We'll discuss ethics and energy later.

Ishmael's relationship with his mom might seem like the most shocking. He's been feeding her life force to keep her cancer at bay. All children have a deep link with their biological mothers. They gain their intelligence, their initial gifts, and their implanted warning through birth. The experiences of their moms—whether surviving a concentration camp or being born to a movie star—are encoded as warnings and proclivities in their children. This is great if mom's talent is one you adore, or terrible if the deep stresses your mother went through leads you to tendencies for food or alcohol addiction. This link/energy boost happens by biology—and the Vampyre can decide what to do with it, which we will discuss in future chapters. Beyond biology there is a second link, that of nurturing. Vampyres receive a coating of energy from active fathers, grandparents, teachers, coaches, and so on. This energy is conveyed as dreams/hopes for the young human. The most aware humans can give the most usable energy ("I hope Bill grows up to be happy"). Less aware humans give tainted energy ("I hope Bill grows up to be just like his dad"). Learning to be aware of this energy—and how to direct/use it—is covered in future chapters as well. Ishmael knows that once an energy account is opened, it can always be two-way. He knows his mom's biology is bad, so he props her up by giving signals to the energy account—he plays the music she played him in the car on the way to school, he takes her to the ice cream place she used to take him, and he responds to every gesture she makes—from telling him to wear his sweaters to listening to her conservative political rants. He receives some energy from her (which makes him younger—see erotic crystallization inertia in future chapters), but mainly he gives her energy. She, too, seems younger. He knows in the end it is a battle that he will lose, but he knows the Vampyre truth that all battles on this earth are eventually lost—it's the Vampyre's game to change the time parameters as much as possible.

We will close this chapter with twenty things people say about Bill. The next chapter will look at what a Vampyre is.

1. Bill is awful with paperwork; he's so helpless, I'm glad to stay after work four times a year and do it for him.

2. You know, you wouldn't think it—but one night there were a couple of thugs giving the women grief in the parking lot. I was dialing 911, but Bill walked over to them. . . . I can't explain it. I mean he just walked, but something about the way he moved, and they got scared and ran.

3. Yeah, Bill and me and this other chick were pretty hot and heavy for a few months. She'd never even been in a threesome. Then we broke up. What? Come to think of it, I don't know why.

4. I'm pretty sure he's twenty-five. Thirty-eight? Are you kidding me?

5. We all wanted to spend time with that writer last month, but for some reason he went to dinner with Bill instead. It kinda sucked, as we arranged his signing. But he was "taken" by Bill for some reason.

6. It's weird, he's been in lot of places from Prague to Glacier National Park. He loves to travel, and he knows people from everywhere.

7. When he wants to leave, he just vanishes.

8. He's the best guy on the neighborhood watch—he'll take foggy nights, stormy nights, you name it.

9. Come to think of it, I don't know anything about him, but I always feel I can tell him anything about my life.

10. One night his car broke down at midnight. He called me and I

went and picked him up. I'm normally not that nice, but he can push my nice-guy button.

11. In grad school he made some brownies once—I won't say they were "magic," but dude, we kinda had an orgy that night.

12. I think he's into ghost busting—he always knows about the haunted buildings downtown.

13. I didn't know Bill was supersmart, but one night he and my dad were discussing Epicurus—my dad's got a Ph.D. in philosophy. They kept it up in email for the rest of my dad's life. Dad even told me that Bill had written some stuff for a journal.

14. Every year Bill helps the neighborhood kids build a kick-ass haunted house, even though he's off to a family reunion over Halloween a lot.

15. There're two great things to do with Bill—go to thrift stores and old bookstores. That man can find anything.

16. He's never the number one student at the dojo, but the sensei says he knows the most.

17. I'm always finding books or knickknacks to give him. I mean it's dumb. He'll say, "I'm looking for this missing book for my Lynn Thorndike set," and I see it for sale, but I can't even remember the names of the books I'm looking for.

18. Sometimes when I'm with Billy it's like when he was a kid and none of the bad stuff happened. He's the best son.

19. When he let's his cat out at night he says, "Ink, come back at nine." Then at nine the damn cat is back.

20. That guy? A weirdo. Most of the folks selling plasma need the money bad. He comes in, makes his deposit, looks like he's doing yoga or something, then I see him again next month. Really different from the alkies this place runs on.

2

THE VAMPYRIC EXPLANATION

We're going to start with what a Vampyre *is*. Then we'll talk about the five myths that create the first door of the Vampyric Way.

A Vampyre is a self-created energy being that is aware of the energy structures that maintain human life. The Vampyre seeks to obtain greater than normal energy, safeguard the energy she has, and use her energy to increase her pleasure, power, wisdom, and, most importantly, to change her relationship to time. To do this she changes her awareness of the world and how she interacts with the world using a variety of techniques from acting, tantra, neurobiology, magic, and hunting. The Vampyre awakens in the human body-mind-soul complex through an energy imbalance, a moment of awareness, and a mythic model. The Vampyre's enemies are not crosses, garlic, or mirrors. The Vampyre's enemies are self-importance, conventionality, disease, pollution, fear, and dharma. The Vampyre is the mode of freedom in a world where everyone is in chains. Let's begin with the chains, then energy, and finally myths.

Every human is constrained by custom; some of these constraints empower the tribal group. For example, we learn not to smell by pheromones—we are better not knowing when the boss is horny. We have traditions for passing on knowledge—if I teach the next generation how to make bronze there will be a generation after that. We will feed the children in times of need. We limit our freedom to give energy (usually in the form of money) to the state, so the state will give us roads, and inspect our milk, and make war on other states that use a different color scheme on their tribal banners. Most of human control is internalized. We don't take a piss on the boss's desk; we don't push the old lady out of line at McDonald's; we stop our car at stop signs (even if we know we are alone in an abandoned complex). This is the social aspect of control.

The social aspect for control leads to post-primate-band forms of government—democracy and various flavors of totalitarianism. These work well for human societies but not as well for individuals.

Beyond the social aspect of control where internalized rules produce automatic behavior, there is a perceptual aspect. We model the Cosmos based on internalized rules. For example, you're taking a shower and you can half hear a song on your neighbor's radio. It's a song you like, so you sing along. Then you turn off the shower—it's a completely different song—you "heard" what your mind predicted you would hear.

Most stage magic tricks work on the power of internalized rules. The internalized rules not only make us good worker bees and consumers, but they also literally keep us from participating in the Cosmos. Let's have a little fun with that idea by running a couple of experiments.

Experiment one: The next time someone asks you how you are, answer, "Pine and yew?" Don't smirk or give away what you've done. Most humans will be just as happy you are a tree. On nice days remark, "Isn't it nice we have weather?"

You probably played with these notions when you were in middle school. Try something a little meatier. This second experiment came from Frater U. D. It will literally change your life. Pick any event that you know will be covered in multiple news outlets. Go to the event, watch it, take notes, record it with such devices as you have. Note its length, and how much time was really spent on various topics. After you have made your record then watch the account of the event on a right-wing media outlet and a left-wing media outlet, listen to the event on the radio, and read about it in the newspapers. How was the reported-on event different from the real one? What does it mean that 99.99 percent of your fellow humans consumed the energy of this event from their favorite media channel?

Energy, as grade-school science tells us, is the "ability to do work."

Any energy that the Vampyre can absorb from biological, emotional, mental or magical sources can be stored, transferred, or transformed to increase the Vampyre's power, pleasure, longevity, or evolution. All humans can absorb, use, store, or transform energy. All humans can play basketball. Vampyres play in the NBA. Some humans have natural gifts in the biological, emotional, mental, or magical realms. Vampyres acquire skill at energy manipulation in all four realms.

The predigested world is very low energy. Vampyres cannot subsist on it. But "normal" people not only can—they are addicted to it. When humans manage to change their perceptions—from right wing to left wing, or humanist to racist, or Christianity to Buddhism, and so on—there is a brief burst of energy. They are happier, healthier, and more powerful. They may expend some of the new energy in trying to convert members of their tribe to the new point of view. But they adjust to their new feeding grounds and return to their normal state. They briefly form "thoughts" in their brain such as "When I was a Republican, I was Asleep but now I am Awake!" Novelty brings not only energy but also dangers. For example, their old Republican friends now call them "libtards." However, their new "enlightenment" fades into a different social control orbit.

Likewise, if a human's perceptual feed is voluntarily changed, there is a burst of energy. Try a vacation, a trip to an art museum, or a new lover. Some humans try to create a constant stream of novelty by becoming swingers, travel writers, or (sadly) art critics.

The average human has two (accessible) parts: the body and the rules-based parasite. The parasite takes care of the body based on the rules it knows. When the body dies, the rules-based parasite decays a few years afterward.

The Vampyre has two entities with which it must deal upon Awakening. First the body, which is the major source of energy, and second, the social parasite.

The Body. The body is about homeostasis. It likes whatever balance you give it. If you give it heroin, it likes heroin. If you give it twenty minutes of brisk walking a day, it likes twenty minutes of brisk walking a day. Vampyres take care of rescue cats to learn how to take care of the

body. If I neglect my cat's shots because it doesn't like needles, I will
lose my cat. If I don't play with my cat every day, my cat is sad. If I don't
clean up its environment . . . you get the idea. The body tries to trick
the Vampyre into thinking its wants are "thoughts."

The Social Parasite. Human society created the parasite to keep
the body in control. The social parasite—the socially constructed
human—is very important to the Vampyre.

The social parasite is an accumulation of social and language training that acts as though it were a living part of your personality. A classic example is that when you are asked, "How are you doing?" it is the
parasite that responds, "Fine." You are taught by social experience to
not complain or brag, and although you may break with your conditioning and produce an accurate answer, you will feel a strange internal
resistance to do so. When your social parasite answers, your will is connected with the answer. "How is Gary doing since Sue died?" "I asked
him and he said, 'Fine.'" Magically, knowing someone's social parasites
is as potent as having that person's fingernails or hair for a magical
working. In the realm of advertising (a common form of sorcery), you
can appeal directly to those infected: "Tired of saying 'Fine'? Buy Zoso
soda and say, 'Great!'"

The parasite keeps us safe when we are resting. The human servant
in the vampire myth is the social self. When the Vampyre first Awakens
the initial thought is almost always, "I'll never be unconscious again!"
Whatever has kept the Vampyre Asleep—drugs, an abusive relationship, and so on—will be removed, and there will be smooth sailing. Of
course, this lasts days, maybe even months, and then the Vampyre nods
off again. You have seen it in your human friends and acquaintances: the
woman who has a string of abusive boyfriends; the man who becomes a
workaholic despite heart attacks; the animal rights activist who hasn't
managed to be happy in twenty years; the pedophile priest. From the
Vampyric perspective all of these are human parasites (just like the one
you see in the mirror)—some are just more toxic than others.

The parasite tries to control us through self-importance. Before the
modern age it used other means. Think of the story of the Buddha—
Sanskrit for "woke guy"—as a good example as he almost made it to

Vampyric consciousness. When Prince Siddhartha Awakened, the forces of Maya (the parasite police) sent three things to stop him. The first was fear—ghosts, monsters, bill collectors, gang members, immigrants, radical feminists, Nazis, and so on. "Look, you can't wake up—if you wake up you'll see all the crap in the World of Horrors! Numb back out!" Well the prince (being royal) said, "No! By being Awake I have an edge over these things! I won't pretend they aren't real, but I will not compromise my self-sovereignty to them!" The demons, ghosts, evangelists, and so on, screamed and relented. Of course, you are beyond fear or you wouldn't have read this far in the book, so your parasite already tried that.

The second "temptation" was lust. Now Desire himself (Kama) sent his three daughters: "You Might Get Some," "You Are Getting Some," and "Remember When You Got This—It Was the Best." Now either Buddha was gay, or he worked out the idea that "Desire is secondary to Being!" In either case the three sirens wailed, gnashed their teeth, and were reborn as post-Disney performers.

So, the forces of Maya sent their most deadly temptation—Dharma/Duty/Self-Importance. He looks just like your dad when he gave you that talking-to when you lost your first job: "Son, in this world we've all got a job. You are a prince. Your job is to rule a kingdom, marshal troops into war, throw out the first baseball at the start of the season. What would happen if nobody did these things?" This is Self-Importance at its worst. It tells you that your role in society is more important than you. What would happen if people knew that a solid security guard like you thought he was a Vampyre? You might not be a good mom if you spent time daydreaming about magic. You can't be a real advocate for the gay political cause if people found out you were an occultist.

The Buddha overcame self-importance and could've made it to the Vampyre Way except for the fourth lure of the parasite: nirvana. This is the most powerful force of the parasite police; namely, the notion that since existence can hurt, there is a mode of happy nonexistence where the red fire of life and the black flame of Self could be "blown out." Nirvana comes from the verbal root *vā*, "blow" in the form of past participle *vāna*, "blown," prefixed with the preverb *nir*, meaning "out." Any notion of a non-active afterlife—the Christian cloud sitting and harp strumming, the "Hindu" (sorry to use a colonialist term) idea of the static union of Atman and Brahman, the atheist oblivion, or the Buddhist nirvana all lead to the ending of the Vampyric self. Why play the immortal game if there is no meaningful leveling up?

So, the Vampyric being has a herd of two to start with: the body, which she controls through healthy pleasure, and the parasite, which she controls through disciplined fantasy. It takes constant effort to yoke these unruly beings to the Self. However, there is a curious side effect to yoking these beings. You will attract the beings of others. On the physical side this may seem like sex appeal—but it can also be the appeal grandmother's cookies cast on children. On the social side it can be seen as charisma. Other humans' parasites are quite happy to let you lead them. This side effect is both what draws people to Vampyrism and can make them get lost in it.

One of the main sources of energy is attention; our own is the strongest, and through it we work the "miracles" of magic and the more understandable feats called "accomplishments through hard work." The next richest attention is that of healthy human love—partner-to-partner being the strongest, then parent-for-child, then other blood relationships. Then comes magickal attention we gain from our teachers, those gifted humans who truly want us to succeed. Then comes friendship from magickal peers, then normal human friendship (when healthy), then attention from animal companions. Then comes our energy that comes from students, then energy given from Sleeping humans, and last, energy taken from Sleeping humans. The last four sources are meager and may lead to grave distortions of the Self.

The energy we receive from animals (although necessary for a certain level of self-change) should be strongly tempered by consciousness. The newspapers are sadly full of the story of the cat hoarder or the man who kept twenty-five pit bulls in his backyard. These humans do not enrich their animals and have usually lost any way to gain energy from the world. Energy from one's students is the basis of megachurches and the occult industry. As humans step away from the parasite there is a boost in their energy that they are not able to store. They radiate out new life—if this is met by an initiatory current this energy is transformed and redirected upon them. However, if it is merely absorbed by the "teacher"—it leads to delusions of self-importance. The follower feels that she is "chosen," and the teacher feels that he is "worthy." This leads to a sort of sexual scandal that is consumed as "news"—basically feeding on what was already rotten.

Energy given by Sleeping humans comes in the form of adoration or fear. Each of these is spiritually deadly in large doses, but the latter is more hateful. Thousands of screaming rock fans can keep that band on tour even if the logical consequences of their lifestyle should have buried them. Fear produces an even lower grade of energy that can be seen anywhere from abusive relationships to certain political regimes. This energy dulls both the giver and the taker and is so hateful to the parasite police that social actions may be taken.

The taking of energy from Sleeping humans is the most controversial aspect of Vampyrism. You can take attention from those who are unwilling to give it. This may be done in four ways, and each must be weighed ethically. First is by shock art. It's easy enough to do: disfigure any icon. This could be done for noble causes (attacking a billboard advertising a church with a message about sexual abuse by clergy) or ignoble causes (spray painting a swastika across a synagogue door). The energy is mainly released inside the body-soul complex of the transgressor. It is a limited boost and sadly requires greater and greater transgressions to maintain the energy flow—quickly turning a playful moment into an angry fix. The second method is psychic vampirism, the destruction of the joy of others. This garners little force yet is approved by the parasite police; psychic vampires are common, and I've devoted some later pages about how to overcome them. Humans who derive energy from these means must be eliminated from your environment. The third mechanism is passive sorcery—simply creating magical devices that absorb human surplus energy—as, for example, the cheering drones at a political rally—and feed it to you. Some of these methods will be mentioned later in this book. The fourth method of Vampyric attack requires hard work. It requires that the Vampyre have a deep link with her target and an expenditure of a great deal of attention. Only in cases of dire situations should this be used. It is mentioned here, however, as one of the aspects of the Vampyric being.

So far, I've hinted at how the romantic notion of the vampire, that product of nineteenth-century sexual repression and folklore, is somehow related to the Vampyric Way. It's time to study that notion in depth. Let's look at the five layers of the vampire myth and how they relate to becoming a Vampyre.

MYTHOLOGY OF THE VAMPIRE

All spiritual paths have their myths. To the followers they appear sacred; to the dumber followers they appear objectively real. A young Catholic is told stories about saints. Some of the stories seem horrific to non-Catholics. Saint Perpetua was offered pardon if she refused her faith. She held on to her faith, only asking if she could give birth before being killed. A couple of days after her delivery she was taken to a field to be slain by a wild cow. The cow gored her, but she did not die, so an executioner was summoned. The executioner's hand slipped, and the sword pierced between her bones, failing to kill her. Perpetua then grabbed the man's hand and guided the sword to her own neck. It was later said that she was so great a woman she could not be slain unless she herself willed it. Saint Symeon tried living in a small cave, but that didn't focus his mind on God enough, so he moved onto a thirteen-foot-tall pillar in Syria. While living up there, his only sustenance came from boys in the village who would climb up the pillar and provide him with bread and milk. Throughout the next thirty-nine years, he continually moved up to higher and higher pillars. Eventually, his last pillar was more than fifty feet tall. Of course, the smarter child knows that no one stayed on a fifty-foot-tall pole for nearly forty years, any more than vampires sleep in coffins or turn into bats. The smarter Catholic could derive instruction on the relationship of priests to laymen (provide nothing and require tall buildings) and the desires of God (in terms of performance art).

There are five levels of Vampyric myth. As we go from the most accessible to the least: current visual media, older visual media, written material, folklore, and the archaic myth. Each offers clues to the archetype, but only the last is a magically workable form. Let's step through the layers.

Modern Fiction

Current vampire media focuses on apparent teen drama—teenage-looking vampires are in our high schools. Whereas the idea of a 105-year-old man with a teenage girl should be repulsive, it's somehow okay if the guy looks young and hot. We discover the power of an archetype when it violates our supposedly deeply held values.

This reveals three things about the archetype. First, it reveals the empowering nature of the "forbidden." If it's "bad" it's "good" when the "bad" is not about pain or hurt. Second, it deals with phenomena of erotic energy and time. This mystery, which both Anton LaVey and William S. Burroughs write about, was named by the former erotic crystallization inertia (ECI). The human body creates erotic energy. In most cases this is utilized by the social parasite to create guilt and motivate lust. (You want the girl? Buy a better car! Enlist!—and so on.) However, this excess energy begins to feed the Vampyric self. As such, most humans' self-image corresponds to the way they looked when they were getting some. Likewise indulging in the cues associated with that time of life—such as listening to the music of your youth—can cause humans' health (and even appearance) to improve. This is a threat to the parasite's control powers, and older humans who engage in this practice are seen as silly or even creepy. Finally, the teen vampire myth tells us about the power of a secret. Humans are both loyal and energized if there is something they know that others don't—whether it's the secret Masonic handshake or that Edward is a 105-year-old vampire.

Classic Films

In the next level of popular mythology, found in older movies, we pick up certain other clues: the dread of mirrors, animal affinity, shape-shifting, cultural distance, and nobility/wealth. The dread of mirrors begins with the simple fact that our image (beginning with the interaction of sexual energy and our Vampyric selves) is different from our actual appearance. To exude a glamour, one must begin with self-visualization and a self-conception that has subjective elements. The mirror not only reminds us of our image without glamour, it also feeds the parasite's powers of self-doubt. The parasite sees the body as a non-magical meat machine whose purpose is to limit bravery, creativity, or leadership.

Animal affinity is the power that the Vampyric self must draw from the energy/neural activity of other bodies. The Vampyre as she masters her body's flow of energy can begin to use the flow of other energy as a means of perception. A Vampyre can know from his dog that some-one's in the backyard or can tell that someone is gravely ill from her cat. Vampyres are often told by their friends: "That's odd! My cat hates everyone. It won't even sleep in my lap like that!" These are not innate abilities but are gained because of practice.

The more startling ability of actual shape-shifting comes from discov-ering animal patterns dormant in the body (or in the magical inventory of humanity) that can be energized and utilized. Many of these practices were discovered by trance artist Austin O. Spare. He called this process atavistic nostalgia (we'll get to this in the training sections of this book).

Cultural distance—the vampire is from elsewhere/elsewhen—has a threefold meaning in the Vampyric Way. First, humans are both fasci-nated by and fear foreigners. Folks that aren't seen as part of the status quo are great to reveal secrets to, great as one-time sexual encounters, and harder to manipulate. Second, the Vampyric Way is based on con-serving energy. One of the great leaks of energy comes from humans being "involved" in human drama that they cannot affect. As an exer-cise, read through magazines or websites from eight to ten years ago. What were humans up in the air about? What caused fights, ended friendships? What celebrities were everyone talking about—because they were pro-gay? Or anti-gay? Pro-Israel? Anti-Israel? Of that vast amount of energy released—what happened? Vampyres are not drawn into energy-wasting topics. If a Vampyre decides to affect an issue, it is not by hot air. Third, the break from the issues/fads of the time forces the Vampyre to seek perennial values. In antiquity this would be seen as a virtue but looks odd to the modern (and postmodern) eye—for exam-ple, in an era where humans look to celebrities as examples of virtue, the Vampyre looking upon Cincinnatus's return to his farm as an example of virtue is certainly out of place. Vampyres are often seen as being very right-wing or left-wing in some of the truths they may pursue. They are seldom sought out as "influencers," and if they choose this role there is a whiff of brimstone that seems to surround their good deeds.

The last aspect of the older movie vampire, the nobility/wealth axis, seems like a hard thing to fake. Sure, I would like to be Count Dracula and buy up a ruined abbey instead of living in a condo—but the meaning of the myth is that the Vampyre must have alternate ways of producing wealth. He or she must be able (and willing) to live outside the matrix. Even if these skills are never called on, the notion of independence must not be simply a fantasy but part of the ground of being as well.

Classic Literature

The written versions of the vampire myth—particularly *Dracula, Carmilla,* and *The Vampyre*—offer four other clues: dirt from the native soil, the Scholomance, dreams, and seduction. These books drew from existing folklore and are an important part of the modern occult tradition. Long before Joseph Campbell, these books present a method: draw from mythological sources, weave a compelling tale, and graft the tale onto psychological needs, particularly regarding sexuality and disenchantment with the modern world. Since these stories require the reader to use all of her brain to create a vision of the world, they draw the subjective universe of the reader into a magical act of creation. As Vampyres begin their Awakening, reading these books has a profound effect that passively watching films and TV can never have. *Dracula* is of course well known to modern readers. Its predecessor volumes, *Carmilla* and *The Vampyre,* are perhaps less well known. *Carmilla,* by Sheridan Le Fanu (1872), deals with the seduction of a young girl by a lesbian vampire. *The Vampyre,* by Dr. John Polidori (1816), was the first to use folkloric aspects of the vampire myth to create a dark romance.

The first clue of the Vampyric Way offered here is in the connection with the tomb or graveyard dirt. This complex symbol has at least three meanings for the Vampyre. First, although the Vampyre must exceed/transcend the biological processes of their body, they must still maintain a direct link with the earth: they must have a way to draw energy from the earth and as immortals must have a sense of guardianship over it. Second, Vampyres must have a link with the pre-Christian myths and practices of their people. Their connection with an older developmental center (mythic/magical) needs authentic roots. Third, the Vampyre does not deny/repress her trauma. She is rooted in the "dirt" of her past. The psychological shock that most modern humans hide from themselves must be transformed consciously into a source of strength—not a wound or weakness.

In Bram Stoker's *Dracula* we are surprised to find that the count did not become a vampire by being bitten by another vampire but by studying at the Black School. Stoker had based his account on the Scottish writer Emily Gerard's "Transylvanian Superstitions," presented for the reader in Book the Fourth. Students at the Black School studied the speech of animals, magic spells, and weather making. Of every ten graduates the devil himself chose one as a dragon-riding aide-de-camp. This book you are holding could be read as a re-creation of its curriculum. Dreams (and associated phenomena like hypnotism, sleepwalking, and night terrors) are part of the initiation of the vampire's victims. This book will offer some practical advice on the Vampyric dream, but it is recommended that readers pause and consider some of their own experiences with some of these states, as their initiation began before picking up this book. Dr. Polidori received his degree for the study of *oneirodynia,* the medical term for sleepwalking and nightmares. Finally, the motif of seduction separates the Vampyric Way from more politically correct modes of neo-shamanism. Deep in the core of the myth is the seduction of the body by the Vampyric self. The Vampyre must seduce both the social parasite and the body. This may or may not be projected onto an outside process either as the seducer or the seduced.

Folklore

The folkloric layer is oddly accessible to the postmodern Vampyre. Even an evening with the internet will provide valuable clues. However, let's consider the motives Stoker, Polidori, and Le Fanu may have had in mind. The vampires of folklore were smelly, hairy, fat, and bloated with blood. They were not something you wanted to fuck. They were gross and by the nineteenth century almost emblems of the kind of superstitious thinking that modernity/British imperialism was going to eradicate. Of the three men, two were bisexual (Stoker and Polidori) and two were Irish (Stoker and Le Fanu)—so all were outside of the host culture. All looked to a prerational state, a pre-Christian primitivist state. Yet vampires are frightened by crosses—by the symbol of universalist/Catholic thinking. In many ways this was a Roman hacking of gnostic Christianity, turning a theology of personal liberation into a philosophy that suggests one should seek older paths of liberation as part of modern practice. The Vampyre will be drawn to folktales, and certainly not just European ones, as maps for liberation.

The etymology suggested for *vampyre* points toward the shamanism of the Lake Bikal region. The Old Russian word *upyri,* meaning "someone who thrusts or bites," shows up in the *Word of Saint Gregory,* an anti-pagan tract of the High Middle Ages with the interesting condemnation that Russians used to worship the upyri as gods. The folk memory of the shaman who can detach himself from his body and become bird or beast was banished from the central narratives of the community by the authorities but, like the Vampyre herself, cannot die.

The folkloric vampire offers the two biggest clues to Vampyric existence: the need for constant energy, and extreme vulnerability. The folkloric vampire's need for blood, its hunger for energy, is the key to its existence. Vampyres have only two true enemies—the first is boredom. The Vampyre understands that once she has become an energy being, she requires food. She enters every situation as a hunter. She respects her situation and stays alert to everything around her. She doesn't waste her movements or her energy nor does she indulge in unnecessary thoughts. There are no off days, no days not to keep her attention sharp.

The second enemy is the lack of planning. Our society is structured to draw excess energy away from humans through social media, advertisements, and the consumption of fast food or cheap alcohol. The Vampyre knows these things look like energy to the social parasite and knows she must be vigilant. Otherwise she's like everyone else: staring at her smartphone, being food rather than feeding.

All folkloric vampires have extreme vulnerabilities. These come in two categories: the unconscious attack (stakes, beheading, or burning the coffin) and the sensory attack (the smell of garlic, bright light, or counting spilled seeds). The former requires the Vampyre, unlike the average New Age seeker, to have a safe home—not only in the sense of good locks on the doors but also in the sense of being inaccessible. The Vampyre doesn't take the on-call 24/7 job. He knows that when he is using his energy in dreamwork he is vulnerable. This is also why he seduces his social parasite rather than destroying it as many spiritual paths suggest. The sensory attacks are harder to deal with; as you will see in your training, Vampyres cultivate their sensory awareness. Learning to cut your awareness down to minimal is a vital sensory skill. Otherwise anything from traffic problems to a crowded mall can bring on a severe headache or worse.

Archaic Myth

But each of these layers point to another deeper state, the Archaic Vampyre. Thinkers such as Jean Gebser (whom we will return to more fully in a later chapter) describe the intellectual states of humankind as both historically progressive and inherent in all humans. Gebser's states were the archaic, the magical, the mythic, the mental, and the (now-arriving) integral.

Most of our civilization works in the mental (rational, scientific, logocentric) state, whereas most humans are still in the mythical (political parties, banners, logos, FOX, and CNN). However, mankind spent most of its development in the first two states and has a great nostalgia to return to these states. The nostalgia has been expressed in racial memory (seen in such epic scale in *2001: A Space Odyssey*), in places as diverse as the hippy movement, Marvel Comics, and vampire fiction.

The archaic state is an undifferentiated state in which man is overwhelmed by neither a past nor a dreaded future. The human state most similar exists in those humans with the oldest DNA on the planet, the native people of Australia. They use various terms for it, but *altjira* is perhaps the best. Misleadingly, this term is often rendered in English as "Dreamtime." But it is a state of energy existence extending both beyond/before birth and after/beyond death. It does not question the boundaries between dreams and waking or firmly held beliefs and later reasoned-out beliefs. It connects human deeds and thoughts not to the social-rule-based parasite but directly to energy flow. This mood appeared in fictions as soon as nation-states arrived and with the coming of the corporation has exploded into popular media.

The Vampyre does not seek to abandon the gains of mental consciousness but rather to fully utilize all existing modes of consciousness to recover the totality of herself, free from the constraints of body, culture, and time.

3
WHAT IS ENERGY

Energy, as your grade-school science book taught you, is the ability to do work. It can be transferred to an object to cause motion or to heat the object. Great-grandfather Aristotle gave us the term ἐνέργεια (*energeia*) in the fourth century BCE. He meant it in a broader way and had no trouble equating it with pleasure or happiness. Humans, who generally have little grounding in the sciences, have the laughable notion that our bodies have vast amounts of energy. Actually the energetic output of a given human is about 80 watts. So the notion that tons of humans could be tapped for usable physical energy isn't good science, however much we love *The Matrix*.

But the Vampyre is an energy being, so where does it get its energy, store its energy, and what work or heat does it do with its energy?

Let's begin with a very simple example and build from there. Consider these four scenarios:

Scenario number one: I get up at six on Monday morning; it's going to be a shitty week. I drive to work seeing the same old crap I see every day. I discover my assistant has once again taken the day off (claiming her child is ill—again). I drink the coffee in the break room. I spill coffee on a report I've been working on for weeks. Of course, there's no backup. I Google causes of suicide in middle-aged males. I drive home; my AC breaks; the traffic is crazy. I eat some Cheerios and hang out on Facebook exchanging memes about How the Government Sucks™. I go to bed by eight with a ringing headache.

Scenario number two: I wake up at six on Friday. As I walk to my car a mourning dove sings to me from the live oak tree in my front yard. At work my assistant has brought doughnuts (as a peace offering). I give a great presentation. I go to lunch with a cute coworker. The boss lets us leave at 3:30. I pick up that book I've been wanting from the library. I eat a healthy, light dinner. I read until eight then call up some friends. We go to a funky old bar until about eleven, then we go for coffee and pie, where I run into the cute coworker. Turns out the cute coworker is reading the same book I am.

Scenario number three: I get up at six on Monday morning, it's going to be a shitty week. I drive to work seeing the same old crap I see every day. Half asleep, I nearly hit a car that was running a red light—missing it by literal inches. I pull over to catch my breath. Suddenly every color, every sound is in sharp focus. I drive to work noticing a new (well—new to me) Japanese fast food place three blocks from work. I hear my assistant's kid is sick. I call her and offer my good wishes. I think of an entirely new angle to put in my report and invite the Big Boss to my presentation. On the way home I buy a slice of red velvet cake to celebrate. I spend the early evening chatting with old friends. I go to bed a little later than usual. Damn, the cool sheets feel great. I have my best sleep in weeks.

Scenario number four: I'm having a middling Wednesday. I'm watching the clock all day at work, even though my evening plans are built around watching Netflix for three hours. At the afternoon break, Suzie (from accounting) tells us a riddle.

Bill, Phil, and Will check into the El Sleazo Hotel. To save money they decide to share a room. "That will be $30," says the clerk at the front desk. So everybody forks over ten. A few minutes later the clerk regrets charging the trio so much for their roach-infested room. He gives the bellhop $5 to return to the guests. He does so. The boys each take a buck and then give the bellhop $2 as a tip. But later that night, Phil (awakened by scurrying bugs) says, "We've been robbed! We each paid 10, but we got a buck back. So we each paid 9. Nine times 3 is 27. Then we gave the bellhop $2. $27 and $2 is $29. We've been had, I tells ya." So where did the missing dollar go?

So I went back to my cubicle, and, having done all my real work that day, I mulled over the riddle. Then I got it! It was misdirection. Phil was confusing two different sums. In reality it was 3 × 10 = 30, and $25 (the amount the hotel kept) plus $5 (the bellhop's starting figure) also equals 30! I felt great; I called Suzie and bragged. On the drive home I figured out my personal finances and felt even more relief. I even went to the gym—the first time in ages (and didn't feel guilty about my monthly fees).

The four scenarios show that "energy" doesn't mean biological energy but something more subjective yet entirely observable in its effects. In the first scenario our narrator lets impressions from the world keep him in a low energetic state, so he remains in a miserable orbit.

The second example is similar. The narrator is ruled by the world—his attitude toward work and the oncoming weekend. But it shows work being performed. He is "lucky"—he gets off early, the desired book shows up, and by "accident" he meets the coworker.

The third situation demonstrates the release of stored energy. The near collision realized some of the narrator's stored energy, which probably prevented the collision and immediately channels itself into perception, compassion, search for sacramental pleasure (spotting the Japanese food place), breaking chains of thought (the new angle on his presentation), and finally boldness (inviting the Big Boss)—all of these are high-level manifestations of survival skills. These three depend on luck or, more precisely, eudaemonia—we'll talk about that later.

The fourth involves the solving of a problem. Now, although the problem came by accident, our narrator applied himself to solving the problem. The energy came in bursts—first, the energy that comes from untying a knot, second, the burst from social approval. The two energies are blended and allow more personal (and therefore anxiety-producing) knots to be untied. Notice that this isn't a "natural" process—energy was voluntarily spent, but it produced a good deal more.

I'm going to give three more examples, and then we will talk about the nine sources of energy, the seven ways to store it, and its four uses.

Scenario number five: I've just spent eight hours with my girlfriend and *her* girlfriend. Having lost a fun game, I must go get food. I am beat, smelly, and have a smile that I'm sure tells everyone my level of ecstasy. I know one thing—I couldn't in a million years want any more sex right now. I step out of my apartment and glance upward to my neighbor's porch. The angle of my gaze happens to be up the skirt of my flight attendant neighbor and on to her pink polka-dot panties. Immediately I am aroused and fantasize about calling her down to join us.

Scenario number six: I have a long hard day at work, and coming home provided no relief since I had to fix my toilet. Heading toward bed, a full hour later than usual, my phone rings. It's my best friend since junior high. He tells me in a sick, hoarse voice that he has a 102° fever—and he hasn't eaten today. He knows it's a pain, but could I buy him some groceries? As I drive over to his home I find myself singing in the car—ready to spend hours taking care of my friend.

Scenario number seven: My friends have taken me to the Denver Museum of Art. It's my first day in Denver, and I'm a little weak and sleepy from the change in elevation. We wander from room to room, with annoying kids being, well, annoying, but then suddenly I am face-to-face with *Linda,* an amazing sculpture by Denver artist John DeAndrea. It seems alive, as if she might open her eyes and speak to me. It is not just beautiful. It is Art. My fatigue, my annoyance, my day-to-day traveling concerns are banished.

Each of these scenarios deals with the relationship between humans in a voluntary context: the first, the seeking of sacramental pleasure— energy can always come to seek more energy; the second, the unlocking of tribal energy stores; and the last, the mystery of exchange (see p. 44).

So let's explore energy: Energy is the state of activity of the authentic (or we may say in this context Vampyric) Self. It is the real Self doing something to ensure its survival in the objective universe. Energy seeks to further itself—either in the Self or those people/forces that define or remember the Self. The Vampyric self is made out of layers of energy structured in primordial times when mankind learned to self-create a being not bound in time. The relationship of this being and the day-to-day observable world is the concern of philosophy and religion. Allowing this being to directly interact with the observable Cosmos is the concern of magic and art. Learning to access and empower this being while still incarnate is the Vampyric Way.

Energy has certain properties. First, it is based on the processing of lived or imagined experience; that is to say, a hundred people might listen to the final movement of Beethoven's Ninth and have a hundred different levels of energy, ranging from a slight drain ("The only music I love is Johnny Cash!") to transformational ecstasy ("Lovely! Lovely Ludwig!"). A very, very few can achieve the effect by imagining it or remembering it. Second, energy can be diseased or stale. A sign of mastery in the Vampyric arts is energetic alchemy—turning bad energy into good energy. Third, energy from human sources is structured, it has personality. If your mother-in-law hates you, her energy will hate you. If your mother-in-law loves you, her energy will love you. Fourth, energy is bound in causality, which makes it appear space-bound. You can send/ receive energy from your mother even if she is on the other side of the world because you and she are entangled, but you can't strike down a dictator even if you are a mile away from his fortress. Fifth, energy is gained at a cost of energy. If you are deeply depressed you won't suck in energy even in the best of environments (see below), but if you are full of energy you can find the miraculous in the least likely of places. The five properties of energy are symbolized by the pentagram. If two points are upraised, it is a sign of sending and receiving energy, the Vampyric Way. If one point is exalted, it is a sign that one waits for a higher power to give you energy, perhaps in a stocking at Christmastime.

Finding Energy

Let's look at the ways energy can be gathered. In general, they are ranked from the least to most skill involved.

Natural Environment. The Vampyre can draw energy directly from the natural world. The environments that feed him or her tend toward the sublime (as the Romantics used to say); that is, they balance fascination and terror—the edge of a canyon, water crashing on rocks, saguaros in bloom in 100°-plus deserts. Areas that provide solitude are particularly powerful. Here the Vampyre can literally breathe out bad/ stale energy and breathe in the good. Eventually such areas will instill a sense of guardianship of the world. The bond with the familiar begins in this stead.

Fear. As Mr. Lovecraft noted, "The oldest and strongest emotion of mankind is fear, and the oldest and strongest kind of fear is fear of the unknown." Fear energizes, as in the example of the near miss of an auto accident mentioned earlier. Activities that rely on fear—from riding roller coasters to hang gliding—are popular among Vampyres. However, this is a dangerous source of energy: what scares you one month may bore you the next. And trusting the Vampyric self to save you every time is a dangerous gamble. Causing fear in others is a form of dominance; sharing fear is a form of submission. Triggering fear—that is to say, energy—in those who see you can be dangerous if they are underdeveloped beings.

Taboo Breaking. Taboo breaking is a major source of power early in a Vampyre's career. Large amounts of energy are held in the social parasite. Breaking its rules releases huge energy packets. Symbolic evil from flipping off the boss when he's not looking to trampling a consecrated wafer during a Black Mass remind the Vampyric self that it is free. Many humans fall into the trap of compulsion, however. They need the rules to be broken every time. The thrill of wearing a black T-shirt that advertises a band that your parents hate may be liberating when you're sixteen but a draining addiction when you're fifty-six. Taboo breaking also requires a strong ethical sense—kinky sex with a consenting adult is very different from sex with a minor. Playing at being a Nazi in your home is very different from expressing those attitudes in the voting booth. The social parasite loves rules, and it's willing—far too willing—to learn *any* set of rules. Taboo breaking is both powerful and limiting (like fear).

Kama. Kama, sexual desire, is a great source of energy in all three of its aspects. It can create energy in anticipation, achievement, or memory of achievement. Three guidelines must be present—it must be made intense, it must not harm or limit any others, and it must be self-expressive. If your kama is only prepackaged—based on media—then it will fail to provide you energy. In fact, if all of your kama is based on fantasies involving an unobtainable celebrity, you are providing energy to him/her/them. Being an object of desire is a form of dominance. Since it triggers desire—that is to say, energy—in those who see you, this can be dangerous if they are underdeveloped beings.

Aesthetics. The energy that comes from an aesthetic source such as music, painting, or architecture is heavily filtered by education, culture, and the circumstances of presentation. What works for you may not work for your friend. However, actively seeking to expand your taste by going to museums, gallery openings, or seeking outside of your culture and class will open you to new sources of energy. The thrill of creating art is a way to add new layers of energy to one's energy being. Artists who use art to coat their energy selves despite great hardship— for example, van Gogh—tend to have great appeal to Vampyres.

Dominance. The word *dominance* may call up visions of BDSM. Whereas both sides of that kink are usable for Vampyric Work, the simple "will to power" that Nietzsche speaks of is a source of energy. Power itself has little energy, so a billionaire's sin running his real estate empire has no special energy and, in fact, may have the energetic vulnerability of insecurity or the imposter syndrome. However, the human that begins at the lowest ranks and becomes a boss has a substantial source of energy. The outer world reflects the growing sovereignty of the inner one. Changing landscape or public policy is a great source of energy. Of course, mindless power provides lesser energy than rulership. Dominance must be allied with telos.

Submission. To many, the word *submission* may seem even more surprising. In BDSM, submissive participants have power because not only do they determine the limits of a scene, but they also hold the safe words. But a deeper idea is embedded here. When my barber trims my beard and hair, I am clearly submissive, sitting quietly in a chair—yet my Will is being done. If a dentist or surgeon acts upon me, my Will is likewise in control. The acceptance of limits—whether you're wearing a ball gag or lying still for waxing—is a very powerful way to force the social parasite to give up power. But, as with taboo breaking, if overdone it changes from energy source to compulsion. If a human is at an especially low ebb, he or she can begin to build up energy by following a very precise ritual in hygiene or while going to bed—in effect submitting to her- or himself.

Wonder. "Wonder"—mystical awe—does not happen for all humans. Wonder is the reaction of seeing energy at work in the objective universe. Its most common form is in the pleasant shock of observing synchronicities. As energy accumulates, synchronicities become more common, it becomes a matter of discipline to observe them and to avoid explaining them away. At a higher orbit one can begin to manifest synchronicities as the result of magickal workings, and it becomes necessary to give them respect and neither deny them nor explain them away. The Vampyre will also notice how synchronicities fail to manifest around people with terminal energy blockage. Dream work is another source of wonder and will be dealt with more fully later. As with desire, causing wonder—that is to say, energy—in others can be dangerous if they are underdeveloped beings.

Vampirism. The last two sources can only happen for humans who have taken up the Vampyric Way. The first, vampirism, is the drawing of energy from one's biological self, a "battery," an egregore, or another human. The first sort—summoning energy from one's body to deal with a trying psychological state—is common enough. It is hard on the body, and many humans treat their body with intoxicants to further this process, which is in general a bad idea. The creation of a battery to store energy is a basic form of Vampyric work and will be discussed later. Egregores can be created by a velvet* of Vampyres to act as a group storage and healing device, but more often egregores are attacked. A group of persons seeking you harm can have their harmful group spirit drained of force; however, this is an advanced technique and a dangerous one—since energy is laced with the intent of its creators. A group that supports or loves you (such as your family) may be a source of energy in time of emergency, but ethically any energy taken thusly must be repaid quickly and with interest. One can harvest energy from others by causing fear, desire, or wonder in them—or one may use a direct attack. The direct attack is the fearsome art. One can unravel the energy layers of a human opponent and absorb them. Like carrying a legal gun in the United States, it is not casual or fun, and we may

---

Velvet is the term for a group of Vampyres, like a murder of crows.

hope it is never used. Early in their careers Vampyres may use this skill in a lighthearted fashion until the first time they see results—either in their target or in themselves—and then one of three things occurs: they freak out and run as far from these practices as they can, they decide on developing a strong moral code, or they play at being a gunslinger until someone takes them down. This book is for option two.

Exchange. Exchange is the highest form of energy work. It can take place in waking (or rarely dreaming) states between two or more Vampyres. It involves the voluntary sharing of energy. All involved walk away with a profound state of being energized and deeply calmed. Like all peak experiences these states help Vampyres move to higher states of self-evolution. This is great for balanced humans dedicated to self-evolution but can create traumatic instability in humans who are not ready. Exchange was the ancient human method of initiation and is still practiced in certain Shaivite, Sufi, Polynesian, Australian, and American Indian traditions—as well in some modern Left-Hand Path traditions. It is not the vulgar notion of telepathy. It isn't linear communication of facts, nor is it a heightened sense of emotional sharing. Exchange between living people can result in post-incarnate exchange as well. Tread lightly; the ice is thinner than you think.

Storing Energy

Now that we've surveyed the major ways that energy can be obtained, let us consider how it may be stored. Most energy, when it is obtained, goes directly to the Vampyric self. It renews/replaces existing energy. As the Vampyre comes into being, she gains both a greater capacity to store/use energy and a greater need for it. This is the frightful aspect of the Vampyric Way. It is not a take-it-or-leave-it approach to self-evolution. The rapid gains that can occur are offset by the need for more energy. Many humans cannot deal with this in a balanced way, so they either plunge into addiction to one of the methods listed above (becoming something as socially acceptable as a tree hugger or as socially unacceptable as an extreme masochist) or they develop issues with depression.

So why are we concerned with storing energy? Like hunting, there are times of luck. We may either by design (or by accident) find ourselves with a great surfeit of energy. Visiting a certain environment—like Maui or the Grand Canyon or Stonehenge—may flood us with more energy than we can apply to our energetic selves. Or we have great sex, or huge wonder, and so on. So here are some basic storage devices.

Art. Since energy surplus is easy to shift into creativity, making art—painting, jewelry, music, tattoos, and so forth—is a natural storage device. Interestingly, the art object becomes a gateway for other Vampyres. They can't steal your art, but they will find their own access to energy in viewing it or hearing it. Cultural conditioning may apply.

Egregore. Placing your energy into an egregore—whether a naturally occurring one like your family or self-chosen tribe or a magically created one—is a very simple wish. Humans inherited this skill as part of their primate status. The famous opening scenes of *2001: A Space Odyssey* illustrate this well. Of course, energy placed in an egregore becomes available to all members of a tribe, which established the link among tribes, shamans, and survival back at the dawn of humankind.

Perfume and Incense. Humans store memories with olfactory clues. Thus, if one is flooded with energy in the presence of a certain smell, this smell becomes a personal gateway to energy. This has misled occultists for centuries to think that certain perfumes had power and is also the reason that Vampyres must never, never use cheap cologne. Wise Vampyres will learn to use expensive cologne with the smallest possible dab of an occult oil to create their own scent.

Story. Stories are the method by which the Vampyric archetype reasserted itself after the Enlightenment. Creating your own narratives is singularly powerful.

Mudra. The body is the Vampyre's most powerful tool. The use of mudras, or hand gestures, to control energy exists in most magickal traditions. The secret is not in learning someone else's prepackaged signs as a source of energy but in learning to use these signs as a way of storing your own energy. If a gesture spontaneously occurs in an energized state or is revealed to you in dreaming, it is worth far more than looking up and copying other people's gestures. Likewise, yoga postures and dance are useful ways to store energy.

Tiki. Creating a tiki, fetish, or idol to store energy is a powerful method. The energy transfer is easily accomplished by the laying on of hands or by breath. There are three considerations. First, would you like the fetish to be public? It could be a troll doll in your office, if you are accepting of its aesthetic. Second, if you enter into a symbolic agreement, you are bound by that agreement. Vampyric energy is not an objective force of physics; the troll will not test differently in a lab after you have charged it, but its theft will mean a loss of energy for you. Third, energy has personality/structure. If you charge a pink teddy bear for your niece, it won't also hex that bad mayor, nor will your Chucky doll fix mom's cancer.

Using Energy

So, we've gained energy, we've stored energy: What's the energy for? There are four uses for Vampyric energy, from the easiest usage to one requiring the most skill and wisdom.

Gaining More Energy. The first manifestation of gaining energy is both the ability and the need to gain more energy. This is the myth of the vampire: always wanting more and bound to flesh that dies. The ugly and fearsome side of the vampire is sensed here. As this state occurs spontaneously during initiation, for some humans this created the entire myth in modern occultism (we'll come back to this when considering the word "Thelema" in a later chapter). If Vampyres do have at least a theoretical understanding of the other uses of energy, they should not seek this path, for they will merely become monsters.

Magic and Sorcery. These will be discussed fully in chapter 4, but both require changing the subjective universe to produce a change in the objective universe. Vampyric energy is not the fuel or medium of magic, but it can quicken or supercharge magical effects. For example, a highly energized Vampyre can cause great effects tossing a penny into a mall fountain and making a wish, whereas his ritual magician counterpart might spend hours agonizing over correct hours and correspondences. This energetic potential can have negative consequences as well. The Vampyre might easily stir things up by his presence—entering an old temple or handling an accursed object that a thousand other people had handled with impunity. Of course this is because Vampyres wish for the unknown—at least until it shows up.

Immortality. Immortality is the great goal of the Vampyric art. To enter into the state of being a powerful essence that supports both models of yourself and influences/explores the Cosmos is the Great Work. All humans have immortality, but Vampyres have access to a more conscious, joyous, and focused immortality. Sensing this difference in the Vampyre is a cause for hatred from the average human, but this can be overcome if the Vampyre takes her place as a healer of the world.

Alchemy. The last item, alchemy, or more simply, heating, is the most subtle of the arts. As humans Awaken into the possibility of a powerful immortality, there's a problem. We suck. Now, the Vampyric Path shows us how to lose those parts of us that aren't ours. Get rid of that hovering voice of your stepfather that claims you are lazy or of that college romantic partner that insists you are dumb. But then there are the parts of yourself that are you. And some of them aren't pretty. The social parasite says you can just repress them. Like most of its strategies this can work only for a short time, and then the undesirable behavior and perceptions are back—but stronger this time. The immature Vampyre may simply accept them. "Sure I'm a monster. We're all monsters!" But the mature Vampyre knows about heat. By constant heating of the Vampyric self, impurities and flaws burn away. The lead of your makeup can be turned to gold. We'll return to this in Book the Third.

The Vampyre is a self-created energy being. You've got a glimmering of what energy is—how to get it, store it, and use it. Let's look at another part of the Vampyre's arsenal: magic!

4

MAGIC AS A WAY OF KNOWING

The Vampyre is a modern dream (or a postmodern nightmare) of the shaman. In films, in books, we don't need an explanation for it; we understand this fact mythically. In the much more constrained world of life, we need guidance for learning this most difficult of human endeavors. In this chapter we will approach magic with different lenses; like the blind men encountering the elephant in the Jainist fable, we will encounter bits and pieces of a phenomenon that stands just outside the realm of language. Magic does not fit well in the modern world of discourse, and various modernist definitions and explorations have moved us even further from that puzzling elephant. After circling as close as it can, this chapter will give you a frame rite (see p. 61) for formal magical workings. We will begin with a working definition, then analyze magic in terms of seven precepts. Fair warning for this chapter: it is an emic description (that is to say, written from inside the belief system) based on three and half decades of practice and conditioned by philosophy, linguistics, anthropology, and ludic studies—or, in other words, this is not written to bolster prejudices that the modern world has thrust upon you.

FUNDAMENTALS OF MAGIC

There are two valid definitions of *magic*. The first is, "Magic is the process of producing a change in the subjective universe that causes a proportional change in the objective universe, depending on the passion and precision of the magician." This is called the Aquino-Flowers theory. The second is, "Magic is managing synchronicities." This is called

48

the Webb theory. Non-magicians scoff at the first, not realizing how hard it is to change the subjective universe (try thinking of anything but a white bear for the next 10 seconds). Or they do not understand how resistant the objective universe is. The second theory seems unlikely to non-initiates. How can you control a synchronicity—isn't it the grace of God or the Cosmos? Both of these theories are most important if considered as guides to the feedback loop called Becoming. Let's look at certain properties of magic.

Magic is a truth process. The idea of a truth process is borrowed from French philosopher Alain Badiou. (Now, Badiou and I stand extremely far apart in politics.) He postulates that there are four areas of truth that do not exist as points of reference but instead as processes that create truth. One does not get all the answers in science, love, art, and politics. One produces truth by seeking these answers. Science did not produce the truth of the fundamental nature of matter by defining atoms. That led to the definition/discovery of electrons, protons, and neutrons. But that truth led to quarks, and so forth. One does not find truth in a political change—say *Brown v. Board of Education*—but rather by following that change in future struggles. Truth processes are the opposite of revealed religion—they demand participation in an endless game.

Magic is a fundamental truth process, but it is alien to Badiou's modernism. If one finds truth by magic, one will continue to use magic all of one's life; that's why there are many bad magicians, or why you have kept to magic despite variable results. Magic not only empowers by granting your wish, it also empowers by not granting it. Let's look at that.

Mike Mulvaney, age seventeen, armed with a used copy of *Wiccan Woo-Woo for Whitefolks,* decides to cast the love spell on Bootsie Collins, with the understanding of love only a seventeen-year-old can have.

It fails. No loving. He buys the more expensive *Setnakt's Spell Sockdolagers.* He repeats his spell with more luck on the more attainable Angie McPhearson. He has a great senior year. He decides he is unworthy of Bootsie and begins self-improvement. He begins stalking Bootsie until he meets Bootsie's dad. He spends more time with PornHub.

Or it works! Plenty of loving. He tries to get out of the relationship for the next six months. He discovers he really wanted her brother, Brad Collins. He decides Bootsie is unworthy of him and plans to go college out of state. Because he has Bootsie, other girls find him interesting. He buys the tarot set keyed to *Wiccan Woo-Woo for Whitefolks*.

In either outcome, Mike has increased his self-knowledge, made choices that will determine future development, and expanded his power in the world. The process has changed Mike, not just the goal. Now, the feedback aspect—Mike sends his Will into the Cosmos and the Cosmos answers—is the grounding of wonder that replaces faith in conventional religions.

Magic alters possibilities, not the laws of physics. Very few true believers can come to grips with this. For practical effects in the objective universe, timing and real-world constraints come into effect. This also means that the "sense" of magical success is subjective. If Mike becomes the object of Bootsie's affections, he can never know objectively if it was the effects of the love charm.

Magic is a different sort of truth process than science, which obtains hard (that is to say, objective) data. However, the subjective sense of magical accomplishment will change Mike's subjective universe and make him a more powerful magician. In this self-creating property, magic is exactly like Vampyric energy. This has another effect: if Mike's world is grounded only in subjective success, he may feel that he is becoming a more powerful magician every day. That is why the folks who do well as magicians tend to have real jobs, raise families, go to college or trade school, and so on. We will talk more about that in the third part of this book.

Magic differs from sorcery. This matters little to the casual practitioner but is the key issue to an initiate. Now, Vampyres can and should use both. *Magic* is the art of transforming the self—the body-mind-soul complex—to gain power. Magic is the process whereby willed subjective change becomes objective change. *Sorcery* is the manipulation of symbols to produce an effect in a situation. The sorcerer is essentially the same both before and after the operation.

For example, Mary Sue Machworter is broke. She performs the Vampyric money sorcery detailed in part 2 of this book. She takes four dollars and writes "Success" on them in money symbols in gold or green ink: $¢¢$$. Then she hands one of the charged bills to a beggar to the south, east, north, and west of where she lives—holding on to the bill for just a tenth of a second so the beggar has to pull slightly. A neighbor offers to buy her seldom-used barbecue grill later that day. She has not changed. Or Mary Sue tries a magical operation to make her more aware of her economic values. She performs a meditation on the rune Nauthiz, then scratches the rune on wood and scrapes the rune off into beer and drinks it. She realizes that she never puts the fact that she knows ASL on her résumé since she had just learned it organically from living with her grandmother. She signs up for a refresher course and helps out as a tutor for deaf students. Within a year she both gets certified and has an impressive job as an on-call night translator. Here she has changed in self-perception, ambition, and outer training.

You can see that this idea is embedded in the etymology of the words. *Magic* is probably derived from the Latin *magus,* from Greek μάγος, which is from the Old Persian *maguš,* which referred to a ruler with magical and religious abilities—you may remember the three Magi in the Bible. The root idea (in reconstructed Proto-Indo-European) was **magh,* which means "to be able." The notion relates to sovereignty and responsibility and is grounded in the type of feedback we discussed above. *Sorcery,* on the other hand, comes from the Middle French *sorcerie,* which ultimately comes from Latin *sors* (fate) with the idea of drawing lots. Its likely Proto-Indo-European form was **seh* (to sort, to line up). A great example would be finding a penny and feeling lucky. Sorcery is tied up in procedure, spell work, or ritual, for the most part. Magic, since it changes the magician, becomes less external. The magician needs to do a few things in the outer world and responds by sense and intuition. The Vampyre usually begins with sorcery for the most part and moves toward magic.

Magic is a form of communication. Magic is expressed in symbolic manipulation. The late Stanley J. Tambiah, Ph.D., created a good model of magic based on J. L. Austin's idea of "performative speech." A performative speech is a speech act that makes something so. For example, a judge can say, "I now pronounce you man and wife." A performative speech requires three conditions: the speaker must be empowered to make the utterance, the action takes place in the correct setting, and there must be a medium for the action to be enacted. In the case of the wedding we would need the judge (or ship's captain, rabbi, etc.), the setting (courtroom, ship, synagogue), and the medium would be the official license correctly obtained.

For a magical act, the magician's authority comes from belief and experience in successful workings. The setting must be conducive—the ritual chamber, a sacred spot, and so forth—and there must be a medium through which the act can take place. Now, the matter to be communicated needs to be communicated in a form pleasing to the magical consciousness—a form that encodes the message in a manner significant to the magician or his targets. This can be a traditional linguistic form—such as the runes or the Enochian language—or an artistic or even substance-based form (see p. 53).

The message, once sent out, must interact with the mysterious other side of the universe—just as a letter dropped in the mailbox must first travel to the recipient, who then must open it, read it, and respond. The other side of the universe responds—this can be in Mary Sue's neighbor's offer to her, or in Mary Sue's own self-remembering of her deaf grandmother. Very few magicians make use of this model because it requires three things:

1. You have to have established yourself in your own subjective universe as a magician. This can be helped by verbal formulas such as "I, the Vampyre Setnakt, do command the forces of Darkness to . . ." Or by external titles such as Adept, Witch, Druid, and so on. But mainly the authority comes from experience, which is why journal keeping is a good practice.

2. You have to find a form to encipher your message that is either pleasing to you or your targets (see discussion of lesser magic on p. 55). Learning a system of magic is helpful, but understanding the magical side of the universe is helpful as well. The magical side of the universe reacts/responds with dream logic and psychological archetypes. Colorful and mysterious actions are needed. Mary Sue didn't

say, "Hey, magical universe, I need an extra $257.32 this month to fix my radiator! Chop! Chop!" She used symbols (even if as ordinary as $ and ¢), colors, and emotionally laden deeds: being brave enough to approach the beggars, triggering their emotions, and a level of difficulty—finding beggars in four cardinal directions.

3. The medium needs be related to the message. Mary Sue used money and need in her sorcery. So, the money came from her area in cash form. The answer was more or less given to her and, like the guy hustling on the street corners, won't last very long. In the magical working she activated the Nauthiz rune, which contains the idea of being prepared; symbolically it's two sticks rubbed together to make fire. She created the message with labor and took the message into her being. The answer came in the form of something within (memory) and something without (work needed in the outer world).

Magic can be language/performative based or substance based. Although Mr. Tambiah's semiotic model is strong, this does not mean that ritual- or language-based magic is either more accurate or more powerful. Magic can be expressed by art or music or even cooking. The Vampyre must learn the magic of cooking and perfumes at a bare minimum.

Magic has some rules. The subjective universe has structure. All traditional systems—Celtic, Aztec, Germanic, Egyptian, Tibetan, and so on—have soul craft. Vampyric magic has a simple soul craft. You have a body (product of genetics and environment), a social parasite (product of culture, family, economic class, education, paragenetics), sub-selves created by experience, the Vampyric self, and the unnamable timeless source.

For the most part the social parasite rules your mind, producing the internal monologue that you incorrectly call your thoughts. This, plus the emotional states produced by your body (mainly) and your assorted selves constitute your emotions, which limit and confuse your internal monologue. Through Vampyric practice you may learn to transcend the internal monologue enough to master (at least for brief moments) your subjective universe. Some guidelines or rules apply.

THE SEVEN RULES OF MAGIC

1. Magic takes the path of least resistance. If you do a money working, you'll find that quarter under your mattress. This is dealt with by gratitude (thanking yourself) and mindfulness (asserting: "It is beginning.").

2. Magic enhances action; it does not replace it. If you are performing an operation for love, you should attend to making yourself attractive, charming, and available. In general, scantily clad folks of the desired gender will not come knocking at your door. (Experience shows that when this occurs it does not end well; see no. 4.)

3. Magic has little effect on the minds of drunk people, stupid people, or folks whose inner life is gone. The uncharged cell phone receiveth not the call.

4. Magic users and mystics are easy to influence with magic. This does not mean that these are superior folk—many of these humans have open holes in their psyches. Humans who are undergoing growth—especially growth they've put off or repressed—are very sensitive to magic. This is why human society developed rites of passage. Humans naturally seek magic to change their fate. Likewise they develop great faith in whatever external magic or sorcery changed them. This is why humans developed religion and politics.

5. Magic that has worked before will work again. Magic that you *believe* worked before will likely work again.

6. A magical operation does not begin and end with the ritual. The moods and circumstances leading up to the performance, the details of the performance, and the moods and circumstances after the manifestation (if any) are part of the operation. The part your social parasite labels the "magic" is the tip of the iceberg—and certainly not the dangerous part. Well-wrought magical operations never truly end.

7. Never deny what magic has given you, or it will be taken away. If the subjective universe is forced to disbelieve in what it has wrought it gives up to the social parasite. One can and should be skeptical; one cannot be materialist.

COLORS AND FLAVORS OF MAGIC

Magic can be divided in many ways. This is the American Left-Hand Path schema of three flavors and thirteen shades. The Catholic Church originally divided magic into "natural," which consisted of using planets and properties of herbs and minerals, and "demonic," which was anything else, since if God wasn't doing the special effects it must come from the other side. Trickier was "angelic" magic: if you could talk an angel into doing something it was probably okay, but this left the church a tad squeamish. Why wasn't YHVH doing the chain-of-command stuff?

Then popular fiction came along and gave us white magic and black magic. The white stuff was good and included healing, blessing, enlightening, protecting, and the black stuff was bad—cursing, vaporizing, compelling. All religious groups and occult groups, of course, said their practices were white and the practices of the Other were black. And really edgy magicians could say they were gray.

Then Anton LaVey came along and turned this on its ear. White Magic was stuff you did for your group's acceptance and approval, and Black Magic was what you did for your own damn self. If you healed your foot from gout, it was Black Magic. If you sent thoughts and prayers to the starving Christians in China—especially if you did it loudly on Sunday and dropped some coin in the collection plate—it was White. He divided Black Magic into shades—Greater and Lesser.

There are some drawbacks to this terminology (as we'll see later), but what's done is done. Lesser Black Magic was using psychology and symbols (or scientific principles) to control others for your Will. If you seduce your date by telling her Geminis are smart and artistic, you've performed Lesser Black Magic on her. You make people leave the conference room because you caused the air to be positively ionized—that's LBM. You discover and use the cologne your girlfriend's father uses and you get laid—that's LBM. Powerful stuff.

Greater Black Magic is formal ritual—candles and gongs, or even Tesla coils and strobes. LaVey also said that magic came in two broad flavors—operative and illustrative. Operative was for changing something. Illustrative was for changing your point of view or insight about something. In LaVey's schema a rite of passage ritual would be illustrative. For example, a somewhat oppressed housewife creates a pyschodrama to illustrate the household that she runs and gains insight into achieving such a household through illustrative magic, or she does a spell to hasten her husband's doom through operative magic. LaVey, although himself a misogynist, recognized that women were getting the raw end of society's deal, and that meant that they would have ample magical power.

Guiniviere Webb added a third flavor: receptive. Receptive magic is a mood of intense openness to signal and power. You perhaps recently performed a receptive working by spotting this book and deciding to give it a try. Receptive magic is difficult—very few magical how-to books deal with what you do as you get your wish. You may think about that.

Michael Aquino took Anton's two shades of black and added a third. Medial Black Magic. Greater Black Magic was a blend of structure (invocation and opening rites) and anti-structure: you did something initiatory in your heightened state—something unscripted, inspired, and transformative. In the medial shade you used existing/explored channels of power to effect change. In the example above, Mary Sue's rune casting would be medial. Lesser would involve conveying your Will to others without them knowing it.

I've expanded the schema to include Red, Purple, and Gold. So here are Uncle Setnakt's "thirty-seven varieties." Scoops Ahoy, eat your heart out.

White Magic

White Magic is the magic of union, submission, and obedience. It presupposes that the self is an illusion from a greater whole or that its worth be reckoned as a sacrifice to that whole (or its owner/boss). Lesser White Magic, the power of the social parasite, is reinforced by symbolic display—either sincere or for purposes of signaling conformity. This would include displaying the Gay Pride flag, the Confederate flag, a pro- or anti-Trump bumper sticker, engaging in school prayer or wearing a T-shirt advertising your favorite Mexican restaurant.

Medial White Magic, the easiest magic to perform, is the cultivation of trance states (either inhibitory or excitatory) for the purpose of invoking a prepackaged Other to do magical work for you. Examples would include saying the Lord's Prayer, the Hare Krishna mantram, davening, Dervish dancing, offering incense at a Shinto shrine, prayers to the Goddess, and so on. The human admits the powerlessness of his or her self (which is identified with the social parasite) and projects his or her magic through a socially created intermediary. Emotional fervor rather than skill is the main energy source.

Greater White Magic is the sacrifice of the social parasite to the Other and is often accompanied by sacrifice of possessions or social power, or physical privation. Examples include the suffering of Christian saints, Islamic terrorists blowing themselves up, Buddhist monks immolating themselves to protest war, the selfless devotion of certain nurses, and most forms of samadhi wherein union with a god or God/Brahma/Tao is sought. If you like fancy Sanskrit terms this is *śaraṇāgatī*.

Black Magic

Black Magic is the magic of self-empowerment, ranging from the least evolutionary forms of the will to power to the most noble forms of self-deification.

Lesser Black Magic, the most outwardly powerful form of magic to master, is the art of covertly conveying one's Will as a guiding principle in the behavior of another. It is also called meta-communication. Examples would include applied psychology, manipulative neuro-linguistic programming (NLP), advertising, pheromones, ELF waves, or telling Aunt Tilly that she will be haunted unless she gives you Uncle Irwin's old Cadillac. Guile, psychological knowledge, or *metis* are the source of power in this operation.

Medial Black Magic, the actions the average human considers "magic," requires both knowledge and passion. Examples would include Chaos Magic, rune casting, goetic magic, hoodoo, making a wish by tossing a penny in a mall fountain, or *sārūpya*. (For my Setian readers, we call sārūpya Xem, 'cause that's how we roll.)

Greater Black Magic is the process of causing the nameless, timeless self to become manifest in such a manner that evolution, enlightenment, and empowerment of the manifest self is evident both in ecstasy and enstasy (at the time of the operation) and there is marked change in the thoughts, words, and deeds of the operator. Examples would include the attainment of the grade of Magister Templi by Aleister Crowley, the Alone Working of Lilith Aquino, the experience of Cosmic Consciousness by Richard Bucke, or the Enlightenment experience of Phillip K. Dick.

Red Magic

Red Magic is willed submission to an authority/regimen to transform or purify the manifest self. This is a dangerous practice for Sleeping or semi-Awake humans in that it usually becomes White Magic.

Lesser Red Magic is the observance of form to regulate the binding of time. Examples would include jogging in the morning, attending Alcoholics Anonymous meetings, writing in your journal, or wearing a uniform.

Medial Red Magic is the use of mild trance states to focus the social parasite to signals from outside its programing. Examples would include *Liber Resh,* reciting the rune row every day, mala-bead rosaries, and ritual banishing. The needed forces here are Will (do it no matter what) and mindfulness (do not forget why you are doing it).

Greater Red Magic is the ordeal that strips the power of the social parasite and allows the direct perception of the manifest world by the unmanifest self. Examples would include the Chaos Magic pilgrimage, the Sun Dance, or going through basic training in the Marine Corps. Without mindfulness, Red Magic becomes White Magic; without Will, Red Magic becomes a non-transformative masochistic entertainment.

Purple Magic

Purple Magic, which Victor Tuner calls *communitas,* is the magic of the circle, the isolated group of initiates. This involves elements of social risk, fraternity, and group willingness to discover/create another reality. Notably, this can shade into White or Black magic. In the examples above, carrying a Gay Pride flag in the streets of San Francisco is pure Lesser White Magic. If two guys carry the same flag in the streets of a backwater town in the American South it is Lesser Purple Magic. Purple Magic often, but not always, is about honoring a symbol of spiritual dissent such as the Prince of Darkness.

Lesser Purple Magic, or the Way of the Trickster, is the championing of an antinomian principle in an ambiguous circumstance. Examples include Nosferatu on Board bumper stickers, Halloween decorations, Mr. Rogers sharing a kiddie pool with Officer Clemmons in 1969, Zuni clown dancers, and that device that makes your toilet seat talk.

Medial Purple Magic is the subordinating of the social parasite toward the dual end of invoking an antinomian principle while seeking (and hopefully achieving) communication with the unmanifest self. Examples would include the activity of the Church of Satan (especially 1966–1974), early feminist Wicca, wearing unpopular religious jewelry, or the ritual activites of Anita Hoffman, Jerry Rubin, Abbie Hoffman, Tuli Kulpferberg, and Alan Ginsberg.

Greater Purple Magic is the sārūpya (becoming the god) of a Trickster figure in a group setting.

Gold Magic

Gold Magic is the simultaneous performance of all the above. Examples would include Crowley receiving and teaching *The Book of the Law,* Aquino's *The Book of Coming Forth by Night,* or Flowers's transmission of the Odhinnsmal's Runa. This would include, for example, all of Stephen Edred Flowers's life before hearing the Word Runa, his Hearing the Word Runa, seeking education to transmit the Word, passing through the degree system of the Temple of Set, founding the Rune-Gild, and writing forty books. Gold Magic is also called life work.

These forms are useful to clarify intent. Magic, which begins in the subjective universe, is strongly flavored by intent. The same external action can have different meanings and effects. Bill, Phil, and Will left water in coolers for illegal immigrants on a hot Texas summer day. For Bill it was Greater White Magic: moved by his understanding of the word *agape,* he spent his not very abundant dollars and time and took the cooler out. Phil was engaged in Lesser Purple Magic: he drove the guys (and the coolers) from Austin to the border with his FUCK TRUMP bumper sticker and matching T-shirt. Will was doing Lesser Black Magic: he shot a selfie of himself leaving the water, which would become a poster when he ran for city commissioner in the very liberal city of Austin. That's easy to follow. But what if Bill, Will, and Phil were the *same* guy doing a complex action?

VAMPYRIC MAGIC FUNDAMENTALS

Now let's set up for some ritual Vampyre magic. Most Vampyric work is done without formal ritual. It is an "empty hand" technique improvised on the spot; however, learning to design rituals and deal with maintaining one's intent in trance states is among the easiest ways of accessing/focusing/amplifying the Vampyric self. Magic grows in a feedback loop, so repeating simple procedures is the best way to capture attention and build up confidence in one's action. We'll start with some guidelines, then get to the rite itself.

———— Four Guidelines for Vampyric Magic ————

1. Vampyric magic is focused. Decorate your chamber sparingly; think about each new item. You want to train the Will with as few props as possible.
2. Timing is highly important. If you want to manifest something big (like the perfect job), do the magical work early—maybe six months in advance. If you are working to influence another human, work when they are at a low ebb—for example, ninety minutes before they rise for the day.
3. Keep records of your work, repeat that which is successful.
4. Do not tell others of your work unless their knowledge of it is part of the energy you're channeling.

————————

What follows is a frame rite and, within it, the Vampyric Invocation. Frame rites might be thought of as being power outlets. You design your intention as a set of verbal and symbolic actions, and you "plug" it into your frame rite. This is very basic. Start with this. You will be called on to repeat the Vampyric Invocation many times throughout this book, so mark the page or copy the invocation for your reference.

Here are your steps.

FRAME RITE

0. Design your work—consider its opportunities, dangers, possibility of manifestation.
1. Choose the time and place for the rite.
2. Prepare your chamber. At the minimum you will need an altar draped or painted flat black set on the northern side of the room, three candles (two red, one black), a holder for incense, a source of music or white noise, a goblet, a symbol of magic (an image of the Big Dipper, inverse pentagram, etc.), writing materials to record results/impressions, and a shiny surface— hand mirror, polished obsidian, etc. As you develop your style you will add to your tools.
3. Dress for your work. It need not be ritual robes; it can be your power dress or your best suit.
4. Turn off all connections to the outside world—cell phones, computers, etc.
5. Perfume the chamber; fill it with ambient sounds. I prefer copal and thunderstorm sounds. Let your taste be the judge. Fill the goblet with icy water or an appropriate nectar. Never blood!
6. Place the three candles in a triangle with the black candle being the focusing candle. If you are working to receive energy or illumination, face the triangle South. For gathering information from the past or strategic advice, aim the triangle East. If you wish to change the political landscape, aid or influence another human, or communicate with an invisible entity, North is preferred. If you wish to drain the energy of another

or work justice or vengeance, West. Light the candles—red, black, red. As you light the candles say:

I gather energy, I purify energy, I send forth energy.

7. Gaze upon your symbol until you feel it Gazes upon you.

8. Say the Vampyric Invocation:

In the Name of Arkte, mother of life and death, I arise from the tomb of mankind to the sacred night. I stretch my soul into the Up and Out, and I am freed from time and convention. The One Becomes the Five.

In the South, I am the Mummy, wrapped in Magic and Sorcery, living from Aeon to Aeon. In the East, I am the Owl, great of Metis, who picks the best strategy each time. In the North, I am the wolf, loyal to my pack who unerringly knows friend from foe. In the West, I am the Vampire Bat, swift, ruthless, and bloodthirsty. In the center of the world I am the unique intimate spark of fire that blends the Red Flame of Life and the Black Flame of Mind.

The Five speak, and all things that aide us are set free, all things that hinder us are bound, the best of the ancients and the moderns inform our Will. I am the Vampyre [VN] (i.e., your Vampyric Name), and I re-create this world as the place of my Hunting and my Play. Look upon my Deeds with Awe, with Envy, with Worship. As it was when humans sharpened flints and feared the Children of the Night, so it is now.

9. Offer the food or drink.

As Lord Dattatreya offered his flesh to his students as a blessing, I offer this food to those who rule the world in the Name of the Great Vampyre. As the receiver of this offering I offer thanks for my nightly sustenance.

10. Make the statement of intent:

I, the Vampyre [VN], child of Setnakt, child of Lilith, change the Cosmos this night. It is my Will that . . .

11. Insert your working here.
12. Closing:

> *My Magic prevails without mercy. My Magic finds its warriors with rapid accuracy. My Magic manifests by the wisest path. My Magic endureth from Aeon to Aeon. My Magic is incarnate in my words, my thoughts, my deeds, my dreams, and my circumstance. Hail the ancient dreams! The Five Become the One and enrich the One!*

13. Meditate on what you have seen—both with your inner eyes and in the chamber. Close your eyes and try to "swallow" your memories.
14. Extinguish the candles in reverse order from your lighting of them, and say:

> *My Energy existed long before this body, long before this Rite. My Energy brings me Power, Pleasure, and Wisdom. My Energy will exist after the passing of this dying world.*

15. Turn on the lights, put things away. Write down your record of the rite.
16. Immerse yourself in another activity that totally engages you (from a nature walk to sex to meeting friends for cake and coffee). Under no circumstances speak of the rite to anyone unless they are a fellow magician working with you.
17. Before going to sleep, stand (preferably naked) before a mirror and say:

> *I send my memories to the wonderland of dreams this night, so I may know more marvels.*

Drink a goblet full of water while staring in the mirror. If you recall any dreams—regardless of how silly their contents—record these the next day as well.

Now you have a basic frame rite. Let's have three examples of using it: workings for love, employment, and illumination.

SAMPLE WORKINGS

A Love Working

The Vampyre Miracalla wants the physical and spiritual love of Dorothy, a work colleague. They meet in a large social group every Friday. Miracalla wants to tip the odds her way before asking Dorothy out. She performs the following pre-working activities. She asks Dorothy's help in a project twice and then rewards her with chocolate chip cookies delivered to her office, thereby conditioning her to have a sense of exchange and pleasure. She observes Dorothy's favorite colors and dress style. She obtains a doll with similar color hair and dresses her to resemble Dorothy. Here is the ritual working she inserted into her frame rite.

She rises at 3:00 a.m. to do the work. Normally she would point the triangle north, but instead she aims it toward Dorothy's flat.

Gazing at the doll she says, "Dorothy, you adore me. You sacrifice yourself willingly to me. Your heart, your brain, your pussy are attuned to me. You tremble at my touch."

She marks the neck of the doll with two dots of red fingernail polish. She visualizes herself flying into Dorothy's flat and biting her in the approved Hammer film style.

"I draw your Essence into me. It changes my thoughts, my words, and my deeds. It remakes me in the shape of your dreams. When I come to you, I am the perfect lover. I am reborn by the arts of Hecate and Inanna as your perfect lover. I cast away my imperfections and weaknesses. I am the Angel of your hopes and the Demon of your darkest desires."

She closes her eyes and imagines feeding blood to Dorothy. "Oh, Beloved, I have taken but I give more. My essence changes you. It opens forgotten memories of love and pleasure. It gently opens dreams of magic and lust. It remakes you in the shape of my dreams. You will be my perfect lover."

She lays the doll upon the altar and then masturbates to climax, saying Dorothy's name at the moment of greatest intensity. Gathering her breath, she picks up a red candle and lets a single drop of wax fall upon the doll.

"By Ereshkigal, Queen of the Great Below, I seal you to me. You see no other, think of no other, lie with no other. You prepare yourself for me. For I am Miracalla. I am Ereshkigal."

She picks up the black candle and allows a single drop of black wax to fall on her left hand.

"Love is a rose with the fragrance that awakens memory, the red that quickens passion, the softness of the bed chamber, the many layers of misery, and the thorny pain of separation. I accept the pains and pleasures of Love. Hail Eros!"

She ends the rite as above. She covers the doll in black silk. She begins wearing the red fingernail polish and gently flirting and joking with Dorothy. On the Friday one month after the working, she asks her out. When the relationship is secure, she takes the doll out of the black silk and says, "I thank you creature of Art. You fulfilled your place until the real came along. I send you to bliss in the court of Ereshkigal, free from ties to me or my beloved." Then she disposes of the doll in a respectful, yet mysterious way, such as throwing it into a nearby creek or burying it in a rose garden, but not tossing it in the trash.

A Working for Employment

The Vampyre Jacobus desires employment in a state agency. He has researched the hiring procedures, verified that although it might be a stretch, he is qualified for a top-tier job. Before the rite he saw a postcard from the 1960s that showed the agency's building downtown. He bought it for fifty cents. He inserts the following words and deeds into the frame rite.

He points the triangle to the north.

"Time bows before my Will. Time is a Fire in which I burn, but by my awakened Will, I am that Fire." He passes the postcard through the flames of the candle. "Time is a River that sweeps all away, but by my awakened Will, I am that River." He takes a single drop of water from the goblet and wets the picture side of the postcard. "Time is a Tiger that eats all men, but by my awakened Will, I am that Tiger." He slaps the postcard down on the altar and imagines himself a tiger.

He takes a nice pen and writes himself a thank-you note for working at the agency. He mentions salary, retirement, mission, and challenge.

He addresses the postcard to himself and puts a stamp on the postcard.

He says, "Humans give to the gods that they might give to humans. Gods give to humans, so that they might be cherished. I give my future self perception, hard work, and hope. My future self gives me pleasure, power, and a platform to do good work. I am a god, the creation of humans. I am a human, the descendant of gods."

He closes the rite in the manner described above in the frame rite. The next day he goes to the agency's building and drops the postcard in the outgoing mail. After he receives it he lays it under his black altar cloth and pursues the agency's listings via the internet. On the day of his retirement he burns the postcard and scatters the ashes around the agency building, thanking himself for his experiences.

A Working for Illumination

The Vampyre Saturnus has been fascinated by the philosophy and science of time and duration. Years of reading and countless hours of meditation have given him some deep theories. Before the working, he buys a plastic one-minute timer from a thrift store, the closest replica he can find to his mother's egg timer. He buys some black fingernail polish and practices painting figures before the rite. He chooses three texts to read after the rite: *Infernal Geometry* by Toby Chappell, *Being and Time* by Martin Heidegger, and *The Labyrinth of Time* by Anthony Peake. He had read them years before and found they suggested useful ideas to him.

He places the books, the egg timer, a blank notebook, and the nail polish on his altar. He faces the triangle south. He plays the theme from *Time Tunnel* as his compression music. He inserts the following words and deeds into the frame rite.

"Human opens his eyes and knows there is Above and Below, Left and Right, Forward and Behind. And he says, 'I am god, king, unconstrained.' Then an evil voice whispers, 'You are too young to know good and evil, then you will be too old and feeble to do good or evil. Then you will be dead and forgotten.' And the human says, 'I am a slave, dead, a speck of nothing.' Then an eviler voice whispers, 'You came from outside the circles of time. You play in the streams of time as part of a Great Rite of the Nameless God. You return to the timeless zone you never left from.' And the Magician arises and says, 'I am human and not human. I am Vampyre, and time grows faces to teach me the rules of the Great Game.'

"There are twelve zones alternating between Life and Death, binding all save for those called Vampyre. For those called Vampyre they are a game board. Tell me the rules, O Urdhr, Verdandi, Skuld. Show me the dice, O Anake, Aion, Moros. Give me a get-out-of-jail-free card, O Zurvan, Heh, Shai. Sell me hotels, O Etu, Purysho, Shiva."

He takes the timer, and on one end he paints the astrological symbol of Saturn, a god of time. On the other end he paints the yin-yang symbol.

"I will reread these books and then play the Great Game for thirty-three days. I will share what I learn with other Vampyres."

He closes the rite in the normal manner. He rereads the chosen books, making notes on his computer as he does so. When he is done, he plays the following game: for three minutes a night (measured by the timer) he free writes his ideas on time in the notebook (without looking at his notes or any book). When he has done this for thirty-three days, he smashes the timer with a sledgehammer. Then he reads his notebook and his notes. He creates an article (or perhaps even a book) that he shares with the world at large—or perhaps just a certain esoteric circle.

Note that each working is not just about the wish but also about inner changes and future plans. Miracalla doesn't just enchant Dorothy; she seeks to become Dorothy's perfect lover and enacts a time when their love is not merely dependent on a spell. Jacobus doesn't just wish for a job but for the ability to enjoy the job and do good work (for mankind) there as well. He honors his magic in secret rather than in a brag. Saturnus doesn't expect the ideas to just come to him and does the hard work of organizing his illumination and sharing with others. You have begun to see the scope of magic and its relationship to the Vampyre. Let's look at the virtues and vices of the Vampyric Path and some of the modes of life that it suggests, empowers, and even demands.

5

THE GOOD, THE BAD, THE NECESSARY

Any path, as opposed to a static set of practices, requires certain conditions in its travelers, has certain obstacles to be overcome, and travels through certain territory. The path is not a highway, there are not maps, most of the time you will go alone, and the rate of progress is your own. This chapter will deal with the path. First, we'll talk about the four totems mentioned in the invocation. Then we will deal with the seven strengths needed to take the path of the Vampyre and the seven weaknesses that can stop your journey. Finally, we'll deal with the question of how you can tell you are on the path and the eight territories you will likely pass through.

THE TOTEMS

In Christian Europe, the blessed dead were buried so they would rise and face the east, the presumed site of Jesus's (a solar god) return. Those who took their own life, practiced sorcery, or otherwise pissed off the church were positioned to face the north. The totems are arranged around such a rising undead: the mummy behind her, the owl to her right, the wolf running ahead, and the bat in the darkness to the left. Each represents an aspect of the Vampyric self.

Mummy. The mummy is representative of four ideas. First, Egypt has had a tremendous grasp of Western magic since late antiquity. Romans, Greeks, and Victorians all agreed—Egypt is the source of magical tradition. Sorcery is based on common belief—accurate or not. Blavatsky and Crowley based their systems on Egypt and India. Florence Farr, Crowley's teacher in the Golden Dawn, attempted to astrally link with mummies in the British Museum—so when Crowley honeymooned in Cairo, it was the natural thing to head to the Great Pyramid on the spring equinox. Second, Egyptians believed that virtuous practice was needed in this life to gain entrance into the next. One had to do good deeds in one's community and be remembered to continue both in the afterlife and have influence in this life. Third, the Egyptian did not see his or her afterlife as a gift from the gods or solely as a reward for good actions. Lore and spells learned while alive were a prerequisite to having a powerful postmortem existence. Finally, the Vampyre's political and ethical views are not tied up in current states or economic systems—just as an ancient Egyptian would find our life baffling, our consciousness will survive into a world we find baffling.

Owl. The owl, companion of Athena, is chosen for four reasons. First, it is a symbol of wisdom—in particular for the Greek word *metis,* which is often translated as "cunning." The owl knows which intelligence to use—emotional, logical, musical, and so on—in a given situation. Second, in both European and Native American cultures its cry is a warning to the wise and a curse to the foolish. Third, it likes solitary, even desolate, settings. Finally, it is a well-established icon of Halloween, another example of sorcery.

Wolf. The wolf is chosen for four reasons. First, as a creature of the pack, it is known for its loyalty. Second, wolves (and their domestic cousins, dogs) have an ability to size up humans as good or bad, fearful or calm, quickly. Third, wolves are seen as a metaphor for warrior initiation in many cultures. The wolf reminds the Vampyre of the virtue of Red Magic. Finally, wolves are sometimes used as mounts by European witch figures—the Vampyre must cultivate warrior friends for times of trouble.

Bat. The fourth totem, the vampire bat, is chosen for four reasons. First, its bite is numbing. When the vampire bat bites a sleeping target, the target does not waken. Second, it derives its nourishment from the physical analogue of energy. Third, it perceives its environment by its own signal. Just as the vampire bat uses echolocation, the Vampyre finds her way by "seeing" how others react to her signal. Finally, this totem has the strongest connection to the Vampyre in popular mythology—even though it was the last added to the popular mind.

VAMPYRIC VIRTUES

The Vampyre uses the totems as a quick guide for action in developing situations. But there are seven virtues that guide long-term actions.

Daring. The Vampyre will choose novel situations and leave her comfort zone. This leads to better hunting in the now, and it also prepares the Vampyre for the most novel of all human states—the afterlife.

Curiosity. The Vampyre knows that the purest energy comes from making the unknown known. She will place herself in situations where questions arise and can be discovered by truth processes.

Balance. Nothing is as unbalancing for a human than surplus energy. As soon as there is more than enough energy for survival, humans' natural impulse to Sleep will cause them to pour that energy in an established channel. We've all known (perhaps even from the mirror) a human who has more than average energy and pours all of himself into his job, or his art, or a hobby. The psychiatric disorder called bipolar is an example of a Sleeping human with a touch of Vampyric ability. He pours all his vast energy into work or sex or spending money until he is forced back into the "coffin" of depression. The Vampyre learns to analyze his life and energy usage.

Eagerness. The Vampyre is constantly aware of the passage of time. He begins practice at once. He doesn't wait to read every book, buy the best magical tools, and so on. He begins with what he has. One of my best students began practice while serving on a nuclear submarine—using tiny tools fashioned out of trash.

Common Sense. The Vampyre lives in the real world of jobs, school, parenting, and so forth. She knows how to balance her practice with real-world concerns. For example, she may read about night-walking techniques later in this book but lack a safe neighborhood to practice this meditation, so she finds an alternative by becoming a power walker at a shopping mall. Or unable to use incense because of asthma, she becomes expert at essential oils.

Persistence. More than any other esoteric path, the Vampyric Way requires constant practice. Since the Vampyre must deal with times of surplus energy or times when energy is low, the temptation to stop practice—or take a break for a few months—is always there. The myth of the vampire lying in his coffin for years until reawakened comes from this reality.

Gratitude. The Vampyre always thanks herself, her teachers, her allies, and the Cosmos. Gratitude is literally healing for the brain. It kills self-importance, loneliness, and depression. It stores energy in the form of memories. It cooks away flaws.

SOCIAL PARASITE SINS

Like the Catholic Church, Uncle Setnakt has a list of seven sins as well. These are defense mechanisms of the social parasite. At times—particularly during trauma—these may have saved you, if by nothing other than allowing you to fit into the herd. When these manifest in your life, be gentle in removing them. Even thank the social parasite for developing them in the first place.

Cowardice. Fear is essential for survival. If used properly in initiation, it is a source of energy. Cowardice is a reaction of the social parasite. Here is an example: Robert wanted to see the new vampire movie. His movie buddy John called at the last minute to cancel. Robert decided not to go because he would feel weird being by himself at the movies. Robert can't walk around in a graveyard (in a good part of town) by himself. Robert can't buy a book on sex magic from a bookstore, so has made Amazon richer.

Solipsism. As humans begin to discover the power of their subjective universe there is the slippery moment that lets them think they are gods. Everything is caused by them. They choose their own reality. This is a very poisonous form of thought. Not only does it end practice, it can lead to dangerous irresponsibility in both life choices and relationship issues. Various magical ideologies promote this idea.

Self-Hatred. Solipsism's ugly cousin, self-hatred, is a dangerous by-product of Awakening. Every human on this planet has done many stupid things. We all have persistent patterns of behavior that we know are wrong, hurtful, or simply stupid. If we do not have an understanding based on the notions of process—this stuff takes time—and nourished by the difficult act of self-love, we will fall into this trap. This mood hits all Awakened humans, but it must be countered by Will in the Vampyre. Self-hatred in the inventory of a human with surplus energy is the spiritual equivalent of drunk driving.

Self-Importance. Many people will be surprised to see this on the list. Self-importance feeds cowardice and solipsism. It begins with the idea that you are essential to the world, and therefore the world owes you a place. I knew a would-be Vampyre who had never missed a day of work for eight years. I suggested that he take a day off to perform a certain pilgrimage. He said he couldn't do this because it would be very cold that day and no one would turn off the water in the outbuildings that night. I asked if this was a difficult or arcane procedure, but he said that he was the only one he trusted for this vital function.

Certainty. The world we create in our heads is the best model we have both of ourselves and the rest of the objective universe. If we treat anything as absolutely known, we both end our hope for change and our ability to effect things magically. It also just makes the universe dull. Aleister Crowley said it best: "I slept with faith and found a corpse in my arms on awakening; I drank and danced all night with doubt and found her a virgin in the morning."

Occultnik-ism. This is a sin we all commit at some point of our development. We read, or are told, or see on a video some "fact": Druids built Stonehenge. Semen powers magical sigils. Egyptians and Mayans came from eastern Atlantis. We hold on to romantic and silly notions. This limits our appreciation of the Cosmos and makes us look silly to the rest of the world.

Returning to Old Orthodoxies. Anton LaVey warned of this. As humans we hold on to ways of processing the world until we force ourselves to revise them. We may think we have left behind some toxic notion—so we (for example) mock our discarded Protestant Christianity but still hold on to notions of predestination and the work ethic without questioning them. Or we declare ourselves to be beyond our parent's racism and then make fun of Asian drivers without a moment of self-reflection. Here's a hard truth: whatever belief system you escaped from, you will carry its infrastructure into your next belief system.

THE VAMPYRIC PATH

So we've got the quick guidelines and the long-term guidelines. How do we know we're on the path? There are four signs you're on the path. They are the extremes, the folks you meet, the bliss, and the longing. Let's look at these and then end the chapter discussing the eight places you may visit.

The Extremes. The Vampyre needs balance as a virtue because her life has extremes. The Vampyre needs a quiet and secure lair but must visit the most active and even loud of human sites. The Vampyre needs both soothing nature and gritty urban scenes. The Vampyre engages in life worship and meditation in the places of death. The Vampyre needs exquisitely mannered self-restrained etiquette at some times and almost bestial release at others. The Vampyre needs the wildest, most mysterious romantic moods and settings as well as moods of logical detachment that most humans would find chilling.

The Folks You Meet. The Vampyre sends and receives a summons on a deep level. The number one sign that you are successfully on the Vampyric Path is that you meet the right people at the right time. You find the book, article, video you need. You may sometimes not do as well with these gifts as you would like, but the basic rule that "energy calls to energy" is a constant in your life.

The Bliss. Despite the troubles, deadlines, and stress in life, the Vampyre has moments of bliss that are overwhelming and often beyond words to share. A certain sky with towering thunderheads, the cry of an owl at night, the view of a city from a jet—these occasionally will allow you to perceive the universe as pure energy. The constraints of your life vanish, and from such ineffable moments you receive not only the energy to carry on but also a wordless sense of what direction you should pursue.

The Longing. The flip side to the above state is a deep feeling—that you once thought all humans had—that the world is not like it should be. Conventional religion tells you this is a longing for Paradise, for Eden. Conventional politics suggests it's a desire for the common good, a prequel to the Marxist "withering away of the state." But you understand that at these moments your Vampyric self is summoning the conditions of your afterlife and that if you can integrate these holy moments of penetrating the future into your practice you are moving to become that which you (and only you) should be.

Our map is about complete. You know how to cling to the path in times of trouble and are aware of the long-term directions and the ways you can spot your progress through the weeks and months. Now let's look at the journey in general terms. There are eight common loci; most Vampyres experience only the first four in a deep way.

First Awakening. It begins with the First Awakening. Most would-be Vampyres are either early or late bloomers. They tend to be imaginative and moody, drawn to fantasy and science fiction, role-playing games, or fantasy art—and, at the worst, popular occultism. These folks have three fates: They may never grow up, being always Peter Pan. They may become the craftsmen of the occult world, the travelers in Renaissance Fairs—or else local "witches." The majority simply become integrated into the regular world. A very few—because of ego-need—become local messiahs, founding their own cults with memberships of two or three. There is a danger of falling under the spell of an unethical adult who lures with sex, drugs, or, most often, religion.

Common Sleep. The second phase is Common Sleep. In this phase, Vampyres fall back into normality, losing their energy (although occasionally being greater than the humans around them). They tend to succeed in their chosen fields. They often become attracted to emotional groups: intense politics (of any flavor), emotional religions, unbalanced relationships (giving or taking too much).

While Asleep they tend to deny their playful pasts. If gently treated with pleasure (for example, buying a hot tub) they can begin a surplus energy feedback loop that takes them to the next phase, usually by causing a synchronicity in their lives—meeting someone or buying a certain book. Occasionally, if they try to deeply repress their Vampyric natures, they will cause a very strong synchronicity that will manifest as life change, trauma, or a magical or mystical experience. This is seen in Joseph Campbell's model of the hero's journey as "denying the summons" or as Eliade's "shaman sickness."

Magician. The step called Magician comes next. Here the human discovers she can alter her subjective universe and produce a change in the objective universe. This can be an end state of megalomania or excessive rationality (both social parasite behaviors) if Vampyres don't spend enough energy to avoid returning to Common Sleep. Alternatively, this state can stagnate as Sorcery or Exotic Sleep.

In Sorcery, all magical practice is used to solely bring about changes in the objective universe; no further personal change is desired. Such people tend to augment their practice with drugs and enter a quiet life of control without evolution. If you look at every large (really large) apartment complex, you will find a sorcerer.

Exotic Sleep is a state wherein the Magician uses her occult lore to convince herself that she is evolving into some super-being. No change is wanted or obtained in the objective universe, and magical power eventually becomes self-hypnosis. This group powers the occult industry by buying a truly staggering number of books. However, if the Magician wishes for a blend of inner and outer results, the teacher will appear, either in an outer formal group like the Temple of Set or the Dragon Rouge, or in internal form. Then an evolutionary leap can occur.

Vampyre. The Vampyre has forged a link with the Vampyric Current; that is to say, the Vampyre has begun a working of Red Magic to train and transform herself by the use of Vampyric archetypes and magical techniques. This can be stated as transforming life into play or the art of objectively manifesting a magical lifestyle. This is invigorating yet has the drawback of needing constant supplies of energy to maintain a subjective universe that is at odds with the rules of the host culture. It may be seen as a gamble against the forces of sameness, stupidity, or convention.

This state corresponds to the Adept degrees of the OTO, Temple of Set, Golden Dawn, and others. For many, perhaps most practitioners, this state is the desired state of being in that it does not require that one self-discipline oneself enough to become an initiator.

There is a need to maintain critical thinking here as well as a peer group—lest you wander into the weeds. If you do not have and cannot maintain a community, this may not be the level you wish to obtain. The Vampyre understands Crowley's IAO formula, which is that any skill you wish to obtain has a three-part learning curve—Isis/Mom: It's fun! It's fresh! It's exciting! Apep/Annoying kid brother Jeez, this is hard! There are more interesting things! Mastery is really hard to come by! I'll just quit. And Osiris/Master: I survived the learning curve, now I can do this like planting crops every year. Sometimes I get a great harvest. Sometimes only enough to get by.

Master Vampyre. If the Vampyre persists and wills it so, she can become a Master Vampyre. She begins to receive energy from higher forces, such as Set, Hecate, or the Great Vampyre. This energy is tailored to the evolutionary needs of the Vampyre but with a hell of a catch. In order to use it for themselves, Master Vampyres must first express this received energy to others as teaching or training.

It works like this: The Vampyre Miracalla needs to understand how to deal with her approaching menopause. Her student, the Vampyre Persephone, has a similar need. While teaching Persephone, Miracalla comes up with the perfect techniques, reflections, and resources. Persephone is impressed; Miracalla is confused—Where did that advice come from?

The formula of the Master Vampyre is called the Abyss/Daath, but I like the phrase the Gap. There's a lag between intellectually understanding something and truly comprehending it with your brain, heart, and guts. In that Gap—that empty space—monsters are born. The Master Vampyre must never act as a monster, but like the "good werewolf" in the movies, knows that she is one. The Master Vampyre lives in that Gap—one foot in a divine realm, one in a human realm. Her processing of energy requires apprentices and furthers certain abstract ideals in the world. This corresponds with the Priest/Priestess grade of the Temple of Set.

The danger here is losing sight of one's vulnerable humanity on the one hand or of one's direct connection to the divine world on the other. There are pitfalls: one may attribute the divine energy to oneself and form a cult; or one may not understand that the advice is summoned by one's need but expressed in teaching/aide to others and die in poverty; or one may fall victim to any of the draining choices of the less-evolved Vampyric states. With practice, the Gap grows smaller and smaller and may become a lens through which one views the world, in which case one can move into the next state.

Sage. The Sage has harmonized the divine and human, the Vampyric self and the lesser selves, her life and the life of her students in a dynamic balance. She can alter the teachings she received in light of her understanding. Her soul becomes quieter in comparison to the Master Vampyre. The Sage is the monster who knows she will never use her monster side because of emotional temptation. This state corresponds to the Magisterial grades of the Temple of Set, the OTO, or the Fraternitas Saturni.

Because of the inner quiet, which by the formula of magic produces an outer quiet, this is a good grade to aspire to and retire in. If the lens of the Sage becomes perfectly focused, she will build up great energy from both her human and divine sides while a developing energy builds up in the objective universe, propelling her into the seventh state.

Scholomanceleher. The Scholomanceleher has either a single idea to teach (magi such as Crowley or Aquino) or a single community to build (like Blavatsky or the Mother). This condition is not as uncommon as Crowley would tell us in *Liber vel Magi,* but then he wouldn't have listed Joseph Smith or Baba Keenaram or ANY women. In this state, called Magus in current Western magic, the energy flows outward from the Vampyre into a meso-cosmos (or tribe, club, neo-family) of his or her creation.

The meso-cosmos is made both for philosophical resonance and with certain magical signs—usually a linguistic unit, say, a word—through which he or she can absorb and articulate this energy. The meso-cosmos then distributes this energy to mankind as a whole usually through art, music, architecture, cooking, and similar outlets. When the objective universe has achieved some balance by enough people filling the meso-cosmos, the Scholomanceleher uses his or her higher energy state to enter into a completely subjective state.

The state of the Scholomanceleher is perilous: if he or she lacks the teaching skill to create the community, he or she will spin out as a charismatic eccentric—a fun guy for the history books like Emperor Norton, but not a force for the evolution of consciousness.

Rex. The Rex (or Regina) is a Vampyre whose task of creating a self-sustaining meso-cosmos that can draw in its energy as individuals and send forth its energy as teachings is done. The Rex begins to live in a Cosmos of his own making.

This can be perilous as he can lose a sense of urgency for the objective universe. This is often corrected by the urge of the Rex to connect his or her work with historical and cultural currents.

Now we have seen the quick course corrections, the long-term course corrections, the signs you are on the path, and the territories you will see. Let's look at the shallow and deep paths as well as the bigger picture of the Vampyre in the cosmic ecology.

6

VAMPYRE LITE: SIMPLE PRACTICE

This chapter addresses the question "But I'm already a (pick one) rune magician, hoodoo practitioner, Wiccan, Thelemite, Hermeticist, and so on—what can I take from the Vampyric buffet?" This chapter will offer basic practices—Vampyre lite, if you will. I'll divide it into daily, weekly, monthly, and yearly practice. If you like the results, you may wish to undergo initiation. If it's too hard or not to your liking, you've still got a scary book you can use to impress your friends.

DAILY

As with any daily regimen, you must customize. The practice of a single mom of two in Chicago will be different from that of a gay farmer in Idaho, a violinist on tour, a graduate student in Mexico City, or a Marine on active duty. This is for a basic day—no magical workings planned, none of the experiments from parts 2 or 3 of the book in process. The cycle begins after sundown.

Preparation
Enter into sacred space, preferably facing north. Incense and quiet music can be helpful. Dim or extinguish the lights. Close your eyes and begin.

Energy Inventory
Make an energy inventory of the day. Think about your activities, your dreams, your interactions with people, and especially any unexpected

moments and opportunities. What fed you? Are you sick or well? What pleasures did you capture for yourself? What/who drained you? What energy did you use? Now you will expel such energy as you deem harmful (more on that practice later). Then thoroughly relax. Let tensions leave your body section by section from your feet to your head. When you feel your tensions relaxed, your breathing slow, your thoughts quiet, rise and say your wish for the next day: "I, the Vampyre [VN], wish that . . ." The wish can be anything you desire—stated as an accomplished fact.

Gratitude Orison

You then offer the orison of gratitude: "I thank myself, my ancestors, my teachers, my friends, and my family for X (your granted wish)." Think of all the things for which you are grateful—from seeing a peacock spread his tail unexpectedly to thinking good thoughts to your health, and so on. End your orison with: "I will live long beyond this body, this time, this mood. I will hunt and play in the stars; I am attuned to forces dark, sublime, and eternal." The gratitude orison is the most important act of the cycle: it records pleasant, unexpected moments into your past, as opposed to losing such memories; it creates happiness in your present and acts against the social parasite's tendency to panic at night; and last, it sets up resonance with your future self. If you live your life "right," you will feel gratitude to your past self—in moments of resonance between ages, intuition occurs as surpluses of energy store themselves across your long-being.

Reflection

Turn up the lights. Journal. At a minimum write down the best thing that happened to you that day (even if it was just finding a quarter in front of the vending machine), your best thought of the day, any magical results, and the phase of the moon.

Plan your next day—include an item to think about (philosophically) and bodily pleasures. Pick activities that decondition the social parasite, such as resolving to spot a new thing on the way to work or putting your left shoe on first. Such silly moments alongside the important ones weaken the social parasite's grasp on behavior. Be mindful of practical needs and energy hunting. Many find it useful to write out the list, leave it in total darkness, then carry it with them the next day. Cross off items as you do so, and thank yourself for your achievements the next night.

Sleeping and Waking

At bedtime pause for a moment to drink cold, clear water in front of a mirror. Look at your reflection. Say the Vampyric Pledge: "Tonight I feed and fly. Hail the ancient dreams!"

As you fall asleep, engage in one of two visualizations. Picture people whom you wish to influence: imagine energy flowing from them into you and a (lesser but more magical) stream of energy flowing from your heart into them. Or choose the ascent visualization: picture yourself rising from your bed and flying either to a Vampyric stead of power (see below) or away from earth toward the Big Dipper. Satellite pictures of your area will aide in this.

Go to sleep. If you lie in bed reading or playing on the internet, rise, shake off that mood before you pledge, and begin the visualizations.

When you awaken in the morning, try lying as still as possible and try to relive your dreams. If you dreamed of a specific location that you will visit today, resolve to be very alert and in control in that place.

After you rise and pick up your task list from last night, say, "The Vampyre sleeps and I guard it. It can awaken at will and moves with the swiftness of the bat. In Its name I summon energy, wonder-giving experiences, and evolution-provoking thoughts to my day self."

Near midday, take a few minutes to review your list and your day so far. This is never an exercise in guilt. Guilt is how the social parasite feeds itself, you must wean it off guilt by giving it the better energies of wonder and the glow of possessing a secret (i.e., that you are a Vampyre).

Take time to try the new when possible, such as a new restaurant or a new route. Or rebel against minor rules or conventions occasionally; this releases energy and deconditions the social parasite.

Cultivating Vampyric Powers

The most common practices for day-to-day life are stalking a space, mastering a space, the Gaze, and invisibility.

Stalking and Mastering a Space. Stalking a space is planning when and how to make an entrance. Do I want to set it up and gain information? Do I want to sneak in and out or make a grand entrance? Do I want to be next to the smart quiet guy or directly under the air conditioner vent? Stalking can be done in advance or on the fly. It is the Vampyre's first action in any situation.

Mastering the space means three things. First, you either invite or ignore others entering your space. This changes the relationship of your energy body to theirs. Second, you play a role (mainly in your head): Do I rule this space? Am I an honored guest, a spy, an invisible serf, or a thief? Third, you ask to enter others' spaces. This part of vampire folklore creates an impression on others. They feel that they are giving you a right to presence, which makes your energy work easier. Obviously if you are entering to be unnoticed you don't announce yourself.

The Vampyric Gaze. The Vampyric Gaze requires subtlety and practice. Practice in shopping malls, coffeehouses, or clubs before you use it on the circle of folks in the center of your day-to-day life. It requires three actions. First, close your eyes for a moment and visualize a crescent moon extending through your head, giving glowing horns on a stormy night. This both dilates your pupils and conjures romantic magical feelings. (Some of you may recognize this from Chaos Magic.) Then look at your victim. Maintain eye contact, mimic their breathing, and mirror their postures. This creates instant rapport. (Some of you may recognize this from NLP.) Third, think, "I am the Vampyre [VN], and my purpose in this meeting is [X]." This helps you be in control of the situation.

Invisibility. The Vampyre controls whether she wants to be seen (and take in energy through others' desire, fear, nostalgia, or admiration) or unseen. To accomplish invisibility, you need four things. First, you must draw your essence into yourself—you imagine yourself as a vacuum rather than an energy field—this is the magical component. Second, you must dress in muted tones, and most certainly in the uniform of the time and place. Third, speak softly—but not too softly to be heard—and avoid your wicked sense of humor or your desire to be clever. Fourth, know your entrance and exit routes. I worked as an industrial detective once, and I crafted an image as a real team player, but when I didn't want the boss to give me extra work because he passed me in the hall, I parked in a small space behind the building most folks didn't know about. My first day on the job, I made friends with the janitors (always a good Vampyric move) and could leave the building through a mainte-nance hallway that most of my coworkers were unaware of.

If possible, watch the sun go down, pull yourself out of your day-to-day thoughts. Think about the philosophical question you've picked for yourself. Feel the planet turning, and break off from news, Facebook, and family. Then go to the first part of the cycle above.

Steads of Power. Vampyric steads of power are of two sorts: exist-ing already or created by you. Existing steads are places of rugged nat-ural beauty or places where the lines between life and death are thin. Some examples would include the Grand Canyon, the serpent mound in Ashland, Kentucky, Stonehenge—or local haunted hotels, theaters, old libraries. Folklore and your own sensitivity should be your guide. Notice if you feel calmer or more sensitive in an area that scares the average human. If you choose to create such sites the work done by Friedrich Marby in his *Marby-Runene-Bücheri* or his *Der Weg zu den Müttern* (summarized in Flowers's *Rune Might*) is useful. For operations that affect all realms (inner and outer, future and past) equally, choose a very slight hill. If you wish to tune in to the future, or receive new ideas, the best place is a tower or platform. If one wants to blend new ideas with a very ancient force, standing atop a tall peak is best. If you wish to limit new ideas and gain insight into both your memories and older arche-types, canyons (natural or artificial) are the best. Finally, if you desire to access only the oldest/most primal energies, totally enclosed subterra-nean spaces are suggested. Although one may pursue formal ritual work in any of these steads, the best work is simply absorbing energy while being mindful of the purpose the energy will be put to.

WEEKLY

The Vampyre has three weekly tasks. First, pick a day for Vampyric work—either a magical working, a visit to a Vampyric stead of power (see p. 82), or socialization with other Vampyres (or at least magicians). Vampyres are not bound by traditional times/days of work but may use the symbolism from the origin of the day names* if pleasing to them. So, Mondays are optimal to affect things that have cycles, Tuesdays for justice/social change, Wednesdays for wisdom, Thursdays to crush or Sleep enemies, Fridays for sex, Saturdays for initiation, Sundays for celebration. Second, you need to review your week—both practical goals (money, health, etc.) and Vampyric education (see suggested reading list in chapter 27). Finally, you should deal with entertainment: What vampire/monster/superhero movies do you want to see this week? What documentaries? What concerts/plays/fireworks?

MONTHLY

The Vampyre has three tasks per month. The first is checking on any holidays that are coming up (see below). The second is considering what energies will be abundant and what will be rare: How is spring different from winter? Fall from summer? And so on. The third task is picking your wishes around the moon phases: if you are wishing to decrease something (either a habit or an external circumstance) wish for its decline three days before the new moon. To increase something, make the wish the day before the full moon and for two days following.

YEARLY

There are four holidays for the Vampyre: his or her birthday, Walpurgisnacht, Halloween, and Yule. Each has certain duties.

Vampyric Holidays
For your birthday celebrate your accomplishments and victories! Some of this should be done with friends and family, but also be sure to spend a few minutes in total darkness thanking yourself for your wonders, your pleasures, your thoughts, and your animal, human, and Vampyre

---

*See *Transylvanian Superstitions* in Book the Fourth.

friends! If things seem sad or astray, celebrate what you can, and tell yourself, "I know I brought myself here for a reason. I had placed resources around and within me!"

Walpurgisnacht (April 30) is a twofold celebration. Part of it should be with rowdy "pagan" friends, meaning folks who are fun, funny, and anti-authoritarian. Part of it should be celebrated quietly. Light the three candles to the north, utter the Vampyric Invocation, and say the following: "I send forth my energy to bless my Teachers who live, my Teachers who are no longer alive, and my Students living or yet to be. I draw in the tides of that time the profane call the 'future.' I am the Vampyre [VN], and I will endure both as memory here and essence in the Great Dark." After the rite, spend some time thinking on what you want to learn, master, or teach in the coming year. Do this even if you have no living teacher or student. The two parts may be done in any order.

Halloween is a time of play in which you can be as obvious about your practice as you like. It is a time of duty when you must help others play.

For Yule, in the busiest part of the shopping frenzy, do a two-part work. In a quiet, dimly lit place answer the following six questions. Be brutally honest. Are you better off this year than last year, health-wise? Are you better off this year than last year, financially? Are you better off this year than last year, Vampyrically? Are you better off this year than last year, emotionally? Are you better off this year than last year, in terms of local political power or community position? What do you plan to do about it? After you have answered these questions, make notes for yourself, leave your dark and gloomy room. Go to a brightly lit busy shopping area. Do not shop. Just wander about feeding on the energies there—pleasant nostalgias to nervous outbursts, love, and anger. Do this until you forget the first part of the work.

7

BRAINY STUFF

There's a three-and-a-half-pound mass of mainly fat, some water, a few salts encased in bone that's processing these letters into words right now using a voltage of about 20 watts, about a fifth of the power in your body. Originally, the brain evolved to coordinate movement, which is why if you don't move, it stops working well (this is one of the reasons I recommend martial arts, yoga, and walking for the Vampyre). Later, this low-powered motion coordinator and, more importantly, motion planner became critical in channeling certain immaterial forces. Everything you visualize is the result of a bowl full of soggy bacon that couldn't illuminate a room.

The brain has 80 billion neurons that each has a resting voltage of 70 millivolts (0.07 volt). Wow, that's tiny, but let's do the math. Calculations suggest that the human brain has regions that possess an electric field of strength of 14 million volts per meter, which is much larger than a lightning strike on the ground. These neurons are connected to each other by axial dendrites, which connect the star-shaped and pyramid-shaped neurons. The dendrites monitor excitatory and inhibitory signals from other neurons. In other words, based on chemistry and "training" they can decide to send a signal along or not. There also may be nonlocal factors involved, as recent research from the University of Vienna points out. The pyramid-shaped cells are involved in learning and recognition; if they are in an enriched environment, they grow more connections—or, as the Vampyre says, they enhance energy. They take care of visual recognition and that weird phenomenon that humans call memory. Their job is to create the illusion of consciousness and provide action/decisions. They are lumped into two big areas called the right and left brain. Between them is a tiny brain called the pineal gland, and more recently the "intestinal brain" has been discovered. Together, these are four of the components that create the biological part of consciousness. We'll talk about the four parts, their relation to the Vampyre, and how their interactions and training create human civilization and the social parasite.

Neurons are cells. They contain DNA in the center that has basic patterns—half of which you got from your mom, half from your dad. The cells are powered by mitochondria, which developed from symbiosis with bacteria. These came from your mom's ovum, not from your dad. She got them from her mom, who got them from . . . So your basic biological energy is a mom thing. The cells also have epigenetic information. This is due to changes in DNA because of stress in the parents. The classic example was found in the Dutch Winter Famine syndrome. Kids born during the famine of 1944–1945 were small—well, no surprise there. But for the next two generations they were smaller (despite no food shortage) and prone to glucose intolerance. Children born of abused mothers have greater susceptibility to anxiety (in part) because of epigenetics. The old wives' tales that the woman's environment during pregnancy can affect the baby is a true one—and this affects your energy field. Now, the neurons grow in density and complexity based on the rearing of the child, so kids born in households devoted to providing a loving, enriched environment will produce kids that have greater energy fields. The neurons grow rapidly until age twenty-five. When the growth rate is slowed, the Vampyric self Awakens using the patterns and images stored in memory. But memory isn't what your social parasite tells you it is.

The social parasite tells you that memory is an actual record. We've all got that friend, family member, or spouse who just doesn't remember stuff right. Maybe it's booze or too much caffeine or their age. Or maybe they're just evil. Memory is just a tape we play, right? Wrong. Memories are encoded in proteins, and proteins don't hang around for more than a few minutes. However, animals encountered a retrovirus (which, like HIV, is hard to get rid of) called ARC that transfers its genetic material between neurons. It's lived with us so long that it's a gene now. In insects it travels only one way, from cell to cell, to create muscle memory, but in you it creates "memory"—that is to say, when you try to recall something, bursts of ARC mRNA travel from neuron to neuron along the pathways you've built up, and you visualize a re-creation of the event or data. You rebuild it if your brain has enough rules. It isn't precisely what happened. So you remember that Uncle Bob took the family to the lake wearing his blue shirt for the Fourth of July, and your sister remembers that he took you to that park in town with a big pond wearing his red, white, and blue shirt. You have that argument until Mom hauls out the VCR and there he is with you kids at the beach wearing his red shirt. You laugh (since you're the more evolved being—hey, *you* bought this book right?), but your sister gets really angry. Why? The social parasite must defend the accuracy of memory as a control structure. That's why you should do the gratitude orison every night: you will encode your experience as an expression of gratitude from your Vampyric self. The social parasite is many things, but it doesn't fight repetition. You will experience your life more and more as a blissful state because you will have reprogrammed yourself. This activity can even affect negative epigenetic traits.

So, let's talk about the illusion of consciousness: your brain's number one job is to weave an illusion that it is in control and decides everything you do. Because of this pernicious illusion religious people feel guilty, magicians feel like failures, and Vampyres learn to say, "Brain, get over yourself!" Here are two often-repeated experiments from brain research. A researcher touches a subject's arm with a hot stick and the subject pulls away. Ask the subject what happened, and she says, "My arm felt hot and I decided to pull it away"—because the brain orders the events. Here is what really happened. The pain stimulus triggered a neuron in the arm to move. The arm moved away. Different neurons sent the pain stimulus and the fact that the arm moved to the brain simultaneously, and, based on the brain's rules, it creates the story. But the real blow to the illusion of consciousness came from Benjamin Libet, Ph.D. Libet discovered that volition and consciousness are not related. He monitored humans who had the task of randomly punching a button. He found that neural activity increased just before a human pushed or didn't push the button. If the human didn't push the button, he said he hadn't even thought about it. If he did push the button, the impulse that triggered his movement happened before the pushing, and then his brain noticed it—and conned itself into thinking it had decided. Libet decided that there is no free will: the "body" did it based on "unconscious" processing. As fellow researcher Susan Blackmore, Ph.D. (see "Recommended Vampyric Curriculum") said, "Conscious experience takes some time to build up and is much too slow to be responsible for making things happen." Vampyres do not accept this as proof of no free will; instead they understand that actions are controlled by the energy they use and not by the brain.

Vampyres are also interested in the recent finding (from Armin Shayeghi, Ph.D., at the University of Vienna) that biomolecules act to self-interfere—nonlocally. The "stuff" your brain uses—especially the chemicals in cognition and memory—show the same sort of quantum weirdness that elementary particles do; that is to say, their "future" affects their reactions as well as input from nonlocal sources. These findings reflect the philosophical notions of Bergson, who thought the brain was a filter, taking in information from a greater and immaterial source and making the weaker tea of consciousness. He had linked this greater source with life force and sexual desire under the banner of élan vital. As such, he is one of the best philosophers for Vampyres to sink their teeth into.

Now let's deal with left brain/right brain. In the 1990s, many neuro-scientists became uncomfortable with right brain/left brain terminology since the field had terms that had been taken over by pop psychology and New Age devotees. Both brains would arrive at more or less the same con-clusion, so perhaps it was just a case of having a "spare brain." However, Iain McGilchrist discovered (after decades of research) that although the two brains would come up with the same answer, the methods each used were very different. The two large parallel processing lobes have different functions. The best book on the subject is McGilchrist's *The Master and His Emissary* (see "Recommended Vampyric Curriculum"). The ten-cent tour is this: The right brain is the big picture—the holistic approach—and includes all of the emotions except anger. The left brain is the detail-oriented dissector of experience. For the fully functional human being, the right brain is in charge, and the left brain follows along. However, in our fast-paced Western world, the left brain thinks it is in charge. Let's look at an experience.

Right Brain: "I love Angelique. I am going to paint her picture. It will create a link between us that will last forever."

Left Brain: "I need stretched canvas. Check my pigments. Need a new brush too. I'll drive to the art supply store after work. God damn it. The traffic is fucking ridiculous. Oh, sale on paint! I'm a fucking idiot. I forgot to buy the brush. Why am I so stupid? Why does this bitch make me do things for her?"

Without a distressed left brain, you could do nothing, but its job of working out the details, combined with anger—a survival emotion that is overused—makes it the home of the social parasite. The right brain is further removed from reality and the least innovative part. It can give joy (but not bliss—we'll get to that). It is the home—the coffin—of the Vampyre. The metaphor of Vampyre comes from this split in your body. The first reason that this is important for Vampyres is for the power in knowing which brain to access: if I want to tap in to right-brain holism, I pick up stuff with my left hand. The body is cross-wired. If I want left-brained details, I use my right side. If I'm doing a work to integrate myself, I hug myself first: right hand on left shoulder, left hand on right shoulder.

The Vampyre also needs to know the effect the split has had on human history, and when the Vampyre was all-powerful, and when he was hunted. To do this we will look at French philosopher and historian Jean Gebser and Canadian media researcher Marshall McLuhan. These two gents, following the lead of Henri Bergson, realized that consciousness and memory and information processing have evolved in the past few millennia while a human's physical structure has been the same. Following are their periods.

At first there was the archaic structure (Gebser), or preliterate tribalism: both brains probably shared control as survival of the small family unit was the basic thrust and there was less left-brain innovation. The magical structure (Gebser) was next (McLuhan does not recognize this phase). Here is when the Vampyre ruled: great leaders, god-kings, and the creation of massive steads of Vampyric power (like the Great Pyramid), most of which have peculiar electromagnetic properties. Gebser feared this phase; he lived through the time of Hitler and observed that humans are often glad to revert to a Vampyre leader who manifests with charisma and an anti-science bias.

The next structure, the mythical structure (Gebser), McLuhan describes as the codification by script that arose after Homer in ancient Greece and lasted two thousand years. During this period, the two brains are in balance: the right brain is drawn to the hero's journey; the left brain enjoys the strong polarities of good versus evil, us versus them, and being able to externalize the forces of the right brain as gods. In this time Vampyres became wizards and priests—or merchants, adventurers, or mighty generals.

Next comes the mental structure (Gebser), beginning with the age of print (running from 1500 to 1900) and mutating into the ages of radio (a hot medium) and television. Here the left brain prevails. All survival skills are based on a detail-oriented fast-paced world. Art and philosophy are seen as nonessential superstructures. Notions of tribe or people are destroyed to build bigger work units. Anger, a left-brain function, is used to ensure that groups do not cooperate unless this is desired by the ruling class. The rulers are not priest-rulers but in fact people whose left brains are hyperdeveloped; they are great at calculating deals but poor at big-picture stuff. The focus on the left brain may be shortening lives and led to the creation of television and movies as right-brain entertainments. This is why (for the Vampyre) movies work.

The last phase, the integral structure (Gebser), or the global village, is coming into being. Because of all the remaining techniques from other ages, the vast amounts of information available to us, and a connectivity that is spanning class and ethnicity, we are seeing some humans using the power of mental-structure techniques to draw from other structures. These new folks are masters of the Way of the Owl—drawing from the right skill set. This new level of human empowerment has been predicted by many esoteric schools, but most of them are so disconnected from advances in technology, medicine, or even the esoteric tools of other traditions that they can't join in this lovely emerald dawn.

Okay, two more brains to go.

I mentioned earlier that the structures in the human brain tend toward symmetry and act as pairs that check/enhance/interfere with each other's work. Not so much for the pineal gland. Now, this little pinecone of mystery didn't even start in your brain. On the forty-ninth day of your embryo's development it began growing in your throat and working its way up to be between the two brains. As it moved it left a little duct into your throat; sometimes when it's excited it sends a bitter little squirt to your throat. In yoga this is called the nectar of ecstasy. The squirt is metatonin—not melatonin—although it makes that too. Now, this structure is in charge of reproductive function and sex hormones, body temperature, immune system, blood pressure, fertility, motor activity, suppressing cancers, and longevity and anti-aging. Oh, and in yoga it's the "third eye."

Listening to the two brains and having a broad range of biomolecules that show the non-locality we've seen elsewhere, this little gland decides when you're horny, sleepy, how fast you age, and sends you on a couple of trips. Remember metatonin? It's hard to find—there's a scavenger in your blood that gobbles it up. It is your body's analog to DMT. For the average human the pineal gland gives two big doses of this: at the moment you came out of your mom, and at the moment you are dying. The tunnel in and the tunnel out. When this stuff is present new (virtual) pathways are produced between neurons, and neurons are hyperstimulated. If the brain is connected to something, this is an upgrade from basic cable to a thousand channels. If the brain were just about biological survival, then it makes sense to show up at birth—but what's the use of the dose at death? Why does the brain want to (a) relive all its memories and (b) tune in to tons more subtle energies?

There are ways to get metatonin without dying: doing a repetitive difficult task, focusing on a difficult formula, having long periods of sexual desire, or simply being under the age of twelve. When this stuff stops being excreted in the brain, kids want to rebel—because their brain wants the stimulation so it can grow. Now, the cool thing for Vampyres is the nightly energy inventory is exactly the sort of activity that releases metatonin: so you've filled your brain with all the ongoing relationships, and, before you make your plans and wish for the next day, this jolts everything up a notch. The bliss of the yoga practioner long seen as a metaphor is a true (and usually bitter) taste. The myth of seeking the Graal comes from an experience in your body. As the Vampyre finds again and again, the greatest magical tool is her body. Now, the more common chemical melatonin helps you dream—that is to say, it helps you create a story (see "Wyrd," chapter 15) that both categorizes your memories as it encodes them but connects them to current perceived patterns and even nonlocal information from the future. This tiny brain is where What Was, What Is, and What Should Be are blended with timelessness and desire.

Three brains down, and one to go.

Consciousness. The enteric nervous system (ENS) is the intrinsic nervous system of the gastrointestinal tract. It is the only part of the peripheral nervous system that contains extensive neural circuits that are capable of local, autonomous function. There are thousands of neurons on the walls of the esophagus, stomach, small and large intestines, pancreas, gallbladder, and biliary tree. It has about as many neurons as your spinal cord. That "gut feeling" you get is founded in a complex system that is not only making sure your food passes through you and your fluids are balanced but also is ordering your body to make a huge amount of hormones. Without getting permission from your left and right brains (although it does talk chemically to your pineal gland) it controls your moods. It also tells the pineal gland to control your energy levels the next day in accordance with the calories it's digesting now. It interacts with the food, the waste, the helpful and not so helpful bacteria, protozoa, and other flora. The Egyptians said that humans stored their magic (*heka*) in the gut, and Gurdjieff said it was one of the human's brains. It can control depression and anxiety.

The Vampyre deals with the ENS by being aware of it and by caring for it: learning good nutrition (see Book the Third, chapter 17), drinking more water, eating more fiber, and so on. But in a more esoteric way, spend part of your energy inventory each night just seeing what your gut will tell you. Become aware of it and ask its help in decision-making. Don't think of your stomach/gut as something you hate; instead, consciously learn to store energy there. Since our society hates our tummies as much as it hates Darkness—love yours. Become aware of the centers of energy in you, and let them all talk.

You are now armed with the basics. If you are happy enough, great. If you want to take a deep plunge, the next section will take you on a nine-month journey—a multiphase magical and psychological transformation called the Vampyric Initiation. Read it through a few times before you pass the threshold. Then, enter, if it is your Will.

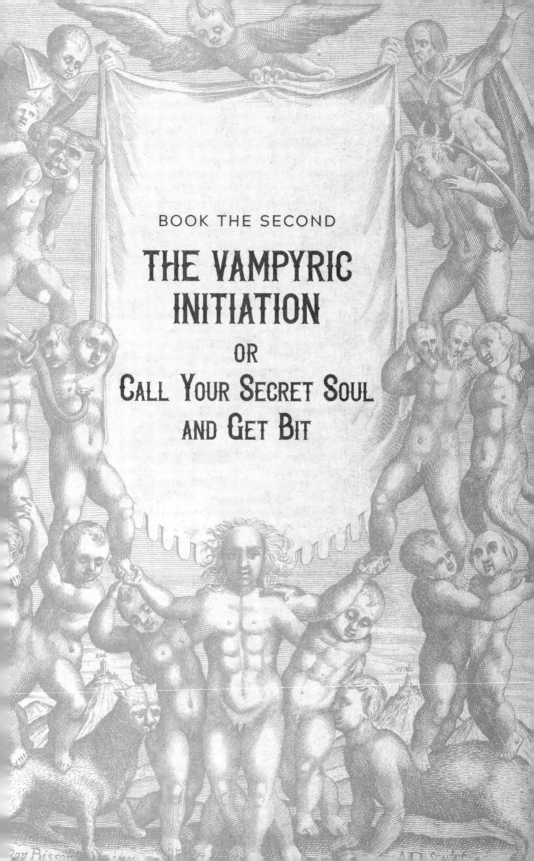

BOOK THE SECOND

THE VAMPYRIC INITIATION

OR

CALL YOUR SECRET SOUL AND GET BIT

The nine initiatic chapters in Book the Second constitute the Working of Scholomance, the legendary Black School where the devil is the headmaster and the art of Vampyrism is taught. The process will take the initiate through the magical developments of nine Left-Hand Path magi. These magi each uttered a word of power, which was used to build a magical philosophy. It is through these words that the Vampyre can come into being. The magicians and their words are:

Paschal Beverly Randolph	—	Try
Aleister Crowley	—	Thelema
Anton LaVey	—	Indulgence
Stephen Edred Flowers	—	Runa
Michael Aquino	—	Xeper
James A. Lewis	—	Remanifestation
Lilith Aquino	—	Arkte
Guiniviere Webb	—	Wyrd
Robertt Neilly	—	Synesis

There are some preliminary steps to take before you attempt these rites. First, you should read through each chapter to see what is required and prepare accordingly. Second, you must have learned the basics from Book the First: the Vampyric Invocation (p. 62) and the Frame Rite (p. 61). This process builds upon the daily, weekly, and monthly forms of Work in chapter 6, so you must also have some experience with those. Third, you should be familiar with the first rank of the reading list in the "Recommended Vampyric Curriculum" (chapter 27) so your mind is armed with some useful ammunition. Fourth, think about the time needed. Each of these nine stages can take many days or weeks to work through, but there is no strict timeline. Make an effort to do one per calendar month. If you have to pause for more than a month between initiations, it will work better if you start at the beginning (chapter 8) again.

Each of the chapters will contain seven things implicitly or explicitly:

1. Background on the magicians and their ideas
2. A rite to open the process
3. Life analysis questions to consider
4. Vampyric analysis
5. Perception exercises
6. Techniques to try
7. An initiatic rite

Throughout, we will look at the benefits you can obtain in each step of the initiation and the drawbacks of which you must beware. Your physical and magical senses will be honed. Your intuition and magical Will will be strengthened. Your Vampyric abilities will be increased, and you will learn new techniques. You will gain some therapeutic benefit—but the therapeutic side of initiation is never a replacement for professional therapy.

That said, let's start!

8
TRY

THE MAGIC OF PASCHAL BEVERLY RANDOLPH

Paschal Beverly Randolph (October 8, 1825–July 29, 1875) changed Western magic deeply and brought into remanifestation some Vampyric principles. He wrote more than fifty books on magic and medicine, was an early advocate of birth control, an advocate for freed African Americans, and a friend of many important people, from Abraham Lincoln to Napoleon III. His work influenced the Hermetic Brotherhood of Luxor, the Theosophical Society, the Golden Dawn, the OTO, Gurdjieff, and Sri Aurobindo. Randolph's name is obscured for two reasons. First, he wrote about sexual magic in frank terms (sperm, phallus, clitoris) at time when such things were discussed either as allegory (fire, serpent) or dealt with as folklore of ancient groups. Second—and most damningly—he was a black man in America before the Thirteenth, Fourteenth, and Fifteenth Amendments.

His white father left the family scene before his birth, his mother died during his childhood, and he came to manhood in poverty. He shipped out as a sailor and visited England, where he obtained initiation in one of the sexual Rosicrucian brotherhoods derived from the teachings of Richard Payne Knight; France, where he obtained more orthodox Rosicrucianism; Egypt, where he obtained an introduction to trance work, possibly from the Coptic magician Paulos Metamon; and the Near East, where he may have received training from various fringe Islamic groups. He returned to America and began a spate of teaching, writing, and medical practice.

He placed as a key to his teaching the Word TRY. This has two important meanings. First, to bravely put aside received wisdom and seek after spiritual adventure and mundane advantage through the use of your body-mind-soul complex. Second, to assay your results. Ninety percent of humans never do the first, drifting along in the sleepwalking traditions that gave birth to and are maintained by the social parasite. Of the 10 percent that do Awaken, 90 percent of them seize upon the first system of coherent knowledge they encounter, and adopt all of its tenets as true. If the system fails to provide the results they seek, they blame themselves.

His system provides seven fundamental ideas for the Vampyre and has two drawbacks. Let's look at the seven fundamental ideas, which are living teachers, multiple systems, the power of sex, the threefold formula of magic, the acquisition of powers, the exotic story, the fight against social systems. Then we'll look at the drawbacks.

Books are awesome. They can give us beginning steps, they are a bulwark against the subjectivity of memory, and they are great tools for our Vampyric selves to work synchronistically through. But they fail to give us two things. First, we can't see living results—with human initiators we see how the system produces results and failures. Second (and most importantly to Vampyres), humans gain initiation through the use of energy. The early stage of initiation is best fueled by the energy absorbed from the teacher, the second stage is the exchange of the student's lesser energy for the transformed energy of the teacher, and the last stage is refining one's own energy enough so that one may teach. Meeting and working with real teachers was the key to Randolph's early rise and his lasting influence, despite the prejudice he faced.

Taming the social parasite is never done by faith. One does not simply pick up a new belief system to break the chains of an old one. Conversion releases lots of energy; perhaps you've seen a friend put aside Christianity for Buddhism (or vice versa)—suddenly they're happier, healthier, and more successful. Their Vampryism is engaged in the ugly form of a desire to convert others. But after a while one of two things happens: they either go to sleep in their new orthodoxy or go through another conversion. The occult industry is fueled by the latter: seekers go through the four-year cycle of "discovering" the runes, Enochiana, and so on, and then getting the next great new thing. If you learn more than one system and can *try* more than one reality tunnel you may never have the smugness of orthodoxy, but you will have the rush of uncertainty.

Randolph discovered the (un)Holy Trinity of Sex, Drugs, and Magick. If you combine Love and Sex—and Randolph is the only writer to unite these ideas—you have a constant path to raise energy. If you maintain sexual desire you do not need the paraphernalia of ritual, just constantly uniting your Will with your Love produces results. And third, the moment of orgasm provides the world-changing moment: you can decree your Will (see below), *and* you experience the bliss of the post-incarnate state as filtered through your body and your emotions. Randolph's word was Try, but his law was "Will reigns Omipotent, and Love lieth as the Foundation." Randolph's system required that both parties achieve orgasm (if possible simultaneously) and that under no circumstance should one party be left unsatisfied. Unlike later systems of sex magic—those of Crowley or Reuss, for example—Randolph's system had gender parity rather than being male-centric.

Not until the development of Chaos Magic was the threefold formula of magic laid as bare as it was by Randolph. Randolph described all magical operations as having three aspects. Using his terminology, these are Volantia (entrance to a deeply calm state—the period of relaxation in the Vampyre's nightly Work would be an example), Decretism (or decreeing something must be so, especially at the moment of orgasm), and Posism (sinking into a receptive mental and physical posture to receive that which has been willed and decreed). This last step is seen as the feeling that pervades the body after a good orgasm, but it is also receptivity in general. Let's say you have performed a working to get a better job, Posism would include making a space for the job—like getting and wearing the clothes you would need, rising from bed and keeping the hours you would keep at your job, or calmly pursuing a routine untroubled by anxiety as you wait for the job to manifest. Most magicians fail at this step because after the end of the external working of magic, the social parasite strives to regain control.

Randolph taught that the goal of magic was not specific operations but the gaining of powers. He proposed that magicians decide the
ability they want—telepathy, precognition, the ability to speak to dis-
carnate spirits—and then for forty-one days engage in workings of sex
magic once every three days in which the desired power was the object
of Decretism. The partners, keeping as much in deep love as possible,
should copulate to orgasms and wish for the state (e.g., "We possess
telepathy!") and then withdraw from the magical bed without speaking to each other, maintaining silence about their goal for the forty-one
days. The idea of a couple obtaining powers together is a very different
moral approach from Crowley's! Since a rather large effort is involved in
this process, a deep planning of life goals is required.

Randolph was a black man when black men in America had huge
obstacles to overcome. It would not be possible for him to say, "Hey,
white folks with money, buy my books. I developed a system of magic and
mysticism on my own!" So, he both mythologized his travels and claimed
deep and secret roots for his teaching. His story, which both deepened
his initiations and obscured to society the fact that he was the one who
created most of what he taught, would also open many doors. This is an
old trick in the magicians' handbook and an unbelievably valuable one
for the Vampyre. In his last book he confessed to creating most of his
system—and perhaps this did lead to his ill luck and suicide afterward.

The Vampyre develops his or her power by resistance to the social
matrix. Randolph was a great speaker for the Abolitionist cause, led
freed blacks in the Civil War, was the principal for one of the first
African American high schools in America, campaigned against the
evils of tobacco (more than a hundred years before the American
medical establishment recognized a danger there), fought for freedom
of the press in discussing sexual matters, and was a huge advocate of
women's rights. He even met his second wife when she was speaking
on behalf of the women's right to vote. Energy comes from fighting
the forces in the social parasites of others that restrict your will.

The drawbacks in his system are twofold. First, he advocates the
use of drugs, especially hashish, to gain trance states. The Vampyre is
free to use drugs for recreation provided that she or he knows both the

biological and legal dangers thereof—but the use of drugs as a means to trance states means that the Vampyre is beholden to a natural substance not under his control and (more importantly) a loss of control and focus will mar the clarity of action.

Second, the overreliance on the exotic tale can lead to huge depression and self-doubt. When one chooses the path of the made-up story, internally a power source is removed; externally, it limits the energy flow to the individual. After Randolph's confession he had ill luck, and depression overcame him, leading to his suicide in 1875. His decline was like the disaster that overtook Anton LaVey after Lawrence Wright destroyed his myth. Like LaVey, Randolph had the greatest outward expression of his Work in San Francisco, forming the Brotherhood of Eulis there in 1875 months before his death. San Francisco becomes a center for many of the currents that shaped Vampyric magic, its fog-laden Lands End is a remarkable stead of Vampyric power. If you want to know more about this amazing man read *Paschal Beverly Randolph: A Nineteenth-Century Black American Spiritualist, Rosicrucian, and Sex Magician* by John Patrick Deveney.

OPENING RITE OF TRY

For the opening, place the candles facing South—that is, toward you—because you are welcoming the forces.

Say the Vampyric Invocation and repeat the Graal Work as follows:

I call the Vampyric current into me as it was remanifested in 1848. From ancient tombs and forgotten nightmares, come O Great Vampyre, I say you are better than my mother: *

> *Dear girl, who believes the firm words of your ever-pious momma,*
> *Who like the Heyduckish peasant folk at Theyse believe*
> *I am a deadly Vampyre, you do not love me—I take revenge*
> *On your unconsciousness; I will drink from you as a Vampyre.*
> *When you sleep softly I will suck rich purple from your cheeks.*

---

*The words that follow are my translation of Heinrich August Ossenfelder's poem "The Vampire" (1748), which represents the beginning of the Left-Hand Path Vampyre.

I will scare you! I will kiss you and kiss you as a Vampyre kisses.
If you are shocked, you will fall dull in my arms
You will swoon like the dead, and with soft voice,
I will ask, are not the Vampyre's teachings better than your
* momma's?*
I bare my neck to the Great Vampyre, I will Try his Teachings,
And if I succeed with them swoon to my old life
And rise anew with the Night!

Now pass your left hand over the flames of three candles seven times.

I will Try the new, I die to what does not empower me. I will Try
my secret wants and set aside dreams, I will Try to remember
myself and forget the lie that that has been told to me. And I will
have faith only in what I discover in this new world of strangeness
and beauty!

Close the rite in your usual fashion.

LIFE ANALYSIS

You should write out the questions and the answers to the following in some sort of bound notebook. It is better to handwrite these things because this process will integrate the left and right brain. You should use red ink. Since you are going to spend a month on the process, don't hurry. Perhaps answer one question a week.

1. At some time in your life you had to figure out something that you had heard wasn't true. Santa Claus doesn't exist, your ex was not working at the office late, a politician lied to you. Try to write in detail your process: How did it feel figuring out the truth? Add sensations you recall, your thought processes, everything.

2. At some time you saw or read about a vampire with some fascination or fear. Can you write an account of what you saw and felt? Did any of it confuse you? (As in, "I know I should be scared, but . . .")

3. You've been practicing stalking a space, mastering a space, the

Vampyric Gaze, and invisibility for a while now. How have these affected your life?

4. Pay attention to people who work in very different environments: in small offices, in tunnels, in towers, on boats, and so on. How does their environment affect them? How much emotion and supposed free will come from a person's environment?

VAMPYRIC ANALYSIS

Here are four questions to think about, or even ask other people. This is about learning to think as a Vampyre. You can write down the questions and answers if you like.

1. Pious Christians have every reason to shun magic as the devil's handiwork. But why do people who aren't very Christian avoid even trying magic? If they're not scared of the devil, what are they scared of?

2. What's the difference between chaos and entropy? Which applies to a crowd of people waiting for the ball to drop at Times Square? What does this mean for the Vampyre?

3. How many people do you know who would be at a loss if they had no TV or internet on a rainy afternoon? Could these people withstand immortality?

4. In Austin there is a double-wide trailer next to a small used-car lot. A sign with a somewhat cartoonish gypsy announces that "Terror" cards (meaning tarot) can be read in the trailer and gives the hours for the car lot. It's clearly not a place of wealth or power. Yet people drop fifty bucks for a reading. What is in their heads to believe? How does that belief work on what they hear? What does this tell you about energy?

PERCEPTION EXERCISES

1. Attentive listening. Listen to what people are saying very carefully. Try not to think about the clever answer you want to make. Don't allow yourself to be distracted or bored. Combine this with the

Vampyric Gaze. What do you notice this does to people? What does it do to you?

2. Learn to identify people, cars, pets, and so forth by the sound they make. Do this until you can hear someone walking up behind you and you know that person's mood.

3. What sounds scare you, soothe you, turn you on, or make you sleep? Can you close your eyes and imagine these sounds?

4. What music gets stuck in your head?

TECHNIQUES TO TRY

Absorbing, Neutralizing, Expelling Energy

When you do your nightly energy inventory you will come across two flavors: pleasurable and painful. To absorb pleasurable energy just recall the incident you experienced. But you need to neutralize or expel painful energy. Let's say a guy yelled at you in the parking lot because you got the space he wanted. Try reliving the incident, but make his voice softer, make the colors less intense. If after four or five repetitions you can play the movie in your head and not feel pain, you've neutralized the energy. Play it one last time at normal levels—and the energy is yours! However, let's say that it still hurts after five replays. Okay; now replay it in your head slowly and see red energy flowing out of you and back to its source. Do this until the hurt is gone. When you become adept at this, you can then take on the big hurts of your life—until all the big fights have been turned into your energy or expelled back to their source.

Flashing Colors and Projection

We're all aware that if we stare hard at something for thirty to sixty seconds and then shift our eyes we see an afterimage. Randolph developed a powerful technique based on this that was inherited by the Golden Dawn. We're going to use a simplified form. We're going to make mental talismans; I'll walk you through how to make one.

Take a blank piece of white paper, say, five inches by five inches. This is for drawing your figure. Affix another sheet of white paper to the wall at eye level—a sheet of printer paper will do.

Now, with a green flair pen, draw the following talisman.

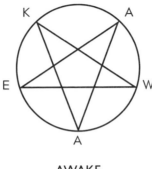

AWAKE

Now stare at the talisman without blinking for thirty seconds. Shift your gaze to the printer paper. You will see an afterimage in red. Good.

Now repeat, but when you shift your gaze, also mentally visualize the same figure in red while you stare at the afterimage. This unifies the red image from eyestrain with a red image from imagination; the effect is surprisingly powerful.

Now do this a third time while yelling in your mind, "AWAKE! AWAKE! AWAKE!" nonstop during both the loading and the staring at the printer paper. Now you have a mental talisman.

You can use the talisman when you need to wake up, say, driving home after a hard day. Just picture the image superimposed on your face. If you need another human to wake up, picture the form on his or her face.

Once you have had some results, try these:

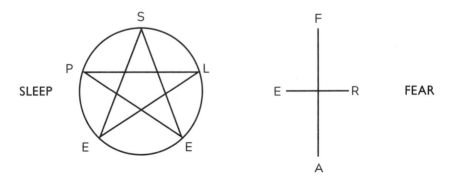

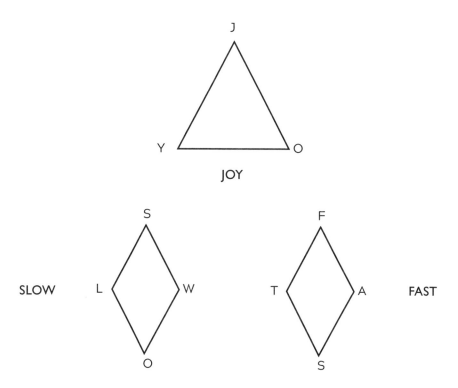

The latter two may be projected on a clock; it won't change objective time but can change your perception of duration. Record your success in your magical journal. After these six you can create as many as you find useful. If the technique doesn't work for you—no worries, you tried.

Mirror Gazing

This is a divinatory technique. At first it is good to practice on items that have very few possible solutions. Obtain a hand mirror; if it has personal significance (i.e., it was your grandmother's) so much the better. You should use the mirror only for magical operations. Sit comfortably with the mirror lower than the midline of your vision. For example, lay it on your desk but look straight ahead. Eventually if you don't look at the mirror but keep it in your peripheral vision it will seem to darken, and if you let your mind wander, pictures may form on the mirror. Reduced lighting may help, a flickering candle is often the best. When you've learned not to look in the mirror, say your need: for example, "Which person should

I put on my team?" You will know the answer when either an image appears on the glass or a sudden thought pops into your mind. Record your results. Once you have had a good result you should store the mirror in black silk under your bed. If you have success with this you will find it a very useful technique.

Initiatic Rite of Try

Draw an isosceles triangle in green ink; in the corners write the letters TRY. In the center write your Vampyric name in block letters in a counterclockwise circle. Aim the candles to the North; you are sending forces away from you and into the Cosmos. If you have had luck with the mirror, place it on your altar. It is best to do this work naked and then to dress in new garments afterward.

Say the Vampyric Invocation and repeat the Graal Work as follows:

Pass the mirror once through the flames, then hold it in front of your face so that you are gazing into your eyes. Project the AWAKE and/or JOY sigil upon the human in the mirror; wait until you feel those forces. Then speak to the human in the mirror.

> *I greet Thee, Vampyre [VN], who ever flies from the timeless place behind the seven stars to stand beside me! I greet Thee, Vampyre [VN], in your unholy name I have opened my ears that I may hear the Secrets of the Universe! I greet Thee, Vampyre [VN], by placing the word TRY in my heart!*

Now turn the mirror away from you.

> *I, the Vampyre [VN], do reflect back to my enemies all energy sent to harm me! I, the Vampyre [VN], do reflect back all forces that seek to enslave or hypnotize me! I, the Vampyre [VN], do reflect back all forces from my past that continue to hinder me!*

Lay the mirror on the altar. Gaze upon the triangle figure you have drawn. Say the following:

> *I shatter the chains that bind me to the world, I step forth as the Vampyre [VN]! I invite the Vampyric Current into the depths of*

my being eternally. I send forth the current of my Will to protect those I love, to summon those who will feed me, to fight that which constrains me, and to return and Transform me when this body dies. What is done cannot be undone!

Bring yourself to orgasm; at the moment of orgasm close your eyes and by means of the flashing colors make the green triangle become red, your unholy name become white. After the moment rushes over you, lie down. Close your eyes and breathe slowly. Do not sink into sleep but come close to it. At the moment of deepest relaxation say:

I receive the Vampyric Current into the center of my being for all time. I will TRY my experiences in its unholy light!

Rise and return to the altar. Say:

The Black Flame of Consciousness is now forever kindled by the Vampyric Current. The Red Flame of Life is quickened beyond Death into Life Eternal.

Blow out the three candles. With as much grace as possible put away your ritual implements. If you intend to go out that evening, shower and put on new garments. If not, shower and go to bed, putting on new clothes in the morning.

You have begun a new chapter in your life. You have passed through the mindless chaos that conditioned you and into a new ordering of life under your own terms.

9

THELEMA

THE MAGIC OF ALEISTER CROWLEY

Aleister Crowley (October 12, 1875–December 1, 1947) probably requires no introduction. A graduate of the Golden Dawn, he created a modern system of magic that incorporated Eastern and Western ideas as well as Randolph's sexual magic. His system has thoroughly penetrated the Western world so that he stands to occultism in the same way that Freud stands to psychology—even if you disagree with him, you are writing under his shadow. He studied magic under Florence Farr and read all the correct and forbidden texts (Nietzsche and Randolph) that the boys and girls of the Golden Dawn did. He created nine important ideas for the Vampyre, and his system has four drawbacks, which we'll discuss shortly. His contributions were the idea of Aeons, the primacy of Egypt, the mathematical insights of Charles Hinton, the integration of personal revelation and work, an understanding of the bicameral brain, the IAO formula, the use of modern thinking, the use of scholarship, and the need of grade testing. Let's look at his contributions first.

The idea of Aeons existed before Aleister as an understanding of the world based on the Christian trinity (the Old Testament was about God the Father; the New Testament, Jesus, the Coming Age, Caspar). Crowley made the breakthrough that consciousness itself was evolving on the planet. He correctly identified magic as a more atavistic form of consciousness but never quite understood the possibilities of integral consciousness. He discovered that politics, science, and art evolved alongside consciousness—and that

110

magic both drew power from and gave power to these truth processes.

The primacy of Egypt had long been part of Western magical thought, but Crowley followed the lead of Florence Farr, who attempted to contact Egyptian priests and magicians (such as an ancient Egyptian priestess of the Temple of Amon-at-Thebes named Nem Kheft Ka), so when Crowley encountered the call of Ankh-f-n-Khonsu, this was a well-known and tested technology. But Crowley took his revelations a step further and saw them as a universal and religious path to replace death-oriented cults such as Christianity. Thus, he cast himself as the Beast 666 from the book of Revelation. This proclaimed a futuristic religion though an atavistic past—the closest thing to integral thinking until Gebser.

Crowley's championing of the mathematical insights of Charles Hinton is seldom commented on. Hinton worked with the topology and geometry of higher dimensions. Crowley saw this as the model of the self, which he called the Khu (Egyptian ahk) a fourth-dimensional matrix that holds the body, its actions, and its thoughts and feelings in a bigger whole. This matrix places the point of perception (Hadit) where it needs/chooses to be to learn lessons that allow it to develop the subtle qualities needed for its evolution. Working in this field, True Will is the manifesting of a certain idea—not as gaining a reward at the end of a task but seeing the daydreaming that leads one to try the task, the reward of the task, and the feelings engendered as a single point. Hinton saw this both philosophically and mathematically in his writings on the fourth dimension. Crowley refers to it to explain his notion of both karma and True Will. As Anne De Witt wrote so well in her (2013) *Moral Authority, Men of Science, and the Victorian Novel*, "Hinton argues that gaining an intuitive perception of higher space required that we rid ourselves of the ideas of right and left, up and down, that inheres in our position as observers in a three-dimensional world. Hinton calls the process "casting out the self," equates it with the process of sympathizing with another person, and implies the two processes are mutually reinforcing" (173). Echoes of this idea will be taken up by both Flowers and Aquino.

The integration of personal revelation and work is a highlight of Crowley's system. He did not consider the religious revelations of

Buddha or Moses as a guide for a human's life. Instead one should obtain one's own revelation. However, these peak experiences are shaped and grounded by disciplined daily work. Crowley theorized that all humans have the capacity for immensely transforming messages from themselves that both grant an understanding of the Cosmos and one's place in it and also magically empower the individual, allowing him or her to succeed in arts, business, or other endeavors. His Aeon would be made of humans that broke free from their social parasites, and, armed by the process of a strong will (see the IAO formula below) and a personal view of the divine would emerge as Nietzschean overmen.

Crowley had an understanding of the bicameral brain. He understood the global big-picture right brain, which he named after the Egyptian star goddess Nuit. He understood the task-oriented atomizing left brain, which he named Hadit (because of a mistranslation of the name of Horus Behedit), and that Cosmos-changing magic occurred when these separated parts were synthesized (à la Hegel) by Love into an entity he called Ra-Hoor-Khuit (Ra who is Horus on the Horizon)—a philosophical amalgam of the Nietzchean idea of creating one's own horizons and the Egyptian god-form of humanity at its highest/royal level. His system resonates with realities of the human animal not yet fully understood when he intuited it.

The IAO formula is the way will becomes Will. At first humans are brave enough to try something new: they feel empowered, the world seems to shine on them. There is novelty and much synchronicity. This is the time of Isis, magic mom. Then the new wears off. Friction occurs. The needs of life press us. Most humans discover this every year as their New Year's resolutions fail. This is the time of Apep, he of "the broken kas," the multiheaded demon who threatens to stop the sun in his underworld journey each night. But some few press on, continue to fight, go down to the gym at five in the morning, and eventually become past masters. They can do the new skill with ease; in fact, what used to be hard now gives them energy. This is the Osiris phase, after the Egyptian god of resurrection. Vampyres who master this undead formula are unstoppable.

Crowley began the use of modern thinking. He considered the insightful critique of current art and study of cutting-edge science to be part of the initiate's duty. Likewise he hired translators to look at important magical texts—unlike the old practice of magicians (like S. L. McGregor Mathers) translating texts, he brought in the use of scholarship.

The need of grade testing is fundamental to Crowley's system. Most occultists, when they hear of a system, assume they're at the top of the heap. Crowley worked his way through the Golden Dawn grades and decided a ritual ordeal was necessary to see where he was. He used the Enochian Aires to see where he was (Magister Templi) and to get glimpses of where he could be (Magus and Ipsissimus). He crystalized each grade, developed a curriculum, and offered means of testing. Now, the seeds for this existed in the guild system of medieval Europe and various Freemasonic systems. Crowley, however, codified the Work and passed through it himself.

There are four drawbacks to Crowley's system: gender bias, limited chain of being, preference for the Kabbalah, and drug use. We've already dealt with drug use in regard to Randolph. The grade system and magical system of Crowley are firmly centered on the Christian Kabbalah, which not only lacks the spiritual force of the real Jewish tradition but also makes no sense in a religion actively opposed to Jewish and Christian mysticism. Forcing pagan gods to be judges by Hebrew misspelling of their names is rude enough, but using the divine name YHVH as your guide to magic is senseless. Crowley did understand the importance of living teachers but thought there were strict limits—there could be only one Ipsissimus, one Magus, a limited number of Magister Templi—hence the system is easily moved toward despotism and (more importantly) limits its range of success. Lastly, his sex magic system is based on the male orgasm and a spiritual adoration of spooge.

If you want to know more about the man, read *Perdabo* by Richard Kaczynski. If you want to understand the mechanics of Crowley's system, read *Living Thelema* by David Shoemaker. If you want to understand the implications of the philosophy, read *Overthrowing the Old Gods* by yours truly.

Opening Rite of Thelema

After aiming the candles to the South—that is, toward you—knock upon the altar loudly: first five times, pause, then six times.

Say the Vampyric Invocation and repeat the Graal Work as follows:

> I, (state your legal name), do understand intellectually that the voice that speaks and the ears that hear these words are part of a five-dimensional entity that currently has forgotten how to speak with itself, but that, fueled by self-love and persistence, it can hear and know all things as angels did speak with the prophets of old. It is my True Will that I will understand this spiritually, physically, and magically and can thereby Work all Magicks as though I held the Tao itself. I honor the Prophet Ankh-f-n-khonsu who heard the Word Thelema, was transformed by Work and Ecstasy, and uttered the Word Thelema to end the Christian notion that the dead "rest."

Raise your hands to the heavens and say:

> I stand in awe of Nuit! Infinite Stars in Infinite Space—always greater than my mind can know! I stand and remember that I am as vast as She, for I know Her. I stand in awe of myself greater than the gods of death who had once chained me with lies that hide my infinite nature.

Lower your hands. With your left hand touch the space between your eyes, your heart, and your genitals. For the speech below use your details.

> I am but a spark of intimate at this moment. I am Hadit living on Earth on the continent of X, the country of X, the state of X, the city of X, at XXX (address) of the street X, apartment X, on this night of (month, day, year). But my Magick does touch all of space and time. I affect my past and my future, my enemies and my friends. I am the winged disk of the sun.

Hold wand or dagger and address each of the directions (West, South, East, North),

I am the Vampyre [VN], lord of life, death, and undying. With each thought, each word, each deed, I unite myself to myself and become an undying star.

Place dagger or wand on the altar and say:

I fill all of my being with this LAW. Do What Thou Wilt Shall Be the Whole of the Law. I will know and fulfill my True Will, nothing can stop me!

Knock on the altar six times, pause, then five times.
Close in your usual manner.

LIFE ANALYSIS

With these questions, note the time you answer them and the big news (what are the headlines screaming?), and the personal news of the day.

1. Tell about a time when an apparent setback turned out to be important, lucky, or necessary to your life.
2. Tell about the single hardest thing you did; talk about how it felt—physically, emotionally, mentally, and spiritually before, during, and after the deed. Then define the word *will*.
3. Tell about a time when your expectations for an outcome really screwed up an outcome.
4. Tell about a time you had bliss or ecstasy.

VAMPYRIC ANALYSIS

1. Become aware of your own outdated programming. Do you shy away from talking to redheads because one dumped you once? Are you mad at bald men because your father used to be harsh with you? Notice where these feelings come from; notice how they affect your breathing, posture, muscle tone. Don't struggle against them, just be aware of them—these things will relax on their own.
2. Pick someone and notice their triggers (like the ones above). Don't

try to play Sherlock Holmes with this, just notice: "Ms. Jenkins always smiles when a motorcycle roars down the street." "Mr. De La Cruz tightens his throat muscles every time a package is delivered to the office." "Mr. Chang squeezes the edge of his desk when that trans girl speaks." Just be aware of other people's spikes in either defensive or receptive energy.

3. Play the "Why am I sitting here?" game. Just trace back to the causes. I'll give you two examples. "I'm sitting here because I came to work early to meet Mr. Chang, but he isn't here. I wanted to meet him early because I'm worried about the agenda for the Wednesday meeting. I worry about agendas because I hate to look stupid. I hate to look stupid because Dad yelled at me for not paying attention. Dad yelled because he thought if I looked dumb, I wouldn't get a good job. Dad was worried about jobs because he was a garbage man. He was a garbage man because he flunked out of high school. He flunked out of high school because he had to get a job to take care of his family. He had to take care of his family because a cop shot his dad. A cop shot his dad, because his dad was a minor drug dealer in the wrong place at the wrong time. Granddad was a dealer because that was the best job an African American could get in Detroit. Granddad was in Detroit because his father moved from Alabama. Great-granddad was in Alabama because of the slave trade. The slave trade happened because the 1 percent back in the day wanted workers to grow cotton. They grew cotton because Eli Whitney invented the cotton gin. Whitney invented the cotton gin because the Industrial Revolution gave him access to machine parts. The Industrial Revolution happened because the new markets in America upped the flow of capital. There were new markets in America because Columbus 'discovered' America. Columbus discovered America because the Spanish had kicked the Moors out of Spain. The Moors were in Spain because . . ." Second example: "I am sitting here now because my office chair is next to my desk. My desk is here because I mainly do work on the computer. I work on the computer because my job is part of the information age. The

information age was a by-product of the invention of the computer to track data in the Second World War. The Second World War happened because of the reparations that Germany was paying for the First World War. The First World War happened because of the conflict between the Central Powers and England and France. England and France were in conflict with the Central Powers because of their control of vast colonial holdings. England had vast colonial holdings because they had defeated the Spanish Armada. The Spanish Armada was attacking England because Henry VIII had divorced Catherine of Aragon. Henry VIII had divorced Catherine because she bore him no sons. She bore him no sons because of the chromosomes in Henry's sperm. Henry made sperm because he was a mammal. Mammal dominance happened because of a meteor striking the Yucatan peninsula in the time of the dinosaurs. . . ."

4. Play with the idea that you were going to sneak up on someone—find some way to choose a random time. This is a thought experiment only—DO NOT STALK YOUR FRIENDS. Let's say you make a list of six people you know and pick twelve hours of the day. If you were going to sneak up on Mr. Phillips at three in the afternoon what would you do? Mrs. McGilchrist at six in the morning? Become aware that everyone has habits that rule their presence and attention. After you've played this game in your head a few times, think about how someone would sneak up on you. How predictable are you? How much of your perception is predictable?

PERCEPTION EXERCISES

1. Pay attention to lifting and gripping things tightly with either hand. How good are you at guessing weight? What does gripping, lifting, putting down, and releasing feel like?

2. Now that you've done that, how well can you imagine it?

3. Play this game: visualize what it would be like to move super elegantly—through the halls at school, driving in traffic, moving through a shopping mall or the airport. Now try to do this: avoid

running into people, practice sidestepping with grace, anticipate traffic jams and avoid them. When you do your energy inventory at the end of the day, relive your best moments. See how much of a dancer you can be in life this week.

4. Play this game: You are a Sith lord with powers of telekinesis. Imagine the Force is helping you lift things, open jars, and is guiding you around people or vehicles.

TECHNIQUES TO TRY

1. Tell people that sometimes you feel you can help out in an "almost magical way." Say that it's prayer or mindfulness or your gypsy blood—whatever they are prone to accept. If they say they have a problem, look off into space, nod. If they ask what you're doing, just tell them its a positive visualization. Then pay attention to their situation. If you hear that things resolved in a good way, ask, "Hey, whatever happened about that thing?" When they tell you the good news, just smile and nod. Don't touch a magical talisman, don't be dramatic. Let them do the rest.

2. When you find yourself rising to anger—for example some fool cuts you off on the freeway—stop your feelings by saying aloud (if you are alone) or silently: "I can use this energy for better purposes!" Imagine the energy flowing into a battery. Take a few breaths and enjoy your calm. When you do your inventory that night you can either leave the energy in the battery or absorb it into your life for health or magical reasons. Try to expand this practice when you are provoked by something in the news or in social media. See how much free energy you gain.

3. Frequently this month—whenever it occurs to you, in fact, say, "I wish I had the guidance of the better hidden parts of myself! Abracadabra!" Don't hypothesize if this means your right brain, your Holy Guardian Angel, your "self ahead of yourself," or so on. When you feel yourself starting to speculate, just stop yourself in the same way you stopped unproductive anger above.

INITIATIC RITE OF THELEMA

Have bread and wine available to consume during the Graal Work. Aim the candles to the North (i.e., away from you). Knock on the altar one time, then pause, then nine times, then pause and knock one last time.

Say the Vampyric Invocation and repeat the Graal Work as follows:

> *I believe in the miracle of the eucharist in that my body shall make this bread into my flesh and this wine into my blood."*

Drink wine, eat bread.
Here is the working:

> *I have seen how the universe has worked through millennia to bring me to this moment. I have learned to dance lightly on this dying world. I ask the universe one boon: that as I finish each task I have set before me, I be in the presence of the best tools to do my next task. In exchange for this boon I promise to teach another my Art.*
>
> *I have taken the Word Thelema into my heart and been transformed thereby. By my Will I am thoroughly aligned with the Vampyric current having been blessed by Ankh-f-n-khonsu to be free from the rest of death. I honor the Sun knowing it is not my enemy, and time bows before my will.*

Face the East and say:

> *Hail Khepra self-created one that rises from the caverns of night. Kophra is thy Word, thy Hidden Name!*

Face the South and say:

> *Hail Re who sees all things and dispels all doubts. In the light of Truth there is no Fear!*

Face the West and say:

> *Hail Atum, the setting sun who brings the wisdom and comfort of a goodly old age!*

Face the North and say:

> *Hail Atef, the corpse of the sun at midnight who is Great in Magic. Undead Sun your Secret Name is written in my black heart!*

Advance to the Altar and say:

> *I return these Lights to their eternal Hidden home!*

Blow out the candles.

To close, knock on the altar three times, then pause, then three times, then pause, then five times.

ᵂ ᵂ

By Awakening your Will—that is to say, the desires of your Vampyric self—you have brought order to those aspects of your life of which you became aware under the aegis of Try. Now you may bring about temporary union with those things and your desire in the objective world under Indulgence and begin to understand your place in the Cosmos.

10

Indulgence

THE MAGIC OF ANTON LaVEY

The most important ideas in Vampyric magic come from Anton LaVey. Anton S. LaVey was born Howard Stanton Levy in Chicago in 1930. He grew up as a bookish Jewish kid. He had an ability to charm women to get them to support his needs—which were modest. He liked playing/listening to cool music, reading spooky stuff, and making spooky rooms. He lived in his parents' house in San Francisco, told great stories, and had a minor hustle giving lectures on the squishy borderland between the occult and the erotic. He apparently visited Jack Parson's Church of Thelema once and was impressed with the naked female altar and had Parsons as a source for occult books until Parsons's explosive death. He did not (initially) conceive of himself as a Magus, nor did he conceive of "Indulgence" as a Word. One of his followers—Michael Aquino—reworked the material into the Western magical tradition. However, Anton did far more than assemble his material (largely plagiarized) into the seminal books *The Satanic Bible* and *The Satanic Rituals*. He synthesized several powerful ideas and literally created a new magical current. Because of the cheese factor, LaVey's work is ignored by the occult mainstream—and that was by design.

Some of these ideas are very useful to Vampyres. Let's look at eleven of these very powerful Vampyric ideas, and then the four big drawbacks. Anton's great ideas: pragmatism is paramount, Indulgence is sacramental, magic must be kept sacred, the Mortensen trio (a.k.a. how Vampyrism works), the three laws of bullshit, the Law of the Trapezoid,

121

the pyramid of control, casting a large net, the pimp principle, the cheese factor, and Vampyrizing the imposter. We will look at each of these ideas—and if you don't find these notions dark and disturbing, you aren't understanding them.

Pragmatism is paramount. This notion was absorbed fully and without credit into Chaos Magic. Occultists love lore and accomplishing meaningless tasks. Okay, hobbies are cool. But RESULTS are what's important. If you are trying to get into Bootsie Collins's shorts, matching her dad's cologne, not the lengthy Venus ritual with the inscribed copper plate, will get you the poontang. If I want my jerk neighbor to stop bothering me, a call to the authorities about his illegal chicken coop is more time and energy efficient than calling up the seventy-two demons of the Goetia.

Anton claimed (probably falsely) that he observed the same men indulging in a brothel, where he played the organ on Saturday nights, and confessing in church, where he played the organ on Sunday mornings. Again and again, Anton (after Pavlov) stated the basic formula, that Indulgence is sacramental. We all get through the week looking forward to moments of Indulgence. Indulgence is the moment the social parasite stops its internal monologue because it is overcome by pleasure. It is the moment when pleasures (big or small) allow the Vampyric self to renew the body, emotions, mind, and magical powers—as well as that of your servitors (both your personalities and humans in your thrall). Indulgence is 100 percent personal and therefore the basis of the Left-Hand Path. For Mike it might be watching *Star Trek* (the original series) on Friday nights, for Ralph and Sue their monthly threesome with Sue's girlfriend from college, for José eating his abuela's chicken mole, for Lance winning a chess tournament, for Lashonda vamping out at the club. Anton noticed that the power of the social parasite was denying Indulgence. (A historical aside: Michael Harner, pop anthropologist and friend of Anton and Carlos Castaneda, told the latter about "Indulgence"—so Castaneda's Don Juan preaches against Indulgence in the author's early books. Bullshitters like to fight other bullshitters.)

Magic must be kept sacred. The longest of the Eleven Satanic Rules of the Earth is the seventh. It is also the only esoteric rule. "Acknowledge the power of magic if you have employed it successfully to obtain your desires. If you deny the power of magic after you have called upon it with success, you will lose all you have obtained." The ONLY principle that Anton proclaims reverence for—other than the vague notion of the "self"—is MAGIC. Not just any magic, but that which has worked for you—the meaning of Randolph's TRY. One of my best pupils, a hot young witch, once told me that she would pursue Adepthood in the Temple of Set, until she got "a great car, a great job, and a great husband." She ticked these items off, and with her new, very Christian husband made a great show of not only quitting the temple and cutting up her snazzy membership card but also publicly repenting of her Black Magic deeds. Within a month the three treasures ended in a rather gruesome way.

Vampyrism works because of the Mortensen trio. Anton was strongly influenced by the photographer who Ansel Adams called the "Antichrist"—William Mortensen. Mortensen (January 27, 1897—August 12, 1965), known for his erotic and/or macabre photos, practically invented Anton's career and aesthetics. He wrote a book called *The Command to Look: A Formula for Picture Success* in 1937. Its formula was that

1. the image must grab the viewer's attention (Vampyrism step one: get their energy willingly);
2. the subject matter must process emotion (Vampyrism step two: make their energy rise by use of sex, nostalgia, or wonder); and
3. the subject matter must hold the viewer's attention by making their eyes move or stop on "hindrances" over the surface of the photo (Vampyrism step three: we must get them to focus their energy in the way we desire).

This is a more powerful formula than even IAO! Anton was primarily a visual magician, his writings were secondary, and the mood of his magic is better approached by watching certain films—*The Black Cat, The Seventh Victim, Night of the Demon, The Cabinet of Dr. Caligari,* or *Burn, Witch, Burn*—than by reading grimoires.

Anton's magic was reactive—gaining power by criticizing the

world's hypocrisy. The most useful idea he had (although he never put it this succinctly) was the three laws of bullshit. Learn these and you will understand 98 percent of the evening news.

> **Law 1:** People love bullshit more than truth. Vaccines cause autism. Hard work is all you need to get ahead.
>
> **Law 2:** The right amount of bullshit is needed in life. We can get some power by living in our lies. Just don't overdo. Reality actually kills.
>
> **Law 3:** People will fight you to protect their bullshit with more force than protecting their family. Fundamentalist Christian, UFO believer, any political thought—people will at the least unfriend you and at the worst ruin your life.

Vampyres who don't know no. 3 have no jobs and tend to get a beating. Vampyres exist by no. 2. And Vampyres rule others by no. 1. Try reciting these rules when confused by ANY news story. There, I have explained the sorry nature of the world.

Drawing from Mortensen (and to a lesser extent color theorist Faber Birren), Anton formulated the Law of the Trapezoid. In a general sense the visual field of humans is trained. People have expectations of what they are seeing. Screw with it a little—make them see the shape of something dangerous (like a lightning bolt) in a non-dangerous form (like jewelry), and they offer up their energy if they are Asleep, or they are energized if they are Awake. A frustrated pyramid, like the one on the back of the U.S. dollar bill, weakens the weak, strengthens the strong. A room with slightly off angles instead of the expected right angles has the same effect. If the Vampyre combines this with the orgone theory of Wilhelm Reich and the knowledge mentioned earlier of Vampyric steads of power, huge energies can be tapped in to.

The pyramid of control is an example of taking modern non-esoteric knowledge and turning it into power. Feelings tend to arise from bodily states, and thoughts arise from feelings. If you control the body with cues of smell, lighting, sound, and proximity—you can control the feelings. If you pitch your desired results to resonate with the feelings, your mark will think the thoughts you desire them to think. This is basic Vampyric technology.

The above is an example of casting a wide net. In Anton's misogynistic guide to practical power, *The Complete Witch,* the bibliography has color theory, history of carnivals, photography, material on cold reading, psychology of smell, and so forth. Power comes from knowledge of the human animal and its motivations—not from occult literature.

Anton liked to claim that his home formerly belonged to San Francisco madam Mammy Pleasant (August 19, 1814–January 4, 1904), a powerful real estate broker, abolitionist, and possible Vodun priestess. A fitting myth for a man involved with the pimp principle. Pick a group (Anton chose women) that is disempowered because of their social parasites—in other words, what restrains them is largely what has been conditioned into them. Teach them most of the secrets you know for empowerment. Then present yourself as outside of the power structure that restrains them (mainly by dress). The now more empowered (and angry) folks love and fight for you. The Vampyre can always do this—look for the disempowered around you, teach them to stand up for themselves, add a few Lesser Black Magic techniques, and you will have an army. This is powerful but ethically questionable.

During the height of the Satanic Panic, when cops in America would literally pick up Goth teenagers for wearing black T-shirts, Anton went unmolested. Why? The cheese factor. This is amazingly powerful: present yourself as just a little cheesy. If someone at work accuses you of Black Magic show up wearing devil horns and a shiny Halloween cape. Carry a red plastic trident, and cast a spell on your accuser: "Mighty Ineffable King of Hell, give me stuff that's really swell! This mortal scoffs at my power, Scooply Whooply make him cower!" Then drop it. You will make 90 percent of people laugh at the idea, and 10 percent will think you need help. Of course, when terrible doom falls on your target, you act horrified that your joke is making anyone think that you hurt your target. Push this idea until YOU get sympathy. The cheesy Vampyre is not the dangerous Vampyre!

By the media-heavy age of the 1960s most humans suffered from the imposter syndrome. Their social parasites told them they were weak or dumb or poor or ugly—and they told lies to themselves and others, thinking this healed the pain. They either worshipped or demonized celebrities. By the age of social media we all suffer. Anton discovered that by being the Other—worshipping Satan, claiming Gypsy descent, posing with naked women in Halloween horns, keeping a lion in his house—he wounded people ashamed of their boring lives. No one ever challenged his lies, even those that could easily be debunked, such as being a police photographer or screwing Marilyn Monroe, because everyone WANTED them to be true. I may not get to photograph crime scenes, but it sounds like fun! I may not get to bang Marilyn, but that sounds like lots of fun. I can't believe in myself, so I believe in Anton! The Vampyre can easily draw energy this way, but see below.

Having looked at the amazing strengths, let's consider the four drawbacks of Anton's system from the Vampyric point of view. These are intellectual passivity, house-of-cards-ism, reactive rather than proactive, and the law is for all. Let's look at each and end this section with some reading recommendations (see p. 28).

Anton had great intellectual passivity. He was willing to plagiarize other sources: big sections from *The Satanic Bible* are lifted from the right-wing rants of Ragnar Redbeard. He was content to get other people to write his major rituals: Michael Aquino, whom we'll meet in a later chapter, wrote the "Adult Satanic Baptism," the "Ceremony of the Nine Angles," and the "Call to Cthulhu." This had disastrous philosophical consequences: Aquino wrote a thoroughly Stoic rite for entrance into the Epicurean Church of Satan that contributed to the Church of Satan's downfall as the leading edge of the Western Left-Hand Path. The other rituals in *The Satanic Rituals* were written largely by other folks, each with their own slant. In later years, the hedonistic atheism of Ayn Rand was popular among newer members of the Church of Satan, so Anton simply proclaimed that he had always been a staunch Randian. This philosophy is incompatible with magical practice and offers a rather immature way of dealing with human growth and emotions; as such, the Church of Satan became philosophically and magically incoherent.

Anton had based his sorcery on various unreal deeds and fakelore.

This house-of-cards-ism has three huge drawbacks. First, if I only impress you because I banged Marilyn Monroe, tamed lions in the circus, and was a police photographer living in Mammy Pleasant's brothel—what do you think of me when you discover I was never in the same room as Monroe, bought (and mistreated) the lion and other household pets, never snapped a photo for ANYONE professionally, and lived in the basement of my parents' house? When the details of Anton's life were revealed by reporter Lawrence Wright, his health and economic status declined rapidly. Second, human memory is a re-creation by our brains: if I tell a lie often enough, I will believe it. Anton's accomplishments were real, but mixed with many fakes; he became the wounded soul with the impostor syndrome. Third, fake magical lore can be used to generate energy for a working or two—but deep research into the mysterious truth can generate a lifetime's energy. On one occasion, when I was friends with his son-in-law Nikolas Schreck, Schreck told me that Anton couldn't stop bullshitting—even to family. He recalled Anton making up a whopping tale of how Robert E. Howard was a member of a secret Texas/Aztec Satanic brotherhood. Nikolas said that he just got up and walked out. He thought that by being family, there might be a circle of truth.

Anton's work is full of great Satanic myths: secret Satanic societies that Thomas Jefferson belonged to, Yezidi thought control towers, and so on. Yet Anton did not advocate self-transformation to become better, nor did he suggest how Satanists might use their power to improve the world. He suggested that the best path was to criticize the hypocrisy of society and retreat further and further into the cave. This reactive rather than proactive approach is anathema for the Vampyre.

Anton never understood that magic wasn't take it or leave it. If you establish a magical law, you are governed by a magical law. Anton didn't know the law is for all. His most powerful creation, the Law of the Cycles of Nine—which, true to form, he borrowed from W. B. Crow in 1948—suggests that history is ruled by eighteen-year periods with nine years of expansion, a catastrophe, then nine years of focusing. This would give us magical years like 1930, when LaVey was born and the Chronozon club founded; 1948, when Achad utters MAnifestatION and Our Lady of Endor Coven was formed; 1966, when the Church of Satan was formed—with the danger years being 1974 and 1975. When Anton proposed selling off the Priesthood of Satan in 1974, a chain of events led to Aquino's founding the Temple of Set in 1975. LaVey's system predicted the year to watch out for—and he didn't watch out. All magicians and Vampyres WILL have this moment when their magic works exactly like it was supposed to—and knocks them flat. The secret is not to do this more than once.

For the Vampyre, I would recommend four books to understand LaVey. The first is the very misogynistic, very pimp-principled *The Compete Witch* (a.k.a. *The Satanic Witch*), which is full of Vampyric theory (and misogyny). The second is the Feral House edition of William Mortensen's *The Command to Look* with a great essay on LaVey's Lesser Magic by Michael Moynihan. The third is LaVey's *The Satanic Bible.* The fourth is Michael Aquino's fiftieth anniversary rewrite of *The Satanic Bible.* Aquino is a much more structured thinker than LaVey and has some insights about the period of the Church of Satan's greater Manifestation.

OPENING RITE OF INDULGENCE

Before you begin the opening rite you should watch one or more documentaries about the 1960s. If possible, also watch the film *Satanis* and then during the month watch several 1960s vampire films. You should have a jigger and a half of Jack Daniels to drink for your Graal offering. Point the candles toward the South (that is, toward you).

Say the Vampyric Invocation and repeat the Graal Work as follows:

> *I slay the hypocrisy I have lived with all my life! I proclaim that it is better to rule in Hell than serve in Heaven. I proclaim that each pleasure I partake of is a sacrament that loosens the power of God upon me. Indulgence instead of Abstinence!*

Slowly walk counterclockwise through your room, pausing when you speak of each sin and arriving at the altar again at the end. Say:

> *I walk against the sun and the natural order. With LUST I take my Vampyric pleasure with whom I will, when I will. With GLUTTONY I feed upon the fat of their dreams and fruits of their struggle. With*

GREED I snatch away their wealth to the last penny. With WRATH I use my powers to destroy men of mildewed minds braying in their self-righteousness! With ENVY I send forth my Vampyric powers to take from the famous, who hold themselves up as living idols. With SLOTH I recline on purple cushions and dream my enemies' dooms. With PRIDE I set my throne on their new graves!

At the altar raise both hands in the air and feel the energy streaming into you.

Satan lives!

Blow out the candles.

So It Is Done!

LIFE ANALYSIS

1. When is your earliest memory of wanting to do something for fun that your classmates or family found odd? What was it? Did you get to do it? Did you ever lie about it?
2. What smells make you happy? Especially weird ones, like gasoline? Why?
3. What turns you on during sex that's so individual you never talk about it? Where did that come from?
4. Think of a person who was considered a witch or magician in your early life, like the old lady down the street with too many cats, or the bald janitor covered in Polynesian tattoos—why were they considered magical? How did that affect their lives? How long have they been an archetype in your psyche?

VAMPYRIC ANALYSIS

1. Who in your life is scared by you? Who in your life is sexually attracted to you? Who do you wish were in these categories?
2. What subtly strange thing is true about your car, or house, or office cubicle, or appearance? The Law of the Trapezoid isn't invoked by massive strangeness but rather by subtle, almost unnoticeable things.

3. Look up 1966: Can you find at least three other Wyrd things that happened besides the Church of Satan being founded? Try 1948, 1930, 1912. If there is a secret pulse, what could you do with it?

4. How can you make your lair more secure? How can you make it reinforce your energy?

PERCEPTION EXERCISES

1. Erotic crystallization inertia. Your body was most in line with your Vampyric self when you were first really enjoying sex. If you surround your body with cues from that time—the food, music, entertainment, clothes—you will become younger. You will have younger thoughts, feelings, energy levels. This is why old people who move to smaller cities often become more healthy. This uses the Mortensen trio—especially nostalgia about the self—positively. Play with it. By the way, you can also use this to heal others.

2. Get a new image of yourself made, looking either sexier (if that's your strength), magically threatening, or showing grandmotherly calm. After looking at some of Mortensen's photographic work, Photoshop the picture. Put it out on social media. For the first seven nights afterward say the Vampyric Invocation and then imagine your new image with the words FEED ME written in red above it. You may wish to use the flashing-color technique from Try in chapter 8. Then attempt to forget about this magical action.

3. Buy a cheesy shirt or art object that identifies you as a Vampyre but in a silly way—for example, a Nosferatu on Board bumper sticker for your car. Show it off. If someone asks you about it, tell him or her you are a Vampyre—in a goofy Bela Lugosi voice. Then let it drop.

INITIATIC RITE OF INDULGENCE

Have the candles pointed North (away from you). Play music from your teen years that you loved—extra plus if it's "dark." When you feel relaxed and nostalgic, begin the rite.

Say the Vampyric Invocation. For the Graal Work drink a bright-red cocktail.

Say:

> *I drink the blood of enemies, my name will be on their lips as they perish. Indulgence instead of Abstinence!*
>
> *I am a child of Darkness. I am Rosemary's Baby. I am the absolute Other, and everyone wants to fuck me, or be trampled under my cloven hooves. The Hounds of Tindalos protect me, the nightgaunts carry my message of dreams and nightmares to the leaders of the world, and I am the master of the Cycles of Time! I call my Brothers to bless me!*

Face the South and say:

> *Arise, O Satan, and fill me with Lust, Pride, Joy, and Anger when I need each. My emotion shall shape the world!*

Face the East and say:

> *Arise, O Lucifer, quicken my mind with reason, bestow on me the best fast and slow thinking I need undistracted by the World of Horrors!*

Face the North and say:

> *Arise, O Belial, and strengthen my body for long life and strengthen the bodies I choose for my pleasure when I have offered this one to the fire!*

Face the West and say:

> *Arise, O Leviathan, serpent that circles the world, guide beyond this world into the black and starry realm where I shall remake the Cosmos into a thing of glory to my Infernal Will!*
>
> *I, the Vampyre [VN], reject the lies of men in this world, and I foreswear divine mindlessness in the next! I, the Vampyre [VN], stand for the Devil now, and stand with the Devil then!*

Picture yourself surrounded by red flames that caress and give your body deep ecstasy. Imagine holding a trident in your left hand. Picture yourself standing in various places of power (the White House, the Stock Exchange, etc.).

When the mood fades close the rite in your normal fashion.

🦇 🦇

Having gained an understanding of the world this month, you will come to see yourself as being one of its mysteries next month. You will discover that the difference between the mysteries within and without is an illusion by listening to Runa. You will glimpse that you, too, are one of the great mysteries of the Cosmos.

11
RUNA

THE MAGIC OF STEPHEN EDRED FLOWERS

The word *rune* means "secret." It can refer to a character in a writing system of Germanic peoples, but it can also mean anything that is hidden (e.g., that John is getting a surprise birthday party) or so complex that it can't be easily explained (e.g., humans' relationship to money). Stephen Edred Flowers's divine formula is a sentence in Old Norse: Reyn Til Runa! "Seek the Mysteries!"

Stephen Edred Flowers was a quirky kid from Texas—liking dark stuff and kinky sex and having an amazing grasp of languages. Certain events prepared him to hear the Word Runa in 1974 and then become Michael Aquino's (see chapter 12) student in 1983. Flowers was briefly snared by LaVey's Working (as we shall see) and broke free from the limitations of that working. We'll start with a brief biographical sketch and then consider the virtues and drawbacks of the Word Runa for the Vampyre. His unusual middle name, Edred, came from his maternal grandfather and reflected a Victorian fascination with Anglo-Saxon lore, so his movement toward the runes came from his soul name. The film *The Vikings* (a 1958 retelling of *Ragnars saga loðbrókar*) and *The Alamo* (1960) created lifelong fascination with small heroic bands, honor, the use of myth, and the importance of community. In his senior year of high school he wrote a fifty-page paper on the fact and fiction underlying Bram Stoker's *Dracula,* which introduced him to the notions of the Devil's School, the Scholomance where Transylvanian folklore connected their older shamanic traditions (both Germanic and Dacian) with the lore of Satan. The underground school may be evaluated in terms of the Vampyric steads of power. It and the students remained unexposed to sunlight for the seven-year duration of their study. The dragon that carried away the prize pupil slept submerged in a mountain-top lake, south of Hermannstadt (now called Sibiu, its Romanian name) in the Saxon part of Transylvania—one of the last places on Earth to use the runes as a living alphabet.

Like many a brainy and introverted youth, Flowers did not find high school an enjoyable time and felt compelled to run off to Germany immediately after graduation. He had an interesting year discovering the reality of the German S-M scene and even working to ferry secret papers into East Germany once. A little wiser about the world, he returned to Texas and enrolled in a Dallas community college and eventually in the University of Texas at Austin. His esoteric side led him to a brief membership in the Church of Satan, where he found stimulus in the "Adult Satanic Baptism," "The Ceremony of the Nine Angles," and especially the writings of "John Kincaid," the editor of the church newsletter, the *Cloven Hoof*.

Flowers joined an occult group called the Nexialist Collegium—a group in which folks from different traditions were invited to share what they knew. The group leader took them to a demonstration by a "Tibetan lama" named Norbu Chen (Charles Vernon Alexander II). One of the less credible New Age practitioners, Norbu did some stage mentalism and then would perform "past life regressions" for a fee. The day following his performance the leader of the Nexium contacted Flowers's then girlfriend with the exciting news that a dream had revealed that she, the leader, and Norbu had been lovers in a past life. She was going to drive to the wilds of Harris County and share these joyous tidings with Mr. Chen and wanted some company—her student and her student's boyfriend, Flowers. Flowers, a freshman journalism major, decided to skip classes and tag along. They drove up to a trailer park near the oil fields, and the woman went to knock on Mr. Chen's door. Answering the door in a T-shirt with a Coors in hand, he proceeded to curse at the woman (oddly more in English than classical Tibetan) until she ran back to her car. On the trip home to Austin, Flowers had the back seat to himself, dozing in and out of consciousness, until suddenly "ROONAH!" was whispered into his left ear. Because of reading Grimm and Stoker he knew it meant something to do with the runes.

The next day he went to the University of Texas campus. The library was in the infamous clocktower, site of the 1966 mass shooting. He sent for all the books he could find on the runes—mainly dusty, dry, academic tomes that covered topics including the evidence for the Indo-European vowel shift in Runic inscriptions such as Wolfgang Krause's *Was man in Runen ritze*. Also—oddly—there was a 1955 German paperback by the master of the Berlin Lodge of the Fraternitas Saturni, Karl Spiesberger, called *Runenmagie*. The book contained practical exercises informed by the thinking of the world's most sophisticated Left-Hand Path group. The twofold nature of his quest made itself clear: hard, reliable, academic data on the one side, esoteric practice on the other. Already freed from superstition or a fear of the forbidden by his Church of Satan background, Flowers knew he needed only two things: decades of hard study and quarters to make a photocopy of the text. Returning to the tower, he made his copy while odd crowd sounds began coming from outside. While he was making his copy, someone had committed suicide by leaping from the tower, the ninth person to do so in the tower's rather dark history. The tower was once again to be closed to the public.

Flowers began writing *Futhark,* but a lack of interest in runes delayed its publication for nine years. He allowed his membership in the Church of Satan to lapse and threw himself forcefully into academia, getting his B.A. (major in German, minor in philosophy) in 1976, his M.A. (Germanic languages and literature) in 1979, and his Ph.D. (Germanic languages and literature/medieval studies) in 1984. In 1982 he studied at the University of Göttingen in Germany under the mentorship of Edgar C. Polemé, Ph.D., which culminated in his U of T dissertation, "Runes and Magic: Magical Formulaic Elements in the Elder Tradition." He picked up a few languages along the way: German, Swedish, Icelandic, Dutch, Old Norse, Old English, Gothic, French, Latin, Greek, Farsi, Old Persian, and a smattering of Spanish. It should be noted that Flowers also studied under the great German runologist Klaus Düwel.

Flowers studied and expanded the semiotic theory of magic created by Stanley Jeyaraja Tambiah in his dissertation and later in his magical practice and occult books. The theory is that magic is a dialogue between the self and the other (hidden) side of the universe. The self creates a command, a question, or other communication. The self encodes this message in a manner attractive to this realm by gesture and speech and then receives an answer in the form of events or thoughts, which the self must assimilate into itself as energy or information. Flowers explored this method in several books on runic magic and also proved the theory useful for magicians by illustrating it in books on Greek and Persian magic. His students such as Toby Chappell and I have likewise expanded Flowers's methods into other areas, like the book you are holding now.

In 1984, he wrote seeking membership in the Temple of Set and later founded the Bull of Ombos Pylon, a Temple of Set group that continues to operate in Austin, which has various leaders including Lechuza Mundo and myself. And he wrote, and wrote. At the time of this writing he has forty-two published books. He created the system of practical heathenry I will describe in the "Advanced Practices" (Book the Third) section of this book. Of his many ideas, some are very important to the Vampyre: the Polemé principle, the Polarian method, inner and outer mysteries, information at the right time, share what you know, the importance of scholarship, the etymology of ideas, the nature of divine speech. Let's deal with these first.

Of course, he didn't invent the Polemé principle; Edgar Polemé did that. This is one of the most important ideas for occultists and moderns in general. Anything touched by the mind of man cannot be reduced to simple explanations. You can't explain magic by biology, economics, or psychology. You can't reduce an artistic movement to sociology or linguistics or chemistry. Most theorists will take something complex, human, and mysterious and explain it in terms of their favorite thoughtlike process, whether Marxism or Christianity or objectivism. Anything with real transformational potential is mysterious and cannot be explained fully by a rational framework. This quality, as well as Aquino's notion of the "unnatural" (see next chapter), forms the basis not only of Flowers's work but also stands behind this book's approach as well.

In the Temple of Set, Flowers took the magical name Polaris, partly after Lovecraft's story of the same name. His method, unlike the lazy approach of most would-be magicians, emphasizes research and academic discipline. The Polarian method: Inspiration, Objective Research, Subjective Synthesis, and Enactment. Inspiration is a moment where the Vampyric self overcomes the social parasite, such as Flowers's moment of hearing Runa. The hidden side of the universe sends a message that remains in a form pleasing to itself. Objective Research means discovering the hard facts of the matter to be discovered. You find what exists outside of the psyche (most occultists refuse this labor). Subjective Synthesis is guided by your personal sense of the Beautiful (Indulgence) and means you create your own model of the system you are studying. Through Enactment you change the objective world using your model and thereby change yourself.

We seem to have inner and outer mysteries. An outer mystery might be how Transylvanian folklore became a conduit for sex magical practices. An inner mystery might be why we wanted to be vampires since age six. Flowers teaches us that the apparent difference between inner and outer mysteries is an illusion.

Vampyres who seek after Runa will discover that they will always have the right information at the right time. Signals that are delivered strongly into your life are exactly the signals you need at the moment.

Share what you know, and your power will grow. The sharing of knowledge—through discussion, writing, teaching, and so forth—with others (particularly those near to you in developmental level) will increase your personal power. You will create yourself as an expert to powerful humans, drive away people with shoddy thoughts, and attract the attention of humans more developed than you.

Just as LaVey discovered the need for a wide net, Flowers demonstrates the need for scholarship. The great secrets are not available in mass-produced books but rather in neglected scholarly work. The secrets are not hidden in a book derived from a book derived from the Golden Dawn but instead in academic theses on folklore and linguistics that take effort to locate (Objective Research). When you find an idea, ask yourself: "Why was this idea created? What was it used for?" This is because ideas hold the intent of their creator (see the Polemé principle, on p. 136). The idea will tend to continue to produce the effect it was created for (see Remanifestation). That is why you should inquire as to the etymology of ideas.

Finally, inherent in the semiotic theory of magic is the notion of divine speech. The messages from the other/hidden side of the universe are much denser in information than speech here. They must be unpacked—sometimes for years. It took ten years from hearing Runa until its recognition as a Word by the Temple of Set.

The weaknesses in the pursuit of Runa are fourfold. First, becoming ensnared in a subjective secret—rather than dealing with something expressed in both the objective and subjective universe (e.g., a true rune)—one looks for something subjective only, such as a dream image. Second, the idea of secrecy can be used for manipulation: some matters are too "advanced" for you, Neophyte, or "Women can't get this." Third, some folks spend too long in any of the first three phases of the Polarian method and never get to Enactment. Fourth is the weakness of atomizing secrets; for example, the way white supremacists will pay attention to only one rune—usually Othala (home)—and forget the rest. Systems (I Ching, tarot, runes) are not represented by a single element.

Flowers has produced a huge library of books. I'd recommend *Icelandic Magic, Futhark,* and *Alu* as good places to start if you are interested in the Germanic tradition. If you are an English reader/speaker you will find greater resonance with the Anglo-Saxon Futhorc to send your messages to the Unknown. The fact that those would have been the runes known to Vlad the Impaler, the historical Dracula, adds to their mystery.

OPENING RITE OF RUNA

Be sure to read the Norse stories of rewinning the poetic mead, Baldr's death, and Mimir's well. These may be found on many websites. Arrange the candles to point toward you (South). Have an eyepatch and mirror available. If you have a drinking horn, use it for the Graal.

Say the Vampyric Invocation, then proceed with the working as follows:

> *Three truths I know because I heard them from ancestors.*
>
> *First, when Odhinn had to regain the poetic mead he took the name Doer of Evil. He labored among slaves, seduced a Jottun wife and wore her out through sex, became a serpent to bore through the dense layers of the past and an eagle to fly to Asgard. To gain the ecstasy to do Work, I will do these things: be humble, lie, be lust incarnate, be the Serpent, and be the Eagle who flies to the place of highest consciousness. I become a Vampyre to do these works and learn how one Work leads to another Work and one Word leads to another Word, knowing I must always keep Working. Ecstasy is beyond good and evil.*
>
> *Second, when Odhinn's son, Baldr the beautiful, lay dead on the funeral pyre, Odhinn did whisper one word into his left ear. Rooonah! So his soul did not travel the Road to Hel but by Seeking the Mysteries overcame Death and climbed to Walhalla! The most precious secret is that there are Secrets! I became a Vampyre so that in my beauty Odhinn will whisper this word in my ear.*
>
> *Third, I know that when Odhinn visited the Well of Mimir, which is filled with the reflection of all that has been known to thinking beings since the birth of time, he paid a price, He plucked his right eye from his head and cast it into the well where it floats at the base of the world tree looking ever upward, seeing all. I would pay this price, the pain now, the greater pain of knowing all without denial.*

Press hard on your right eye and then put on the eyepatch. Look at yourself in the mirror, then take up the Graal cup that you have filled with icy water.

> *I drink the memories of all. I drink the memories of all. I do not lose myself in this knowledge, but I sacrifice my prejudices, denials, and false illusions no matter how much pain this sacrifice causes me.*

Drink almost all of the water, then fling a small amount out into your space.

I came into this world of mine own Will to fight sickness and ignorance and poverty. I hide the clues I needed in history and deeply within myself. As I Seek the Mysteries within, I grow wiser, stronger, better. As I seek the mysteries without, I grow more powerful, I move across the Earth to be standing in the place where I need to Work and Fight, I Hear what others do not hear, Find what others have forgotten, and Teach what others scoff at. The Razan of the World call to me. The Runes of the World speak to me. The Mysteries of the Ages are shown to me in the hidden places.

Say the following three times each:

Runa will Test Me!

Runa will Teach Me!

Runa will Save Me!

By making the Unknown Known, I shall create more Unknown! As Dracula pointed the way to Edred, the Vampyre within points the way to me!

Close the rite in your usual fashion.

LIFE ANALYSIS AND PERCEPTION EXERCISES

1. Dowsing with a forked branch. Read a few articles on dowsing. Find an appropriate branch and tell the tree: "I take this to further my powers of life. As I grow so shall you grow. I honor Ash and Elm, the trees that Odhinn made into humans." Learn to find small objects by practice. Be sure to check in on the tree's welfare.
2. Think about a time that you knew a secret—like folks were going to throw a surprise birthday party. How did keeping and knowing that secret make you powerful and happy?
3. When has someone used the idea of secrecy to manipulate you?
4. Have you ever used codes with anyone? Who? Why? What was it like?

VAMPYRIC ANALYSIS

1. How can you appear mysterious to some folks but nonthreatening to others?

2. How do you pick the folks to whom you appear mysterious?

3. How are your Vampyric steads of power like runes?

4. What's the best way to send a message to the universe? How does the method of sending change the message?

TECHNIQUES TO TRY

1. Create a bind-rune, a Vampyric monogram with your Vampyre name. Write your name out in the runes of the Anglo-Saxon futhorc. Many charts of the Anglo-Saxon futhorc exist online, if you do not own reference materials. Then combine the runes into a single symbol and simplify it. Use this as your magical mark to protect/bless your home, your steads, your goods. Mentally project it on the foreheads of people you wish to control.

2. Hide small magical tools in your steads of power, and then "find" them when you do workings.

3. Mention to people that all your life people have shared secrets with you. Just say it one time, then add you don't know why. Your victims will come up with reasons for you. "You're trustworthy, and so on." Then they will share secrets with you.

4. Since Flowers has a vast canon of techniques, buy some of his books and try what you like.

INITIATIC RITE OF RUNA

This is done in two parts. The first in your lair, the second in an outdoor environment of your choice. You will need a thin piece of wood, the thinner the better. You will need an X-acto knife to carve the runes, a red Sharpie to redden them. You will be using your Vampyric Name (VN); if you have not chosen one, then use what you think of as your name. Know the runes you need in advance. The Graal should be filled with the juice of apples. For the second part you will need a small hand shovel, some birdseed, and a trash bag.

Part One

Face the candles toward you (i.e., the South). Say the Vampyric Invocation. For the Graal Work say:

> *I drink to three Goddesses that are loved by all Vampyres, that I may emulate them in my deeds. Mother Earth that sustains all life, I who live forever will protect you. Mother Night that hides all Secrets, I will teach others to hold you sacred. Idunna, whose apples give long life by increasing Desire I will Seek the Mysteries in your Name.*

Drink the juice in a great gulp, then fling any remaining juice into the air.

For the working say:

> *In the Name of Odhinn, Father of Magic, All-Father, the Old Man, I carve powerful runes into the warp and weave of the world. I, the Vampyre [VN], will hide these runes in Mother Earth, and they will return to me in mysterious ways.*

Carve and redden the following phrase in runes:

> *:WEALTH AND RUNES CAME TO [VN]:*

When you have carved the runes, close the rite in your usual fashion.

Part Two

Find a natural spot that speaks to you. Depending on your Vampyric style it could be anything from an old cemetery to a mountain wilderness to a patch of ground in a traffic island. This can be done in daylight or at twilight. Spend some time there finding the correct spot; the dowsing branch may be useful. Dig a small hole and bury your runes. Say:

> *I hide these Runes in Mother Earth, and I become her immortal protector. I will look for these Runes as they return to me through*

my words, thoughts, and deeds. Like the Word whispered in
Baldur's Ear they shall awake me in the tomb.

Pour your birdseed over the spot and say:

I leave an offering to Mother Earth.

Then clean up the area—remove any trash from a circle at least nine yards radius from your spot. If anyone challenges you, say you're just trying to be a better steward of the Earth.

During this section of the Vampyric Initiation you will have glimpsed that part of you that is eternal and outside the world of change. Next, you will begin to sense how that part of you also exists as an active force of self-creation in this universe.

12

Xeper

THE MAGIC OF MICHAEL AQUINO

It is hard to picture a human as different from Anton LaVey than Michael Aquino. Born to an upper-middle-class family and well educated, the guy was also literally a Boy Scout: he was the number one Eagle Scout in the United States in 1965. His father was a decorated World War II veteran, his mother a distinguished sculptor. He was born into a socioeconomic class that by and large didn't go off to war—certainly not to Vietnam. But Michael enlisted.

Shortly before his all-expense-paid vacation to Indochina he was walking by a movie theater in San Francisco that was a few blocks from the pub where Aleister Crowley had declared himself as Magus, a few more blocks from the Church of Satan, and a few more blocks from Randolph's first Rosicrucian hall. A coffin-nosed Duesenberg pulled up with the personalized license plate VAMPYRE, and a bald man and some devotees in robes and hoods scurried into a showing of *Rosemary's Baby*. Aquino was fascinated. Who or what could these folks be?

Part of the publicity for the film *Rosemary's Baby* was listing Anton LaVey as "technical consultant." Anton played the role to the hilt, wanting to increase attention on his Church of Satan, which in those days was conceived of as a local affair. Shortly afterward, Aquino found his way to the Central Grotto, paid his $13, and got his medallion, scary membership card, and some of the flyers that would be assembled into the *Satanic Bible*. Most humans when threatened with death (for example, getting ready to go into combat) fall completely under the spell of their social parasite and perform the self-hypnosis of conventional religions. For the elect, the threat of death has the opposite effect and makes them seek methods of survival under their own power.

Aquino set up an altar in his barracks per the Church of Satan's instructions (a simplified version from Crowley's *Magick*) and immediately felt something. Most of the visitors to LaVey's house felt his great charisma (or, as we would say, Vampyric power), but Aquino sensed something alien—and not quite the guy in red tights and horns. He continued his practice in Vietnam. His superiors forbade it on army grounds because it frightened both the Vietnamese and American soldiers. Aquino was allowed the eccentricity of unusual religious practice because his specialty was psychological warfare (and those guys are all nuts).

His sense that he was dealing with something *older* and less *human* than LaVey's Pan-like Satan led him to adopt his first theorem: that the Prince of Darkness represented consciousness rather than social programming. Like Gurdjieff before him, he declared war on the robot, and he felt it was his mission to clarify this principle to mankind. Aquino set up an altar in the jungle, oddly not too far from the spot where Crowley had completed his Abramelin Working. He decided to write a response to Milton's *Paradise Lost* and began writing "statements" in the voice of each of the "Daimons." His odd practice of writing fan fiction is a major magical technique unique to him. He starts with a popular myth, poses a philosophical question, and then writes down the drama that unfolds in his head. In this case, as each Daimon spoke, the text changed from a Satanic critique of Milton into a very different sort of beast—an encoded magical philosophy. The book was partially destroyed by enemy fire. By the time he had finished the last and shortest chapter, the "Statement of Leviathan," a new magical philosophy had emerged. LaVey had described Satan as a force in man, dark and primal, but natural. In Aquino's work "The Diabolocon," the Daimonic race gives mankind a consciousness that creates meaning and expresses desire free from the natural order.

Unlike LaVey's idea that man was another animal, Aquino held that man was the recipient of the "Black Flame," the principle of isolate intelligence, and therefore was special and beyond good and evil. Because of its self-organizing power, this intelligence was immortal. Immortality and salvation were not gifts from God to the faithful but rather a gift to man to oppose the cosmic injustice of the galling confines of the mechanical universe. The Black Flame had a need: it—being outside of the mechanical universe—needed to witness its effect on that universe as fuel. So man had to begin the truth processes of politics, science, art, and magic. In Aquino's system magic is not the utilitarian adjunct to life that it is in LaVey's system but is instead a source of wonder. The Awakened self took up magic and the other truth processes to survive. Aquino mailed a copy of *The Diabolicon* to LaVey, who worked some of its phrases (but little of its theology) into Church of Satan Workings.

Aquino returned from Vietnam and was a workhorse for the Church of Satan. He organized a grotto in Louisville, Kentucky. He wrote the Adult Satanic Baptism ritual, which LaVey incorporated into the *Satanic Rituals*. It seems as if LaVey had failed to read the rite: it incorporated the nonnatural theology of the Diabolocon and a very Stoic oath to accept the pains and pleasures of existence. Aquino was soon recognized to the second degree (Warlock) and third degree (Priest of Mendes). At this level he began writing most of the church's newsletter, *The Cloven Hoof,* under the house name of John Kincaid. His efforts were memorialized by being the last of the many folks to whom the *Satanic Bible* was dedicated.

Let's have an interlude about the *Satanic Bible.* Anton's publicity bit in *Rosemary's Baby,* a typical William Castle shtick ranking up there with the special glasses in *13 Ghosts,* had attracted a ton of press to an obscure San Francisco cult. Peter Meyer, an acquisitions editor for Avon, suggested that a Satanic Bible would be a hit. He approached LaVey for a manuscript and wanted it ASAP. Well, the Church of Satan had the "Rainbow Pages," which were lectures on "Satanic Sex," S-M, ritual, curses, and so on, but it wasn't long enough. LaVey copied some pages of the Social Darwinist tract *Might Is Right* by Ragnar Redbeard but carefully removed the racist rants. Still not long enough, he took his copy of Aleister Crowley's *The Equinox* (bought from his occult book connection, the late Jack Parsons) and added the Enochian Keys.

That really filled up the pages. Each Key had a title page, a cookbook page, a page on how to use the Key, a page in Enochian paired with another page for an English translation with the original references to the Christian God exchanged with Satan. With nineteen Keys you get seventy-six pages filled! LaVey could have chosen anything from his vast library, so these choices are significant. By including Redbeard, he introduced the idea that a Satanist was an elite, evolved sort of being, but that this wasn't tied to race but to *mind* and *attitude*. This perfectly matched Aquino's philosophy (but didn't fit in with LaVey's carnalism). The Enochian (as well as LaVey's borrowing of the naked chick on the altar from Crowley's *Liber XV*) both legitimized the Church of Satan as Crowley's successor and criticized past occultisms for being squeamish about Satan. With this book in hand, John Kincaid wrote Satanic philosophy until 1975. Meyer's instincts were right: with more than thirty printings and a million-plus copies sold, the *Satanic Bible* is the most influential occult book of all time.

In the meantime, Aquino and LaVey had a lively letter exchange, spurred on by their experiences with *The Diabolicon*. Aquino was sure of two things: "Satan" was not a force in man but a force that acted on man to produce the unnatural aspect of man, the only being that can reflect on its birth, on its life and death. Second, since this force had to be there at the dawn of consciousness the church should look for an older model. He suggested the Egyptian god Set. It seemed a perfect fit based on Aquino's (then) rudimentary Egyptology. Set was one of the two most ancient gods of Egypt, the other being Horus, a god of light. Plus, Crowley thought Set was his own initiator. LaVey wasn't buying, but did write Aquino (since he was a brainy college boy) asking what philosopher was the most Satanic. Aquino replied with Fichte. Now, Fichte has an ugly streak—non-Germans are stupid and women are almost as stupid as non-Germans—but he has two very insightful ideas. According to Fichte, the first thought has to be positing a self. To think, the thinker must divide subject (the thinker) and object (everything else). The thinker has no experience, training, sense data, or reason for this first thought. The first thought is therefore self-creation. The second useful idea is recognition. The self needs, as part of its survival, to find an outside entity (church, philosophy, state, etc.) to recognize its merits and limitations. The first thought (self-creation) needs an external verifier. This fits Aquino's encoded philosophy perfectly.

LaVey sent a letter to all grotto leaders telling them to spice up their rituals by looking for historic or folkloric models. He had begun assembling texts for the *Satanic Rituals.* Aquino bought Budge's *Easy Lessons in Egyptian Hieroglyphs,* a grammar book that used to be paired with a text selection from a temple wall or a scroll that showed the grammatical feature. He noted a brief verbal phrase, *Xephra Xepher Xepheru,* written by Budge using the notation of a Greek classicist: *x* for chi (kh), *p* for phi (f). It illustrated the archaic stative: a verb that is both active and passive (acts on itself) and both past and present. We don't really have verbal forms like this in the Indo-European languages. The verb *khefer* means "come into being." The text is unidentified; in the book it was cited as a text from the Bremmer-Rhind papyrus called *The Book of Felling Apep.* It is a text for killing one of Set's enemies, Apep—the demon of nonexistence—the mental noise and self-doubts that kill the Awakened self. But Aquino didn't have time to dwell on this; LaVey had another job for him: write a Lovecraftian ritual for the *Satanic Rituals.* It should combine Mortensen's trapezoid with Satan's pentagram. So Aquino created a jargon (Yuggothic) and a form for the Nine Angles. (For more, interested readers are referred to Toby Chappell's *Infernal Geometry.*)

After playing with the jargon for his rituals, Aquino's fancy turned to the Enochian in the *Satanic Bible:* What if LaVey's myth was correct in a magical sense—that Western occultism had been approaching the Left-Hand Path since the time of John Dee because its roots lay in the beginning of mankind's involvement with magic and religion? What if the spiritual truth of the *Diabolicon* was not subjective to him but transpersonal? He began a new magical translation of Dee's work called the "Word of Set." But as we saw with Runa, inner mysteries and outer mysteries are always connected. While this intellectual/philosophical pastime was going on year IX* came. Aquino chose

---

*Year I of the Satanic calendar was 1966.

midsummer to contact the Prince of Darkness, and, in the "The Ninth Solstice Ritual," Satan said the mysteries needed to be hidden. At the same time, as noted in the previous chapter, Odhinn was telling young Stephen Flowers to "Seek the Mysteries!" Anton was having a different sort of crisis: the publication of his books had led to movies—you can see him in *The Devil's Rain,* for instance—and a taste of the good life. But there was not enough money for more than a taste. What if he sold priesthoods in the Church of Satan? In an era of occult-chic what could go wrong? Aquino was horrified. The priesthood had been based on merit and dedication—it seemed the only legitimate aspect of the Church of Satan. Letters shot back and forth.

Eventually Aquino rebelled.

He would contact the Prince of Darkness on his own. Like Crowley before him, he had outgrown his mentor. And with Crowley as a guide, he sought to make his own connection with the Prince of Darkness using the Word of Set as his technology. His working in year X yielded the *Book of Coming Forth by Night.* And Budge's grammar illustration yielded the Word of the Aeon of Set: Xeper. Aquino decided that he would throw out the notions of a supreme ruler and created a not-for-profit corporation that could fire its high priest. It could provide recognition by merit in accordance with his Fichtean ideals. For the first time in the occult world, the leader was not the dictator. Most of the Church of Satan priesthood came with him. In keeping with the "Ninth Solstice Message," the group did not seek notoriety and claimed a fairly open theology. The two principles mentioned above that Aquino was sure of became dogma, and it seemed the likely name for the force was Set, somehow equivalent to an ambiguous Egyptian god of long ago. Rebellion is part of the Xeper process: one must outgrow one's school. Within the Temple of Set this is institutionalized as the fourth degree, the Master of the temple, who must establish his or her own school of thought. Aquino ruled the temple for five years—and then astonishingly stepped down. His successor, Ronald K. Barrett, experimented with a new Word, Xem, the aftermath of which we'll examine in the next chapter. Aquino had a foolproof plan: make the temple worthless; it held no real property, no important copyrights, no fancy regalia (except for medallion colors signifying grade), no public face. Who wants to steal nothing?

In the year XVII that answer was that nothing was too small to steal. In a sitcom-worthy plot, three high-ranking members with forged letters and much melodrama briefly elected a new high priest. This mainly had a cost in destroyed friendships and the aches of betrayal, but it also led to a spiritual crisis for Aquino. The conspirators were not alien thugs; they were the best and brightest, they were examples of Xeper. What had gone wrong? Aquino considered the divergence between ideal and real. So he looked for the most flagrant example of ideals and practices that had gone in violently different directions: the warrior-monks of the Nazi SS. On paper these were shining examples of devotion to the homeland and protectors of the folk but, in reality, the most savage terrible werewolves to plague the world. He went to Himmler's castle and, once again using the Word of Set, invoked the Prince of Darkness. He got his answer, the third phase of the Xeper process: rulership. Humans had to rule themselves in accord with the principle they wanted to remain on this Earth after they passed. This was expressed in the Word *Walhalla!*

This word was the keystone of the Order of the Trapezoid, a knighthood that would inspire the other orders with principles of leadership. The Order of the Trapezoid would express itself in the principles of chivalry and would study the runes. Aquino sent his new order into the world by publishing an intra-temple newsletter, *Runes*. And quite coincidentally, Stephen Flowers wrote seeking membership in the Temple of Set. Aquino resumed the high priesthood for fifteen years until he stepped down again (for me). One of the aspects of this phase is that your students become your teachers, you do not fear them because they have already pledged themselves to principle (Walhalla!). Notable, since the Order of the Trapezoid came out of Himmler's castle, is that some folks assume it is in favor of Nazism. Since one of our grandmasters was an African American woman and we have gay and Jewish members, I say that if we are Nazis, we are very, very bad at it.

Twenty-five years passed until the phase of Xeper that I call

Enchanting happened. The Temple of Set being secure, many of its initiates are writers and artists; it has achieved a sort of fame very different from the tabloid-driven Church of Satan. Aquino began writing a series of books to ensure that his thoughts were accessible to the whole world. He created histories of the Temple of Set, a revision of the *Satanic Bible,* a study of Rosicrucianism, even a retrospective of his lifelong love affair with cars, *Ghost Rides.* The depths of his philosophy will seep into the world. His magnum opus in this period has been *Mindstar*—a radical expansion of an essay I wrote about Egyptian soul craft. Taking the essential theme of immortality as inherent in the awakened soul, this afterlife-for-everybody book is the ultimate repudiation of the gods of death.

OPENING RITE OF XEPER

Have the candles pointing away from you (i.e., North); music and incense should suggest Egypt. Use pomegranate juice in the Graal.

Say the Vampyric Invocation and repeat the Graal Work as follows:

I am the source of myself. I am the source of my masks, my behaviors, my servitors. I am compelled to disclose the great world of my Being to myself and the Cosmos by my deeds and words. My truest mask is Vampyre who inspires Desire and Fear.

Turn to the South and say:

In the South the leopard Erbeth teaches me to hunt and whispers one command: "Survive!" Most ancient One who created Life to receive the Gift of Self. I will survive that I may Come Into Being.

Turn to the East and say:

In the East Iaa holds knives that glitter in the light of Khephra, the rising sun, and he brays one command, "Rebel." I will rebel from the lies of mankind, its churches and states and slave philosophies that I may Come Into Being.

Turn to the North and say:

> In the North stands the model of all kings, Pakerbeth. Above him the stars of the Thigh of Set shine as a crown, and he pronounces one word, "Rule." I will rule every aspect of my life. I am as constant as the Pole Star, so that I may Come Into Being.

Turn to the West and say:

> In the West stands the great griffin Ablanathanalba holding the remains of Osiris in his paws. The leader of the Hounds roars, "Enchant." I will enchant the world to make it a matrix for my Will now and after the passage of this body so that I may Come Into Being.

Now cross your arms over your chest and say your personal motto and thoughts. Spin slowly (the idea is addressing the worlds, not becoming dizzy) counterclockwise and begin:

> In the center of time and space stands [VN]; I have Come Into Being, and by my Coming Into Being the process of Coming Into Being is established.

Close the rite in your usual manner.

LIFE ANALYSIS

1. Who have you outgrown as a teacher? Why? How do you preserve the best of what those teachers have taught you?
2. Who have you trained or taught that has become your teacher/trainer? Did you receive this with respect and enthusiasm or were you a jackass?
3. What minor action (like randomly picking a book in a thrift store) became a major gateway for you? Do you think it was fate, chance, or something else? Why?
4. How have locations enhanced your magic? What about modes of transportation?

VAMPYRIC ANALYSIS

1. Who in your life acts as a prophet? Pay particular attention to people who offer good advice but don't believe as you do, dress as you do, or otherwise look like they would be your guides.
2. What utterly non-occult hobby or pastime is a source of energy for you?
3. What landscapes turn you on magically?
4. Where in the world would you most like to do a magical operation? What are your concrete plans for getting there?

TECHNIQUES TO TRY

1. Above all, start with what you've got, but act as though you'll get everything you want. You want to do Vampyric magic in Dracula's castle? Okay, start this week in your crappy apartment, but also be getting your passport and learning what else you need in order to get there.
2. Pay attention to your speech. Do you use positive action words or are they passive? Do you speak negatively, in terms of limits, or positively, in terms of opportunities? How much time do you waste in gossip? As you become mindful of your speech, move toward the positive and the essential.
3. If you tell someone (or yourself) that you will do something—do it! If you don't intend to do a thing, say so. If you want to have magical power in your words, stop being powerless.
4. Henceforth you can tell if you are traveling in a good direction because your life will be full of synchronicities; if there aren't any on a new path you're probably on the wrong path. Life can still be hard or joyous, but from this point on it should never be without magic.

INITIATIC RITE OF XEPER

This ritual is the high point of the Vampyric Initiation. It processes all that came before it and all the rites that follow. Take your time with it—and be sure to reread the questions and techniques above.

THE RITE OF THE FOUR TALISMANS

This is the central rite of the Vamypric Initiation. It charges the elements in the Vampyric Invocation to a greater level of power. You need to obtain the four totems explained in chapter 4—toys or small figurines of a mummy, an owl, a wolf, and a bat. Each week you consecrate one and then leave it in a special environment. I give examples of such environments. If you don't have the perfect place, merely choose a location away from your home in the correct direction: South (Mummy), East (Owl), North (Wolf), and West (Bat).

With each rite, turn the candles toward the North. Scent the talisman with your personal Vampyric scent before the Work. Sleeping with it for three nights before the rite is a good idea.

Mummy–South

> *O creature that ties me to other enchantments, image of the living dead of Egypt, I call you into Being by my Will and give you the power to speak to the dead and learn their Secrets. Because I place you in the world, I have access to the lore of ages. By the Gift of Set, I, the Vampyre [VN], am within and beyond you and free you to walk the dusty corridors of time.*

Place the mummy in a relevant place of power—for example, behind books about Egypt at a museum.

Owl–East

> *O familiar of Athena, sing to me in the night the secrets of wise rulership. Fill me with Metis, that I may always choose the right modes of consciousness. Let me know when to be animal, man, or god. By the Gift of Set, I, the Vampyre [VN], am within and beyond you and fill you with the wisest of counsel.*

Place the owl in a relevant place of power—for example, on a picnic table in a zoo or near a home for predatory birds.

Wolf–North

O creature that taught mankind brotherhood, the need for loyalty in rebellions and war, I give you the dark forests of the world to roam in, that I may always have the strength to help my allies, the wisdom to rip apart false friends when needed. May my Pack grow strong! By the Gift of Set, I, the Vampyre [VN], am within and beyond you and I make you an Alpha wolf.

Place the wolf in a relevant place of power—for example, in an area where wolves or coyotes have been seen.

Bat–West

Flying in darkness, seeing by sound, smelling blood, you are the ruthless survivor. Nothing slows you, nothing hinders you, your victims see you not and I would be the same, a ruthless survivor. By the Gift of Set, I, the Vampyre [VN], am within and beyond you and I charge us both to be the essence of the Vampyre.

Place the bat in a relevant place of power—for example, in a cave or niche that has bats. This can be anything from a natural cave to a commercial haunted house. It can be an actual or a symbolic bat abode.

☞ ☜

You are responsible for the creation of you. This is the great Vampyric mystery: you call what you need to yourself both as experiences (in the outer world) and thoughts (in the inner world). You must assemble yourself from these energies by digesting and refining them. Now that you have tasted Xeper, let's dream about the future through the Word Remanifestation.

13

REMANIFESTATION

THE MAGIC OF JAMES A. LEWIS

In 1948, Frater Achad, Crowley's heir (and rebel from Crowley) Uttered the Word MAnifestatION, or MAION. His notion was that there was a countercurrent in the world. Humans were working their way up the Tree of Life guided by Thelema, but their god-selves were working their way down the Tree guided by MAION. The human consciousness ran from past to future with its goal to experience Kether. Divine consciousness ran from future to past and worked downward to experience Malkuth, physical manifestation. Our moments of enlightenment, which Crowley called the Knowledge and Conversation of the Holy Guardian Angel, were literally you meeting yourself. A few days after this utterance, James A. Lewis was born.

James A. Lewis was possessed of a profound desire to participate in the bigger universe than could be found in his Georgia home. He began in the faith of his father, entering into study of the Roman Catholic priesthood. As a young gay man he had a choice: accept the hypocrisy of being gay in a religion that condemned it (as thousands of Catholic priests do every day) or be honest and accept both social and ecclesiastical damnation. Lewis chose the braver path in a classic fashion. Mounting a hillside, he invoked Satan, and Satan did manifest—in the form of a San Francisco PO box. The founding of the Temple of Set sounded promising. Lewis joined and received his *Crystal Tablet,* the first book received by new Setians, just as he was heading off to holiday. He pulled the shortest section he could from it, the "Statement of

Leviathan" from the *Diabolicon*. He was caught in the image of a force so alien that it acknowledged neither God nor Satan and had cosmic power goals in a deep future. This matched his deep longing for participation in the Cosmos.

Energetic and studious, he moved rapidly through the first four degrees. High Priest Barrett recognized him as a Master of the Temple. He appreciated some aspects of Barrett's Utterance of Xem: the notion that the evolving soul would create its own horizons à la Nietzsche matched the mood of the "Statement of Levithan." But Barrett was a very conventional occultist: he equated memorizing lore and the sort of facts one might encounter in an occult bookstore with growth. His method also relied strongly on the assumption of godforms, which struck Lewis as superstitious. When the crisis of year XVIII came, Lewis took Aquino's side. The Temple of Set had no clear afterlife teaching. However, a young Canadian Priest, Robertt Neilly, gave a talk on Vampyres, and at a working that followed Lewis asked what he felt happened after death. Neilly's answer, "Remanifestation," fascinated Lewis for months. Robertt Neilly we will meet again later as Magus Neilly.

Here was an answer that didn't require props from the past. Lewis began to realize that humans have two sorts of time in them: the cyclical eternal return that shows up in most religions and the progressive linear time of the West. Lewis's breakthrough was huge: What if eternal return is not a reflection of the mechanical universe but instead the unnatural gift that Aquino called the Black Flame? We encounter the same situations over and over in life. Sometimes we repeat our mistakes, but sometimes we learn. What if this was the basic human condition?

In the movie *Groundhog Day* the hero is literally trapped in a repeating day, but he retains his memories. He decides to use each day to get better. To say smarter things, to learn new languages, to have progressively more challenging experiences. Lewis suggests that on a spiritual level we are trapped in cycles—but not mechanistic ones—cycles that reflect our essence. Like the hero in *Groundhog Day*, we can use the cycles of our being to improve (Xeper) or to eliminate what we don't want or need. When we have reshaped a part of the Cosmos so that we don't need the lesson anymore, we move on. We achieve deep empowerment. Eventually our interactions with the Cosmos are not as a trapped soul but as a freewheeling essence, moving through time and space not unlike the British sci-fi hero the Doctor.

Lewis's magical style is to cut free from robes and ritual as much as possible. Power comes from self-analysis and expressing your Will at the correct moment. Ritual should be minimalistic, rational, and most likely rarer as you progress through life.

INITIATIC RITE OF REMANIFESTATION

Aim the candles toward you (South).

Say the Vampyric Invocation and then, for the Graal work, say the following:

> *The Wheel of Time is the Wheel of me. I order my Cosmos with its cycles. I am not ordered by the outer universe. I know what goes around in my life. I know what I can improve as my Wheel turns, I know what I can lessen with each cycle. My cycles are known to me in this lfe, and will be known to me beyond this life. I hold my universe together by swallowing my tail under the mysteries of the perfect number 496, written in Hebrew as Leviathan. I am Ouroboros. I am Jormungandr. I, the Vampyre [VN], Remanifest at my Will, I demanifest at my Will. I increase in might and main beyond God and Satan recreating the whole of the Cosmos in accord with my Infernal Will.*

Close in your normal manner, but involve yourself in an activity that reflects your rationally based plans.

LIFE ANALYSIS

1. Be brutal with yourself: What life trap (abusive relationship, overspending, etc.) do you keep falling into again and again? You know it's on your life map, what are you doing for the next time you're there?

2. Be totally loving with yourself: What life opportunity do you keep getting (travel, love, great teachers)? You know it's on your life map, what are you doing for the next time you're there?

3. What were the strengths and weaknesses of your parents? What are you doing to claim the strengths and release the weaknesses?

4. What are your personal omens? These may be the songs on the radio that show up at important life moments, or movies on TV, and so forth.

VAMPYRIC ANALYSIS

1. Look at question one above when you are wishing to harm a target—what are his or her traps?

2. Look at question two above when you lead a group. Groups likewise have recurrent opportunities that you can manage.

3. Look at the spiritual DNA of an organization—it will inherit the strengths and weaknesses of its founders: What can you do with this information (of which most of the group members will be unaware)?

4. Get your targets/victims to tell you their personal omens; then you have keys to manipulating them if you can control their reception.

PERCEPTION EXERCISES

This month notice serial reoccurences. For example, do you always get caught in bad traffic before a mental breakthrough? Do you always get a call from your mother after a magical Working? Each time this occurs think about the questions: Why are certain parts that make each moment of now—there? Why do I summon time to me thusly?

TECHNIQUES TO TRY

1. Pick a task that you do every day in the presence of others. On a personal level, imbue it with meaning and magic. It can be opening the door of your business, brewing the first cup of coffee, or

washing out the pot at the end of the day. This is just as valid as doing a gesture in ritual.

2. Take a magical practice from your past, even throwing a coin into a certain fountain of your city, and begin it again. Feel a connection to your earlier self as you do this.

3. At times of great pleasure or power say, "This is another level of my Remanifestation, as high as this seems now, many more ladder rungs are Coming Into Being above me."

Initiatic Rite of Remanifestation

Aim the candles toward you (South).

Say the Vampyric Invocation and repeat the following Graal work:

I am the Vampyre [VN], and I travel through space and time powered by my Desire. My Desire is a dragon, and I am the tenth student of the Scholomance, chosen by the Dark One to ride the dragon of desire. My Desire beats its great bat wings and waves of time buffet my enemies. My Desire roars, and those who oppose me flee in fright. My Desire takes flight, and I can visit stars and planets as yet undreamed of. My Desire Remanifests opportunities for me again and again. My Desire Remanifests learning moments again and again, and I learn. The Black Flame of my Desire begins to burn like the Red Flame of the Life Force as my Remanifestations occur again and again. Nothing withstands the dragon of my Desire.

Close the rite in your own fashion and, as before, plunge into rational activity that furthers your goals.

🦇 🦇

You have dreamed about your cycles of existences, perhaps apprehending yourself as the Ouroboros. Now let's plunge into the mystery of the body, the joy of the life force, the love of Earth and her animals as we are born into Arkte.

14

ARKTE

THE MAGIC OF LILITH AQUINO

By now (if you have been doing the Work) you will have some strange thoughts, unusual sensations, amazing coincidences. You will have begun to feel differently—more Awake perhaps, more moved to sudden ecstasy, attracted to art or natural scenes you'd never noticed before. Of course, you have many doubts as well—maybe this whole thing is silly. Maybe you are chasing after a fantasy. This month you will decide to become a Vampyre or just someone who can use a huge variety of Vampyric magic. There will be no outward sign: you won't start sleeping in a coffin or having no reflection. You will just automatically begin to think and feel in a different mode. You've felt it growing, and whichever decision you make—to finish this month or simply to stop now—you have shown great bravery. You've broken beyond your narrow band of perception; you've felt and known things that 99.99 percent of humankind has ever felt. You're also aware that this does set you apart.

Now being set apart may be part and parcel of your life. Randolph was set apart (African American), LaVey was set apart (Jewish, born of immigrant parents), Crowley was set apart (bisexual). And 99 percent of my readers may have noticed something by this point: Where are the women? Nearly 52 percent of the human population seems ignored by the esoteric community. Are they unimportant? Lacking in skills? Or does this reflect some unfortunate trends in civilization connected with the labor of motherhood and males' unfortunate tendency to see themselves as the great explainers? (I am referring to other men, not myself.) I could have easily created the meta-narrative of Remanifestation that I am calling the Vampyric Initiation in all-female terms—Mary Anne Atwood, Florence Farr, Maria de Naglowska, Nema, Diane Hegarty, Starhawk—but I chose the humans that I read (or directly worked with) first. It is hoped that some of my students correct this in their own volumes.

But let's talk about women in Western esotericism. They are usually given one of three roles: eye candy, marginalized pseudo-males, or slightly scary grandmas. As with any archetype, getting on the train gives you instant power, but it also gives you a script—and the world will NOT approve if you don't follow your lines. In this, every Awakened woman in the Western world is forced to do what males in the Left-Hand Path may or may not elect to do. Men must choose door A or door B. Door A: extract the driving force of the counterculture and become the god of that force—LaVey, Timothy Leary, Charles Manson. Door B: be a fighter against one's time and say the words that call a future into being—Aquino, Nietzsche, Tesla. But women often have a much rougher time than men: they often have little humans to protect and rear. That means they must be a hundred times craftier than men, and they are forced to deal with philosophy in terms of transmittal.

The result produces four consequences in female esotericism: First, women have a much greater tendency to express themselves through social/human media (like schools or temples) rather than the written word. Second, women's utterances tend to occur later in life than those of their male counterparts. Third, women (and in a violence-ruled patriarchy this means ALL women) have to learn when to be invisible and when to be commanding visually (yes, all women are in some sense Vampyric). Fourth, women's teachings are more often bound to social and biological realities.

Let's play a little game before we discuss Lilith Aquino and her Word Arkte. The game is called Minus Women. The rules should be self-evident. Randolph's teaching exists because of his first wife, Mary Jane, who created his line of spiritual drugs (mainly cannabis preparations—insert Mary Jane joke) and most importantly his second wife, Kate, who made sure his Rosicrucian writings and brotherhood survived. Crowley's first magical teacher, Florence Farr, bridged nineteenth-century Spiritualism into ceremonial magic by starting the idea that Egyptian tomb relics could be used to get a message from the past to surpass the East-West divide. Crowley's wife Rose channeled Egyptian forces so that he could have his major revelation; his love bunny Leila Waddell helped him synthesize his system into a teachable format, and his most effective world-changing magick, the Thoth tarot deck, owes 93 percent of its power to the artist Lady Frieda Harris. Anton LaVey, who was too lazy to type (and to organize written materials), owes his *Satanic Bible* and *Satanic Rituals* to Diane Hegarty. Okay, so are we up to speed?

Lilith Aquino had to leave home in her adolescence, and like many smart teens fled to the Big Apple. Wanting to make it as a model, Lilith had to develop five qualities: outward self-confidence, discipline, customer service, scheduling/prioritizing, and sorcery. All of the Vampyric skills were in play from the first, and in the early 1960s there was also feminist politics, a beginning ecological awareness, and an occult boom—a mélange of Eastern techniques and whatever out-of-copyright books could be brought out. A man came into her life and, two kids later, left her life—so now she was a working mom trying to make it as a model.

Her inclinations to darkness were perfectly fed by LaVeyan Satanism. But her flavor was very much her own. LaVey's Central Grotto used zaftig working girls as altars—Lilith began using herself—transforming the male gaze into power. LaVey used his parent's home, Lilith had to get another single mom to watch her kids while doing rituals. Lilith was the only woman to develop a leadership position in the Church of Satan and, like her husband-to-be, Michael, one of the few Church of Satan clergy that had relatively minimal contact with LaVey. Taking the name of Adam's rebellious first wife, who had claimed equality in the relationship and superiority in the realm of desire, Lilith made a deep connection with the Qliphothic side of magic early on and, because of her profession, became the master of "empty hand" techniques. If you are interested in the Qliphothic side of the Lilith tradition, consult my friend Thomas Karlsson's *Qabalah, Qliphoth and Goetic Magic*.

She had two major objectives. First, she wanted a Satanic community. Occultists tend to silo off, hiding their struggles and weaknesses. But folks interested in real power will find places to share their struggle. Second, she was in love with a dynamic young Priest of Mendes, Michael

Aquino. LaVey didn't like the idea of people getting together, and after the first Satanic Conclave (in Dayton, Ohio, 1974), he put a kibosh on future large Church of Satan gatherings. The love interest proved permanent. Lilith was the first human to hear and accept Xeper. The first follower is the basis of all things, it determines the way of reception. Her desire for community made sure the Temple of Set was not a book club and was rooted in a tradition of international conclaves. Although the temple initially clustered around San Francisco, Lilith made sure the first conclave was outside the United States, in nearby Canada. Since then Porto, Munich, Prague, Berlin, London, Helsinki, and Toronto have all had their conclaves. The Setian tradition comes from Lilith Aquino.

At the Fourth International Conclave, where the temple had its darkest hour, Lilith once again heard a message, this time from the same gateway as Lewis above: Robertt Neilly's talk on Vampyric magic. Nielly cited a review of Hodder's *The Vampire* from the 1930s (in *The Occult Review*) of an occult order wherein old—possibly *very* old—leaders kept themselves alive through vampirism. Neilly speculated not about feeding on younger members but about the possibility of a tradition of energy users. Lilith's mind then developed the full notion that would become the Temple of Set's Order of the Vampyre, wherein many of the ideas and techniques of this volume came into being.

As the order developed the focus, the image of the vampire bat shifted to the wolf, and Lilith herself (never one for abstract experience) became active in wolf sanctuaries—getting to know, feed, and care for wolves. Lilith sought a word to focus her magical interests and, at suggestions from Stephen Flowers and myself, chose the name of the Greek bear goddess Arkte. Lilith's magical journey from a magician of image and sorcery (in the cutthroat world of modeling) into a dark goddess avenging animal rights was complete. Note that her power is in sensing potential and enshrining it in community.

Lilith is the key figure in galvanizing the idea of the Vampyre. She offers seven essential techniques to the Vampyre: the way of the animal companion, the way of reflection, the way of Circe, the way of the three valleys, the way of the bat, the way of the wolf, and, lastly, the way of Suteck. As the creator of modern Vampyric magic, her ideas are the most essential. Let's look at each and then the dangers that come with the Word of Arkte.

The witch with her black cat is the most archetypical image of Black Magic in the Western world. All Vampyres (if health allows) should have an animal companion. The best choice is a rescue cat. The cat will teach you nightly lessons: energy (food and affection) comes first, play is always important, self-importance must be discarded (clean out that litter box and you are humbled), curiosity is an expression of being, death is a part of being, nature is not about good and evil but consequence, magic is bound in DNA not in book learning, you must still your mind. You may know these simple truths intellectually, but if you wish to BE a Vampyre, you must know them deeply in your body, your dreams, your heart. Nothing you will learn in this book can teach you as well as your rescue cats. If you would know more, consult *Cult of the Cat* by Patricia Dale-Green. Why a rescue cat? They are attuned to Vampyres: they have known trauma and yet by force of Will have survived.

Modern vampire myths focus on the notion that vampires have no reflection. The theory was that silver—which was used to back mirrors—was too pure a metal to reflect something as impure as a vampire. Lilith turned this on its ear. The Vampyre is the master of reflection. She has three modes: reflect the innermost desires of the person you wish to control, make others reflect your most fearsome self if you wish to scare them into flight (or submission), and lovingly reflect the best parts of a human that you wish to soothe, nurture, or initiate. In the last usage Vampyric exchange is possible; this is the (un)holy Graal of the Vampyre—a process that replaces the Graal Work part of the rituals in this book. It begins outwardly with two Vampyres gazing at each other. Biologically, humans have become the dominant species of this planet using mirror neurons. We evolved to learn rapidly: it is the unique (or to use Michael Aquino's term "unnatural") part of the human mind-body-psyche complex. Vampyres, by tuning in to this part of their beings through the Vampyric Gaze, directly activate the most biological *and* most spiritual parts of themselves. The oldest, most stable aspect of this planet is the self-replicating DNA molecule. It has outlasted mountains and seas; it is more stable than governments, religions, science. It connects you to every living thing on this planet and the deep past thereof. It explains why shamans in so-called primitive cultures can find medicinal plants. There are literally millions of compounds in the jungle, the beneficial ones often require elaborate preparation—these were not found by trial and error. Humans in their older, right-brain consciousness use the method of reflection—when Randolph began playing with mirror magic, he was invoking an ancient magic that Lilith Aquino perfected.

Modern magicians (for the most part) follow the way of Hermes. This involves the study of philosophy mixed with magical practice to gain understanding/illumination. Modern sorcerers follow the way of the humbug: dazzle the people you wish to control with lies, special effects, and magical power. Lilith teaches/Remanifests an older way—the way of Circe. First, have an island; that is to say, your own realm. When the forces of seeming chance send people into your realm you must tempt them with their senses. If they are easily entranced you must turn them into beasts—they are happier and more virtuous thereby—but you must rule the ecology of your island (not too many bears, not too many pigs). If, however, you find a human that equals you in power you must seduce him (or her) with sex and the promise of your knowledge over life and death. Once you have gained power over this human, you must allow him (or her) to think he (or she) is the ruler, while you use all of your enchantments to stop time in your magical realm.

The Way of the Three Valleys is first described in the Ming Dynasty (1368–1644) text the *Anthology on the Cultivation of Realization*. It describes a twenty-seven-year path to obtaining immortality. The three valleys are in the human being, and your soul dwells in each as a minor god rules a valley. The top valley is the celestial valley: for nine years you learn and practice the Way. This corresponds to the time of learning magic and acquiring from books and living teachers the tools of initiation. It is the head. Here vitality (life force) changes into energy, and the energy rises. After nine years the celestial gateway opens up and you meet the Hidden God beyond (symbolized by the seven stars called the Great Bear, Arkte in the *Greek Magical Papyri*, or Tezcatlipoca of the Aztecs, or Set of the Egyptians). After this upper channel is opened the spirit dwells in the middle chamber, called the crimson chamber or the valley of repose. This is the heart. Here the spirit attends to governance: the practical matters of running a school, establishing a business, and so forth; unlike humans who do this first, the Vampyre is not lulled to sleep by practicality but becomes a charismatic ruler (although invisible when she desires). Here energy tunes vitality. The Vampyre does not use her body as a source of energy (having learned other techniques) but allows her energy to direct her body. Her eyes are led to certain sights, her ears to certain sounds, and prodigious self-healing can occur. In the valley of repose, time stops. The Vampyre amazes her friends and enemies by the miracle of not aging—her body has become the animal companion of her spirit. After nine years here, a lower chamber opens: the valley of the soul, also called the elixir fields. Here the soul dwells in its depths, looking upward. The techniques become personal and subtle. Energy, vitality, and consciousness appear as one, and although time can no longer be kept at bay, the movement toward immortality is serene, with bodily death as a mere ripple in a placid lake that perfectly reflects the stars of Arkte. In this valley life force is not seen as a personal affair, and the Vampyre becomes a warrior for all life-forms, and this affects and colors her teaching methods as well.

The way of the bat is an example of the mutating legend/myth of the vampire. European vampires didn't turn into bats until the vampire bat was discovered by Western science. The nocturnal bloodsucker gained iconic form because of Bram Stoker. Like most of the leading figures who shaped Victorian occultism, Stoker's roots were in the theater. To create the stage illusion of Dracula's disappearance a high collar and long black cape were used. With little tweaking, they also worked to help with the manifestation of the count into bat form. So the flying bloodsucker emerged as THE image of the vampire.

For the Vampyre the bat has three vital lessons: Strike quickly—if your body is afraid, trust it; your body knows your enemies. Second, strike invisibly—the bat feeds in the dark, secreting an anesthetic to hide its bite. Third, create your own navigation system—the Vampyre sends out her own signal and gets her own feedback; this means she steps out of social rules to assess her victim. For example, you observe that your best friend is being emotionally and physically terrorized by her ex-husband. The social rules are either fight the (possibly) dangerous guy face-to-face or use approved forms like the police when he comes around. But you (for example) know how to check tax records—that guy has a big problem with the county. Using your secret knowledge, you write the right letter to the right authorities. Meanwhile you prepare a magical attack, again using secret knowledge. But you say nothing. You draw no attention to the quick doom that follows. You were unseen. Eventually a reputation will attach itself to you that people shouldn't mess with you. This is your cloak and high collar. Thank you, Mr. Stoker.

The way of the wolf is an older part of vampire myth coming from Emily Gerard in her "Transylvanian Superstitions" article in 1885. Romanians drawing from their Dacian ancestors had always connected their ritual specialists with wolves. For a long while, wolf researcher David Mech had put forth the idea that the alpha male in a wolf pack dominated the others by force—but this idea comes from captive packs of non-related wolves. This bad ethology was adopted by some pseudo-LHP groups, but Lilith (informed by the way of the animal companion) uses better science. Wolves share four great virtues: they mate for life; the alpha pair walks at the back of the pack, overseeing the safety of all members; they are fiercely loyal to their family; and when happy, they dance.

The toughest to master and greatest secret of the Vampyre is the way of Suteck, which is symbolized in the Vampyric Invocation as the mummy. For the average human, desire leads to loss of freedom. We know these humans—the guy who always thinks about money, or sex, or his hobby. Seemingly they accomplish great things if they have Vampyric energy. Driven by their desire night and day, all of their vitality is aimed at one goal. If they have Vampyric energy they excel at the goal—getting rich, having tons of sex partners, excelling in their subculture. Yet they are never free. The Right-Hand Path tells us that desire is bad. It limits freedom. It enslaves. For most humans this is correct. But what if that supremely powerful moment of desire is stabilized? Rather than sending it out to bring you cars, cash, or pussy, what would happen if you froze it? Your godlike moment that makes millionaires or Lotharios could be instead a godlike state that makes you, well, into a god.

For the average human, energy rises in front (from your sexual center); it rises and is sent out through your eyes as coveting. I want this. I want that. So, all of my power is tied up in this or that. If the average human has surplus energy, a good brain, discipline, and great timing he or she gets his or her desires (but not lasting happiness). If the average human lacks any of those four elements, he or she gets disappointment and illness. So those seeking happiness retire to the forest, the secret island, and so on, and eliminate desire. The Vampyre knows the supreme secret. The oldest name of Set is Suteck, the "Stabilizer."

The Vampyre knows how to freeze desire. Instead of sending the desire outward, she identifies with it. In the middle of her lust for sex, a car, German chocolate cake, she pauses and sends a self-command— (Randolph's "Decretism")—I AM DESIRE. Do this again and again until this exceeds your lust for money, sex, or great concert tickets. Do it until it becomes a point in your being. Then when you have this pivot, REVERSE the flow. Make your energy rise from behind, come up your spine (rather than being tugged up by advertisements), and descend down from your head, bathing your strengths, your lusts, your weaknesses with a protective field. The Vampyre does not fear desire, as does her Right-Hand-Path Auntie. Nor does she value herself on the basis of fulfilled desire like her Ayn Rand–reading cousin.

Now we will talk about the vulnerabilities that come with the Word. Every Word has points of vulnerability. For Arkte there are three soft spots. The first is your totem, the second is the cruelty of humans, and third is the greed of certain humans. As you work with animals, one or more will become special to you. For Lilith it was wolves. Whichever your totem, you will overspend, over-fascinate, and even blur yourself with the totem. Your friends will notice—and enable you. For example, one of Lilith's students has put 10,458 pictures of cats on his Facebook wall. Tragic. Another has over 50 owls in her office in various media. Very sad. The second problem does not come with smiles. Since the fuel of magic in general is emotion (as LaVey taught us) the Arkte practitioner can be wrathful or sad when she hears of animal mistreatment. When harnessed into political/social change this is awesome. I remember when Michael Aquino found out that Asian food markets in San Francisco sold live de-shelled turtles. Watching an ex–Green Beret trained in psychological warfare get laws passed quickly in California was like seeing a hurricane hit a beach! But seeing the weeping despair that happens when bad ecological processes are revealed in media is much less entertaining. Suffering comes with Arkte, not mild discomfort. The last soft point is manifest when fake charities rip you off in the name of animals. However, every Arkte follower learns to research charities and movements very well (after that first time you give your birthday money to Save the Gypsy Moth).

OPENING RITE OF ARKTE

This month the candle direction is reversed. Set your candles away from you (North) at the beginning and toward you (South) at the end of the month. You will need to gather these things: several spoonsful of rich loam, a bowl of clean water, incense with a pleasing natural scent (like rose or pine), a new red Sharpie, and four one-dollar bills (or their equivalent in your currency). A source of natural sounds (birdcalls, sea crashing, etc.) should play throughout the ceremony. For the Graal liquid, vegetable juice is preferred.

Say the Vampyric Invocation. The Graal Work is as follows:

My senses thrill, my body is nourished, and I call the Life Force into me, in this body and beyond. The Life Force is my Witness, my coach, my Master, and my Familiar. I will learn its Mysteries and I will hide my Mysteries within it. I will guard it, enrich it, worship it.

Tonight, I will send the Oaths into the natural world through its symbols. By daylight I will send the Oaths into the world of humankind.

Pass your left hand over the three candles nine times. Focus on their warmth.

By fire I vow to be receptive to energy. I will take the Life Force

from my foes, heal my friends and family with it, protect all Life.
This is the Oath of Lilith.

Close your eyes, breathe in the incense.

I will honor the million flowers of the field, the savor of food, the
smell of my lovers. I will honor the memories they have brought by
accepting the pains and pleasures of existence. This is the Oath of
Marduk.

Make a ball of loam in your hands, feel its weight, smell it, taste it
with your tongue.

I touch the pure pagan silt and renew my bond with the thousand
tiny paws that tread here. This is the Oath of Arkte.

Dip your fingers in the water, trace an inverse Pentagram on your brow.

I am washed clean by nature and I must clean her. I honor my
bond with springs and wells, rivers and lakes and the mighty
ocean and all who dwell in these places. This is the Oath of
Tefnut.

Sit and speak these words:

I send my Oaths into the Secret places of Fire, Air, Earth, and
Water. I will live as Vampyre to revel in the ecstasy of the natural
world, but vow to use my powers to protect that world against the
stupidity of humans. I love all life, even human life, and I know the
Vampyric Essence lies beneath all Life. I will worship through the
ever Remanifesting altar of my Self. I forswear human mindlessness
knowing this makes me often Alone. I have sworn the Oaths and I
am set aside as Vampyre for all time. My Oaths travel to the Great
Vampyre and I am judged.

Take the pen, write on each of the bills: "I took the Oaths." In the
coming days give them to beggars, leave them as tips, contribute them
to various charities—one at a time.

Close the rite in your usual manner.

LIFE ANALYSIS

1. What did you feel when you first totally lived on your own?
2. When did you discover balancing common life needs (getting a paycheck) with magical needs (staring in wonder at the full moon)?
3. Who are you when you are alone in nature?
4. What smells excite you? What textures? Do you keep these facts about yourself personal or share them with lovers?
5. Where were you when you first recall hearing the word *vampire*?
6. What did we learn in the late '60s that is part of your life?

VAMPYRIC ANALYSIS

1. See how your friends, enemies, bosses, employees treat their animal companions—this is a much better revealer of character than runes or tarot. Don't sign a contract with a man who beats his dog or starves his horse.
2. Try some animal-time math. Assume that all life spans are equal—from birth to death is one unit. If this is so, divide the unit. What does a minute mean to a gnat who lives twenty-four hours? What does a decade mean to a three-thousand-year-old bristlecone pine? Try to imagine what that feels like.
3. What animals show up in your dreams? If they were your magical totem, what does that say about yourself?
4. Play the childhood game of "If you could be any kind of animal what would you be?" with people. Assume this is a way to get beyond most of their masks. Note that the social parasite is so strong in some people that they will become angry at you for posing the question. This is the person who will harm you someday.

PERCEPTION EXERCISES

1. Crawl around on the floor with your familiar. Sniff what they sniff. Lay in that sunbeam. Lap up their water. Visualize yourself as them,

until something shifts in you and you are them (even if only for a few seconds).

2. Practice running in the woods on full moon nights. (Choose your woods carefully.) Hide in tree shadows. Be so still that birds stop warning others about your presence.

3. Hand-feed rescue animals at a shelter, or wash oil off seabirds, or help hold animals at a charity vet event.

4. Zipline at night.

TECHNIQUES TO TRY

The Bentov Effect

Obtain a watch with an easily read second hand. Sit in the area where you perform magic and close your eyes. Picture yourself in a pleasant place. Be fully there. Feel the warmth of the sun, see and feel the ground under your feet, hear the sounds, and so on. When you are fully in the memory open your eyes slightly. See how the second hand slows? Eventually you will be able to make it stop for brief periods. Do this often.

Arkte Charm from the Greek Magical Papyrus

Copy with the same red Sharpie that you used for the opening rite. If possible, write this on papyrus, if not, on parchment. Keep it with you, it can be used for any wish. I recommend using it first to slow time, then to gain the senses of an animal totem.

To slow time, say the following petition to the setting sun. Visualize the Great Bear often. When the wish is granted, burn the papyrus with frankincense and scatter the ashes at night under the Seven Stars (if you live in the Northern Hemisphere) or at sunset (if you live in the Southern Hemisphere).

> *I call upon You, Shining Arkte of the Seven Faces of Darkness, the Greatest Power in Heaven, appointed by the Ananke to turn with a Strong Hand the Holy Pole, NIKAROPLE'X. Listen to me, Arkte, Ba of Set-Typhon, hear this ancient Holy Prayer, You who hold together*

the Universe and bring to Life the whole World, THO'ZOPITHE'
EUCHANDAMA O'CHRIENTHE'R OMNYO'DE'S
CHE'MIOCHYNGE'S IEO'Y THERMOUTHER PSIPHIRIX
PHROSALI KANTHIMEO' ZANZEMIA O'PER PEROMENE'S
RO'THIEU E'NINDEU KORKOUNTHO EUMEN MENI KE'DEUA
KE'PSE'OI. Add your wish, for example: "Oh Arkte, soul of Set-
Typhon, who rules the sky make time bow before my Will."

To gain the senses of an animal totem, use this petition to the sun at sunset. This formula is to be repeated each day until your wish is granted.

THE'NO'R, O Helios, SANTHE'NO'R, I beseech You, Lord of the
Gates of Twilight, the Gate and the Key to what humans think of
the Inner and Outer worlds, make my Will law in the steads of
Being and Becoming.

Meditation Practice
This will allow you to harmonize your physical body with your mind.

Step one: Dance wildly and in an uninhibited fashion until you have raised both your mood and pulse rate.

Step two: Snarl, bark, make threatening moves until you have scared your timid thoughts away.

Step three: Sit quietly with eyes closed picturing the Seven Stars of Arkte/Big Dipper. Do this until your pulse rate drops and breath becomes easier. If thoughts of a social or business nature intrude, do the animal snarling until they are frightened away. Do not beat yourself up if you find this hard to do, just try.

Spend from ten to fifteen minutes a day with this exercise; if it works for you, it will lower blood pressure and stress; if not, remember that there a thousand other doors for you.

INITIATIC RITE OF ARKTE
You will need the red Sharpie and a mirror. Candles should be aimed toward the West as you are invoking the transpersonal past. The Graal liquid should be bright red.

Say the Vampyric Invocation. The Graal Work is as follows:

> *The tyrant god, father of the social parasite, maker of chains, says that all blood offered from animals should be His, for the blood is the life. I, the Vampyre (VN), pledge my oneness with all life and end all sacrifice and cruelty. I dethrone the tyrant god and His spells. I drink all Life, return all Life to its rightful owners, drain all Life that stands against me. Great is Arkte, and greater still She through me.*
>
> *The modern myth that has been crowd-sourced as the vampire is my Gate, but my Will unfettered by superstition or fear, is the Key. I am no longer a living being with a single death, but Life herself. I am Arkte, Anahita, Inanna, Anat, Nepthys. I am the slayer of the followers of the Death God. I walk knee deep in the blood of the slain, restoring lands with fertility, undoing the works of maddened men. I use their myths to steal the forms of the dead, to borrow the forms of animals, to become the shape of their lurid dreams. I give myself the mark of their myths.*

With the Sharpie, mark some spots on your neck as though you have been bitten. Stare in the mirror at your handiwork. Begin the chant below, starting at a whisper, then louder and louder, until you feel you have become the goddess.

> *Lilith, Nephthys, Ishtar, Anahita, Kali, Freya, Oxomoco, Daji.*

Then blow out the candles and sit quietly in the dark. After a few minutes ask the following question aloud:

> *If I fully Become a Vampyre what justice do I bring to this Earth?*

Close the rite in your usual fashion.

You have been born into the world of Life from "life," and you are now a Vampyre, and that means you are re-created with certain patterns, you are doomed/blessed with Wyrd.

15

WYRD

THE MAGIC OF GUINIVIERE WEBB

Michael Aquino's first recognition was Lilith and his last was Guiniviere Webb, and the path between the two takes a detour among fire worshippers of central Asia about three thousand years ago with stops at *Oprah, Beowulf,* Stephen LaBerge's Lucidity Institute, and nineteenth-century French esotericism, from MILD to a broken spear. Let's consider the strange case—dare I say the Wyrd case—of Guiniviere Webb.

Guiniviere was born in Los Angeles to an engineer father and an artist mother. But this open, hopeful beginning was replaced by rainy Portland and dank fundamentalism. Like many families after the American Bicentennial her family caught religion, a strong and bad case. As she grew up following her natural inclinations toward art and theater, her family warned her not only against these impractical dalliances but also the Dark Side itself. To warn her daughter, Guinevere's mom had her stay home from school on February 17, 1988, to watch Oprah Winfrey's exposé of Satanism. There she saw Michael and Lilith Aquino and heard Michael say, "We are not servants of some god, we are our own gods." Fateful words for a supersmart kid who wasn't being allowed to develop the very traits she had been encouraged for having in a talented-and-gifted program. The cage of behavior tightened considerably, and eventually Guiniviere was expelled to the streets. Street-smart, and able to make money playing the piano at a local club, Guiniviere survived but knew education was her only hope.

Armed with a lady's compact bearing the inverse pentagram of the Eastern Star, she asked that sisterhood for aide. Seeing her real need behind the tale she told of her grandmother, they helped her find her way into a community college, where she thrived. Soon she was directing her first play, Lewis John Carlino's *The Brick and the Rose*. The young director's family showed up, and a partial reconciliation was made. Guiniviere continued with her studies, returning to California for her exoteric education, and the Temple of Set for her esoteric one. In Berkeley, she was introduced to ecofeminism—the notion that folks who mistreat women, most likely also mistreat animals and the Earth—a useful insight for the Vampyre as well as the feminist. Here Guiniviere also began to learn about the importance of narrative and who owns it in political discourse.

She pursued archaeological studies, digging up the Sauro-Sarmatians, the legendary Amazons. As Greek physician Hippocrates of Kos (ca. 460–370 BCE) wrote, "[They] have no right breasts . . . for while they are yet babies their mothers make red-hot a bronze instrument constructed for this very purpose and apply it to the right breast and cauterize it, so that its growth is arrested, and all its strength and bulk are diverted to the right shoulder and right arm." Guiniviere discovered that the Amazon paradise was not the past envisaged by mystical feminists, but she did discover the wide range of tolerance among the folks of central Asia, especially those who worshipped fire—and some of their magic entered her worldview. The Sarmatians were closely allied with the Dacians and are one of the roots for the Transylvanian beliefs that were recast into the myth of the vampire.

Meanwhile, as she was growing as an initiate in the Order of the Trapezoid and the Order of the Vampyre of the Temple of Set, a third powerful force entered the picture, the Lucidity Institute. Founded by Stephen LaBerge, Ph.D., it sought enthusiastic dreamers to learn skills in remembering, reporting, and controlling dreams. Guiniviere both contributed to and learned from its research (including the MILD formula—see her version, WILD, on p. 189). Guiniviere joined an early order that studied Wyrd and dreams and, when its grandmaster left, took over the order. Moving to Texas to live with her wolf-mate (me),

Guiniviere finished her formal education in art history, writing a thesis on feminist, pacifist, and culture warrior Jane Addams.

In Austin, Guiniviere became the recipient of a powerful part of a Setian artifact. When Stephen Flowers became the Magus of the Word Runa, he had performed a working in Hollywood creating an artifact called the Spear of Wyrd. A powerful curse was placed on the Spear by Michael Aquino—all world-changing artifacts have a curse. The keepers of the Spear had great stresses—even temporary madness—and it was disassembled. The shaft was hidden in the mountains of the Sierra Madres for decades, but given at last to Guiniviere. Soon after its arrival Guinivere had a powerful moment resulting in a received text called *The Book of Wyrd* that summarized, synergized, and empowered the ideas I alluded to here. Before we begin to explain her ideas we need to explore two powerful ideas: one so deeply at the root of Anglo-Saxon esotericism that it is almost forgotten (Wyrd) and the second that comes from the heart of central Asia through Gurdjieff, Alexandra David-Néel, and French occultist Joseph-Alexandre Saint-Yves d'Alveydre (Synarchy).

Let's begin with an obvious fact about the English language (and its Germanic cousins like Old Norse and Yiddish). It has no future tense. It has a present (*run*) and a past (*ran*), but future ideas require a helping verb (*will run*). The idea of a fixed future, which you might encounter in Hebrew, Latin, or Chinese, for example, is not part of the thinking of a brain grown in English. And sure enough, the giant women, the Norns, who are the universe's response to the crime of Wotan/Odhinn show this division: Urdhr is all that has "spun out," Verdandi is what is turning out NOW, and third is an altogether different verb, skuld, "that which should happen." Wyrd represents a debt owed by the universe to the intrepid adventurer. But sometimes, as we know, the universe craps out (in the short run).

Wyrd was not a resonant concept with monotheism, it put too much power in the individual, and it took away the future as being the Will of God. Most Anglo-Saxon literature lost wyrd, but it survives in *Beowulf*. When Beowulf fights Grendel, Grendel's wyrd is known—the monster cannot be killed by a weapon. Beowulf, knowing this, strangles the beast. In so doing he pays back an obligation that his father had to King Hrothgar (every wyrd is another's skuld). At this point he is free, and could leave, but decides to help Hrothgar fight a tougher foe, Grendel's mom. Boldly he descends into the cave (the Great Unknown) and Wyrd blesses him with a giant sword from another age for his present struggle. Wyrd often rewards the bold adventurer. Then there's the final battle—the universe should let Beowulf beat the dragon, but he's seventy at this point. So the dragon wins, but Beowulf becomes immortalized in story. Beowulf's skuld played out as well it could. The notion of three women returned as the witches of *Macbeth,* where skuld becomes temptation—the temptation that maddens Macbeth. The last gasp of Wyrd until modern times was in Dickens's *A Christmas Carol,* where the Norns become a method of allowing Scrooge to rehabilitate—drawing strength from the virtues of the past, wisdom from seeing desire working in the present, and the likely future judged by the first two. Thus Scrooge returned to the Wyrd of his past and (as a good sovereign) redeemed all in his care.

The way of working with Wyrd is clearly shown as working with narratives. There are four sorts of narrative we tell ourselves: the disempowering one that births and empowers the social parasite; the heroic family/tribal narrative, including epigenetic material (often lost in childhood); narratives we create to make sense of the world; and the dreams we make for ourselves each night. Learning to stop repeating the first, remanifesting the second, providing hard evidence for heroically fashioned yarns in the third, and the deep magic of the fourth is the Way of Wyrd. Some methods for the last two are shown below. Historical note: the modern *weird* took its form in Shelley's poem "Alastor" to describe something uncanny that lures men onward to their doom. The modern English words *weird* and *worth* both come from the Anglo-Saxon *wyrd.* If you wish to pursue the linguistic/mythic aspects of Wyrd, you should consult James Bauschatz's *The Well and the Tree.*

As James Webb wisely points out, English occultism tends to be a fringe phenomenon, while Continental occultism is allied with the establishment. The notion of a ruling secret group is very attractive— Anton LaVey was drawn to Talbot Mundy's *The Nine Unknown.* Others saw the notion of a secret ruling group in schools from central Asia (as

Gurdjieff taught) or the mystery of Shambhala/Balkh that Alexandra David-Néel propounded, or as the great-granddaddy of central Asian mysticism Joseph-Alexandre Saint-Yves d'Alveydre (under the tutelage of a prince Hardjij Scharipf) purported when he described a central Asian city called Agartha that "radiated" Synarchy to the upper world. Synarchy views society as a living organism like the human body.

As Saint-Yves explained: "The first function corresponds to nutrition and that is economics. The second can be defined as the will, and that is legislation and politics. Finally, the third corresponds to the spirit and that includes science and religion." The belief in a community of free association under the guidance of scientists (for objective universe considerations) and initiates (for subjective universe evolution) is deeply resonant for many esotericists. Saint-Yves d'Alveydre also drew inspiration from the medieval Knights Templar, long held by occultists to have been Europe's hidden rulers during the Middle Ages. He believed the Templars' immense wealth and power came from their adherence to a sociopolitical system of Synarchy. These ideas (present in Plato and in most Indo-European traditions) had a mystical turn: aligning yourself to them gave wealth and a sensitivity to schools of initiation. I mention Saint-Yves d'Alveydre and this idea because Guiniviere Webb came back from Siberia with strong interests in community after a dream initiation (see "Techniques to Try" on p. 190) from a Shaka shaman whose kurgan she had excavated. Guiniviere also notes that all the central Asian fire worshippers—Tripolian, Scythian, Sauro-Samartain, Bashir, and so forth—had the same symbol: the spiral. Now, these groups are considered among the first civilizations of the Iron Age—if they're white (by Russian archaeologists) or if they're yellow (by Chinese archaeologists). But it is clear that in about 2000 BCE a series of ideas radiated out from here: tolerance, worship of mind (in the symbol of fire), shamanism, spiritual liberation being part of rulership, and mystical techniques of dream control. The Russian and Chinese studies are highly politicized, and Americans and Western Europeans don't dig much in the cold deserts.

Guiniviere Webb produced eight methods for the solitary Vampyre (as well as an advanced technique for groups, which I'll deal with in part 3 of this book). These methods are Moving to the Real; the Way of the Owl; lucid dreaming as training, not goal; civic power as training, not goal; the runic secrets of Wyrd; Turning into the Skid; bringing Life to Wyrd; and, finally, the Hallowing of the Stead. Let's deal with these and then with the vulnerabilities that can come from Wyrd. Dreaming and other intrasomatic (to borrow Anthony Reake's useful coinage) methods will be dealt with in the third part of this book.

Moving to the Real comes from Guinevere's training in European archaeology. If you are going to study something (in her case transition from bronze to iron in central Asia) you must do the thing—in her case cast both bronze and iron. If you use metaphors from gardening, you should really plant stuff and be a gardener. If you use metaphors from pottery, better know the feel of clay and the concentration you need at the wheel. The movement toward the real is an antinomian idea in modern occultism: modern occultists prefer to remain in liminal states and never reintegrate into the real world. This makes occultism a form of exotic sleep and makes occultists easy to manipulate for money or political purposes. Without the movement to the real occultists are victims, not Vampyres. Because of this orientation Guiniviere tells her students to avoid dream interpretation.

Guiniviere Webb has a lot in her toolbag—street-smart homeless person, working archaeologist, lucid dreamer, master of the night terror, Vampyre, artist, videographer, manager of a multimillion dollar budget, director of a museum, tree hugger from Oregon, rune magician—and her totem is the owl: symbol for wisdom and community for Athena, symbol of understanding a system just as it passes away for Hegel (i.e., the harbinger of cultural transience), or the symbol of the shape-shifting witch in Mexican folklore. The Way of the Owl is about knowing *which* method to use. Typical of her move to the real, Guiniviere has backyard owls—ninth generation as of the writing of this text. The owl is the symbol of cognitive fluidity, the mystery of twilight and transition, the scary side of female empowerment. It flies from the East, connecting the Vampyre with the mysteries of central Asia, and balances the bat in the West. If you would like to know more about owl folklore see *Owls in Mythology and Culture* by B. G. Marcot and H. Johnson.

Lucid dreaming as a first step, not a last one, is the notion that separates Guiniviere Webb from all other popular thinkers on dreams. Dream control is important, when desirable. But lucid dreaming is only one of many states—from insomnia to dreamless sleep—that Vampyres have in their toolkits. Many humans may delude themselves into thinking that lucid dreaming is a key (or worse still, *the* key) to a coherent afterlife. However, the steps that you need to master in order to lucid dream—remembering your dreams, learning to dream multiple times at night, learning the cycle of dreams that your body has, learning to manipulate your sleeping environment to influence your dreams, and learning to get immediate payoff (solutions to your problems and really good dream sex)—to continue your progress are essential to learning how to use a variety of several discrete states of consciousness. So where most popular dream books tell you that you have reached your destination, Guiniviere says, "Great! Now you can get started!" For a good beginning text try Patricia Garfield's *Creative Dreaming*.

Likewise, just as dealing with the narrative of dreaming is part of Wyrd, dealing with the political narrative of the world is part of the process. Civic power is the training, not the goal. Guiniviere Webb sees community activity first as a stay against delusion. If you're working in the world, you aren't sleeping in mom's basement. But this leads to its second use—the check of real power: Does your magic get you better results? Third, it puts you in the place where Vampyric skills are needed and tested every day, in addition to the more prosaic skills such as emotional control and balancing introspection and action. However, civic power is NOT the goal: the Vampyre does not wish to rule as a tyrant. She rules for justice—for the release of certain subtle energies that can only come from a healthy evolving society (Synarchy). Finally, civil power will cause the Vampyre to examine her own past so that she is ready to fly above it. Hegel's words on Minerva come to mind (from the *Philosophy of Right*, 1820):

Philosophy, as the thought of the world, does not appear until reality has completed its formative process, and made itself ready. History thus corroborates the teaching of the conception that only in the maturity of reality does the ideal appear as counterpart to the real, apprehends the real world in its substance, and shapes it into an intellectual kingdom. When philosophy paints its grey in grey, one form of life has become old, and by means of grey it cannot be rejuvenated, but only known. The owl of Minerva takes its flight only when the shades of night are gathering.

The wyrdling must understand and cure the world in order to fly from it. Wyrd is not a path for the forest hermit.

Wyrd is an Anglo-Saxon word, and as such should be written in runes of the Anglo-Saxon futhorc—the runes used in the Saxon parts of Transylvania—so there are runic secrets in the Word. First, Wyn (ᚹ), the joy/ecstasy that the shaman gets for working for the folk. Next, Yr (ᚣ), the Anglo-Saxon longbow was fatal at great distance and was the notable weapon mentioned in a poem from 1377 called *Piers Plowman*, which mentioned the outlaw Robyn Hode (Robin Hood). The long bow requires accuracy. Then Răd (ᚱ), which is still heard in modern English as "ride." And finally Dæg (ᛞ), again well known to our ears as "Day." Let's look at these runes in the *Anglo-Saxon Rune Poem* and then consider their esoteric meaning as the four-lettered spell WYRD.

> *Ecstasy he enjoys who knows not suffering, sorrow nor anxiety,*
> *and has prosperity and happiness and a good enough house.*
> *Yr is a source of joy and honor to every prince and knight;*
> *it looks well on a horse and is a reliable equipment for a journey.*
> *Riding seems easy to every warrior while he is indoors*
> *and very courageous to him who traverses the high roads*
> *on the back of a stout horse.*
> *Day, the glorious light of the Creator, is sent by the Lord;*
> *it is beloved of men, a source of hope and happiness to rich and poor,*
> *and of service to all.*
> —Translation by the author

Seekers must obtain not only ecstasy (communion with the divine self) but also have their lives in order—economic stability, domestic happiness, and a place to live. This ecstasy must be projected by a technology that requires training and social power and responsibility. As the most famous bowman shows us, this power may be turned against the establishment as well as used to save it. The bowman—always connected with the horse—knows the real work is hard and dangerous. (The poem also mocks those who merely fantasize.) If these conditions are met, the Lord sends insight (day), which benefits everyone—not merely the knight but also the poor in his care. Note lastly that the Gift from the Lord (the sovereign Self) becomes new Ecstasy. The formula has numeric significance by rune tally: (W) 8 + (Y) 28 + (R) 5 + (D) 23 = 64. In Germanic lore 8 × 8 signifies centeredness and prosperity.

Guiniviere Webb's system has one of the best self-control techniques, based on the word *wyrd* (turning). It is called Turn into the Skid. As we seek to perfect ourselves, we become aware of previous fuckups. Almost always a behavior that saved us in traumatic times—such as a huge display of anger—does not save us now. Wyrd, the world of patterning, exists because of energy the Vampyre spent in the past. Do not fight against this energy. Go with it—much as you would turn in to a skid on an icy road. For example, some jerk yells at you in a parking lot, you start to yell back because such behavior saved you in an earlier, rougher part of your life. Don't restrain yourself by fighting old energy with new energy. Go for it. Yell back something over the top, even silly, feel the old energy rush through you and then regain your direction. Break up the moment with a smile. Then later, when you do your gratitude exercise, thank yourself for giving you the defense when you needed it, and thank yourself for changing your life so you don't need it now. You will find that working with Wyrd heals you faster; for details see the rune poem above.

Bring Life to Wyrd, don't bring Wyrd to Life. You can pick a coherent pattern and engage your life force, energy, and emotions with that pattern consciously. You are doing that right now as you work through the Vampyric Initiation. Likewise, you should avoid the opposite: DON'T bring Wyrd to Life. Don't let other humans (or their internalized voice from the social parasite) give you a Wyrd you don't want. Let's look at three examples. You just married Bob. Bob's first wife had big knockers and fiery red hair (just like you). She drank herself to death. Everyone in your life and Bob's begins to act like you are going to drink yourself to death. Bob's dead wife's Wyrd is being thrust on your life. No bueno. Or you've been given a classroom in your new school. The last two teachers who had that room burned out. Everyone has a theory why—too near the boy's restroom, too noisy, and so on. Your burnout is inevitable. Here, people are (consciously or unconsciously) trying to give your classroom and you a bad Wyrd. Better change it. Finally, "everybody" knows that Chinese people (like you) get bad colds in the Midwest; oh dear, you're sniffling. It's not enough to ignore social pressure, you must banish it. Or your precious energy fulfills someone else's Wyrd!

The mystery of the Hallowing of the Stead is a deeply hidden aspect of the magical lifestyle. By exploring the idea of steads of Vampyric power earlier in this book you've received some subtle powers that will help you in this. John G. Bennett's idea of hyparxis is useful here. Let's look at time—which is the weft of Wyrd just as your deeds are its warp—in one sense time is mechanical. Cause A leads to effect B that is cause for C. Repeat. Repeat. Repeat. There is no free will. Let's call that Time. On the other hand, Time is full of possibilities. You can make new choices every second. The least change, like taking a slightly different route to work, could have vast effects—from meeting your wolf-mate to being in a fatal car accident. The future holds all possibilities—let's call that Eternity, the storehouse of all possibilities. Like Time it has no meaning—not because it's fixed, but because it's infinite. But what happens when a Wakened mind draws from Eternity into Time? He or she can then act. He or she has what Bennett calls hyparxis. Or the "Ability to Be." I am going to give you an example of hyparxis, then Guiniviere Webb's breakthrough.

I drive to work every weekday, starting at point A and ending up at point B. If I am not conscious—and most of us are never conscious when driving—this is an event in time. However, in theory I could be doing something novel instead: trying a new route, crashing my car, parking and deciding to quit my job, reciting the runes, masturbating, eating fresh vegetables while I drive—each could utterly alter my life. That would be in the realm of eternity. But most of these choices are deadly or at least awful in consequence. But what if I pulled from Eternity enough energy to make a move toward liberation? What if I chose to—for example—write the Wyrd chapter in my head while driving? Then I have moved out of rigid time but not into meaningless eternity. Bennett called this time stream hyparxis—it is here I grow my soul, my self that is not bound by the mechanical laws of the universe.

Webb noticed that each such action leads to greater possibilities for similar actions AND improves luck—that is to say, those experiences that I think I am not in control of. Every time I Come Into Being, the stead of my Coming Into Being is expanded. This explains the reason why almost anyone who begins working or playing with a new magical technology enjoys more happiness and good luck for a time and then sees this season end as they codify their experience, turning their new energy over to the social parasite. If you wish to avoid this fate, see the runic formula above!

These are among the ideas that come with Wyrd, and like all Words, certain vulnerabilities come with it as well. There are three common vulnerabilities: the bipolar run of dreaming success, the trauma/need of new structures, and the dangers of receptivity. Let's look at each. Dreaming is never a linear process; it usually goes like this: no progress, sudden amazing breakthrough dream, no progress, no progress, excellent results with one technique. The lack of progress is very depressing. The lack of progress after success is even worse. And sudden expertise brings manic joy but also a tendency to think that whatever is now working is the *only* or best path for you. Riding a horse is about balance, and it's tough riding it (instead of thinking about riding it). The trauma/need of new structures is about the Hallowing of the Stead; at first each energy breakthrough is easy to store in the body, but the Ability to Be will outstrip the structures of your emotions and your physical body. Unless you willfully build up new/higher structures you will be prone to panic attacks or migraines. New energy needs a new Wyrd. Choose well. Lastly, let's talk about the dangers of receptivity. The Wyrd Vampyre must be receptive to the new Wyrds she seeks—or the existing Wyrds within her that she wishes to empower. But not everything that presents itself to her is good or beneficial. Some ideas may look good because they appeal to deep layers of the social parasite—for example, a jerk girlfriend may be resonant with an abusive mom. The jerk girlfriend shows up just as you're dealing with the past, and you wrongly think, "I'm supposed to be with her," instead of, "She's a reminder of what I need to get rid of." Experiences don't come to you labeled "good" and "bad"—they come to you labeled "eat me" and "drink me"—and rationality and the ability to laugh at yourself are the only things that save you from poison. Magic is never safe, my fellow knight riding the Vampyric road; I promise only you'll have the bow.

OPENING RITE OF WYRD

Candles should be pointing away from you (North). Light a short candle in the South of the room, place a bowl of ice an arm's length away in the North. Graal liquid should be a vanilla milkshake.

Say the Vampyric Invocation. For the Graal Work, place one hand over the fire—close enough to feel the heat but not be burned—and one hand on the ice.

> In the beginning, the ice and fire streamed toward the great dark, and they made the monster-man Ymir and the Cosmic Cow. He drank her milk, and there was no imbalance, no Desire, no consciousness.

Drink from the milkshake.

> He begat a male and a female. And they begat Odhinn. And Odhinn did evil. He killed the monster-man Ymir and fashioned all the world. Now there was Mind. Now there was Evil. Now there was Death. And out of the East three giant women came. And Odhinn knew he was screwed.
> "I am Urdhr, all that has ever been. Wyrd is my name," said the First.
> "I am Verdandi, what is turning out Now," said the Second.
> "I am Skuld, that which should happen," said the Third.
> "We shall shape Life and Death and Life-in-Death. Fools on the left shall call us Random Chance. Fools on the right shall call us Fate. We stand in the middle as Wyrd, all of the patterns that were, are or may yet be."
> I am the Vampyre [VN], what is my Task?

The Three spoke as One: "Bring the Wyrd of the Vampyre to your life. Let it change all you have been, let it inform you of all that's really happening now, let it make you a partner in power with us for all that shall be."

Are there dangers?

"Many have tried. Many have died. But we will tell you a rune: when your Desire has become your Wyrd, you shall be beyond Life and Death, Good and Evil, Past and Future. Now depart and learn while we lay down the Law as Earth for the Great Tree and water it with blood, sweat and tears."

Close the rite in your usual fashion.

LIFE ANALYSIS

1. What patterns, good or bad, show up in your life over the years? If they're bad, why do they trap you?
2. Have you ever found an item or artifact that changed your life? What happened?
3. What have you done to improve the lot of women in this world?
4. Have you and another person ever had the same dream? Did that precede anything unusual in your relationship?
5. Have you ever felt healed by a pattern of events in your life? Do you think you could re-create that feeling/circumstance?
6. Do your friends tend to have odd stories/life paths?

VAMPYRIC ANALYSIS

1. How many times in your life have you been caught in family-of-origin reenactments? You treat the manager like Mom or Dad; you have a sibling relationship with a coworker. How many of the folks around you are caught in such reenactments?
2. When in your life have you been depressed by "My magic isn't working anymore"? How did you deal with your depression? Are there better ways?

3. How often do you see Wyrd being placed on other humans—where you work, by the media, at family reunions? How effective is this unconscious magic in empowering/controlling social parasites?

4. How often do you see yourself doing a new good thing (like standing up for yourself) but part of you feels it is very old?

PERCEPTION EXERCISES

Reality Testing. If you wish to get good at dreaming, spend a month doing reality testing. When you do something in waking life (such as turn a light on or off, look in a mirror, try to read a book) that produces a constant effect that it wouldn't in dreaming, say the following (aloud if you are alone, to yourself if you aren't): "If I am dreaming the light in the room won't change when I hit the switch." Or, "If I am dreaming the words in the book will change when I try to read them." Or, "If I am dreaming this apple will turn purple." This habituates your consciousness to reality testing, so when you do the same when you are dreaming, you become aware you are dreaming.

WILD. The Lucidity Institute teaches a mnemonic called MILD: "mnemonic induction of lucid dreams." It has four parts: (1) recall your dreams (every morning before you get out of bed); (2) reality testing (see above); (3) lucid affirmations—when you realize you are in a dream, say so in the dream (for example, "The words in this book are changing, so I am dreaming."); and (4) affirm your dreams; comment to yourself that you can lucid dream. Modify this to WILD (wyrd induction of lucid dreams): (1) recall your dreams twice—once before awakening and again during your gratitude work at night; (2) reality testing; (3) lucid Vampyrism—when you realize you are dreaming say, "I, the Vampyre [VN], am dreaming my way to power"; and (4) affirm your dreams—make your verbal affirmation Vampyric: "I, the Vampre (VN), can lucid dream" and when possible enact part of your dream. You dream you are wearing black sunglasses, buy some black sunglasses. You dream you are eating at a certain Chinese restaurant, eat there—and verbally affirm this in your gratitude work: "My dreaming self gave me these cool sunglasses! My dreaming self suggested a great dinner for me!" Mix this practice of the basic Vampyric techniques and you will rocket into a new orbit.

Restraint of speech. Crowley showed us years ago in *Liber III vel Jugorum* the value of controlling speech and thought. Vampyres eschew his harsh method of self-punishment—slicing yourself with a razor when the key word is mis-uttered. Simply take a mental tally of your successes and mention it during your gratitude rite. There are two speech practices: avoid saying the modern English *weird*—in the sense of "spooky," "odd," or "unusual." Say *weird* only when you mean *Wyrd;* that is, a pattern running contrary to the laws of the natural universe that may have so run before. If you fail, correct yourself gently. The second requires tact. When someone places a Wyrd you do not desire on you—"Looks like you're the new Nancy these days," verbally reject it: "I'm glad you see my technical skills as being as good as your late boss, but I am not, nor do I desire to become, Nancy." One simple statement is enough, you needn't be tiresome on the subject. Thank yourself. Thank yourself in your gratitude session for each piece of bravery.

Napping and the hour of wakefulness. See what happens to your dreams if you change your sleep habits. Try napping at unusual times and in unusual (but safe) places. If your schedule permits, try waking up ninety minutes before your usual waking time and engaging in reading about Vampyres or lucid dreaming or sexual play for an hour and then take a ninety minute nap. As you drift off repeat to yourself: "I am having a Vampyric dream. I am having a Vampyric dream."

TECHNIQUES TO TRY

Incubating a Dream

This works, and if you don't recall your dreams at first, it still programs your dreams. Pick something you would like to have a dream about—for example, you're trying to figure out whether you should move. So do the following exercise.

Night one, just before sleeping, look at yourself in a full-length mirror. Practice the Vampyric Gaze upon yourself. When your mind/

breath is calm, say out loud: "I am the Vampyre [VN], and I enter into the realm of dreaming tonight." Then drink a large glass of very pure water or a red-colored low-sugar nonalcoholic drink while looking at yourself. Be sure to try to recall your dreams in the morning.

Night two, same procedure but with different words: "I am the Vampyre [VN], and tonight I will dream of how moving in the past has influenced me."

On the third night say, "I am the Vampyre (VN), and tonight I will dream of how moving will effect me in the here-and-now."

On the fourth night say, "I am the Vampyre [VN], and I will dream of myself a year after this move." You needn't pay attention to the content of your dreams (i.e., a dream your new neighborhood is full of werewolves) but pay attention to the mood (i.e., "My new neighborhood was full of werewolves. It was super-fun!")

You may use this method for anything you wish—great dream sex, flying dreams, finding Aunt Tillie's lost purse, and so on.

Dream Sending

If you want someone to have a dream, you must do two things. First make the message simple: "Be scared of Bill!" or "I make you happy!" Do not try to send a complex message like "You should invest a reasonable part of your savings into Equifax Inc.!" or "Your political views on the matters of gun control and abortion should be reevaluated in the light of statistics published this year." The method is simple. Wake up ninety minutes before your target's waking time. Visualize yourself flying to above their home. Fly down to their bedroom. Repeat the mantra to them for several minutes (ideally as you are falling asleep yourself). Decide to do this ahead of time either for one night—or three nights. For three nights leave a night between each operation. DO NOT SEEK CONFIRMATION— no "Hey boss, did you have any weird dreams last night?" If your target tells you on her own, verbally affirm it: "That sounds about right to me."

Dream Initiations

Beginning with the Bön lineage of Tibetan yoga, there is the notion of dream initiations. The Bön tradition came from Afghanistan—most likely the city of Balkh, which the Tibetans call Shambhala, which means "Source of Happiness." Dream yoga insists that the narrative we tell ourselves in dreams is not unlike the narrative we tell ourselves to explain waking reality. It differs only in its inconsistency.

On rare occasions (such as the high fever on an archaeological dig wherein Guiniviere encountered a Shaka shaman) one can receive initiations from long-dead teachers. These can be sought by the methods mentioned above. One should deal with these states as personal and subjective; that is, don't put in your Facebook that you ran into Apollonius of Tyana last night.

You should seek secondary verification of things—preferably something that you could not have known before (e.g., female Shaka shamans wear what kind of hats?). If on the one hand the initiation is ethically correct and philosophically coherent, and on the other, a definite benefit—economic, emotional, or whatever—comes from it, these initiations may be taken as authentic.

INITIATIC RITE OF WYRD

Draw an equilateral triangle with nine-inch lines in pencil on parchment or papyrus. Inside this draw a counterclockwise spiral in a heavy red line that spirals out and breaks though the triangle. For four nights before the rite, tape the sigil to a shirt over your heart. Use the dream-induction method above. While looking at yourself in the mirror say:

> *I am the Vampyre [VN], and I will pass through an iron door*
> *bearing this sigil in five nights.*

Do this same act every night, counting down each time—four, three, two, tomorrow night. On the night of the work hang your sigil on the eastern side of your chamber. For the Graal liquid use buttermilk or other sour milk product.

Say the Vampyric Invocation, and for the Graal Work repeat the following:

> *I rode in caravan across the desert, and I began to have strange*
> *dreams. I came upon the Kurgans and I say the Red Sign. I said the*

names of the Eight Cities: Tamaghis, Ba'dan, Yass-Waddah, Naufana, Ghadis, Shambhala, Agarttha. Eight are the cities, each with eight gates. I drank the last of my canteen and waited for the Sign.

For the working, sit and close your eyes, visualize a great iron door upon which the spiral/triangle design glows bright red. When you can see it, open your eyes and begin the liturgy.

In the heart of Asia the worshippers of Mind chose Fire as their Symbol of governing humans and Vampyres. In the heart of Asia the makers of Iron chose the spiral as the Symbol to link individual evolution with care of the tribe, saying, "I have Come Into Being, and by Coming Into Being, the place of my Coming Into Being has Expanded." In the heart of Asia the Vampyres created Milam, the yoga of dreams, so that we may receive Transmissions from the long dead and the Undead. I come to the door.

Sit and visualize the door opening. When it opens, step through. If visionary material arises, watch it; when it is done or if it did not come at all, say the second part of the liturgy.

The owls of twilight fly forth from Shambhala. They teach the government of happiness and challenge. The mind-worshippers went west even to England. The mind-worshippers went east into China and beyond into the Americas. The mind-worshippers went south into India and north into Mongolia and Tibet. They taught the path of reintegration between dreams and waking life. Have your dream practice in the real world. By the use of the mind-gate in the center of my brain, I reach into the past to obtain the great Secret.

It begins with ecstasy, the sacrament of the Vampyres. When one aims to become awake during dreaming, the Vampyre learns to become Awake during seeming wakefulness. The elite proceed onward hiding their nature amid the terrors of the World of Horrors. Then a new day dawns for them, a Black Sun arises from Balkh-i-sham, the mother of cities called the Exalted Candle. I will live fully in that New Dawn.

Sit and close your eyes—let feelings and thoughts come to you—and when you feel the moment is past, say loudly:

> *I have re-created the Secret that Vampyres gave humans that they would become Vampyres. I live forever guided by my own pleasure and the need to evolve mankind. This was the ancient pact.*

Close the rite in your usual fashion.

ᴥ ᴝ

You're almost there, your gestation is almost done. But entering the world you need to know what signals to listen to. How can you hear new ideas and be open to them but not be swept along in a crazy thirst for the novel? How can you use the signs of your daily life reliably as a guide? How do you hear whispered truths in a world of shouted lies? For that victory, you need what's called critical listening or, in Greek, *synesis*.

16

SYNESIS

THE MAGIC OF ROBERTT NEILLY

I have built this narrative (this Wyrd) mainly on Americans. I could have chosen Baba Keenaram, Alan Kardec, Franz Bardon, Gregor A. Gregorius, and so forth. But I chose Americans for two reasons: One is that American spirituality is by nature recombinant. Americans tend to engage in cultural bricolage, and the Vampyric synthesis recombines tools and thoughts from several traditions. The second is that Americans want to get ahead. Every schoolchild knows that virtue serves (or is even manifested by) greed for dollars. The Protestant work ethic runs deep here, and it is easy to use it as an analog for the Vampyre's lust for energy.

Robertt Neilly is a Canadian whom we've already met twice in this narrative—first, introducing the word *Vampyre* to Lilith Aquino, and second, literally saying the Word Remanifestation to James Lewis during a conclave working of the Temple of Set. He was the cofounder of the Order of the Vampyre. His path is distinctly different from that of his peers in that it is derived from the modernist myths of positivist occultism. These myths usually make traditional occultists wary, and referring to them as myths makes modernists wary.

Let's talk about positivist occultism, a Toronto experiment with Skuld, and finally how all of this leads to a virtue Uncle Aristotle called *synesis,* the ultimate word that every smart occultist lives by—even if they've never heard it—but which has some deeper ethical and pragmatic meaning for the Vampyre. I will also talk briefly about Napoleon Hill and William S. Burroughs.

Positivist occultism is the Enlightenment's heartfelt attempt to keep magic on the shelf. The occult world and its wacky phenomena are just manifestations of an unknown science (and the language of magic is better served by "field" than "angel" or in these days liberal use of the word *quantum*). In fact, John Polidori, who gave us the word *Vampyre,* was a positive occultist interested in Mesmer's magnetic fluid and Aldini's experiments with electricity on newly hanged criminals. While he was writing his vampire novel he did talk to teenage Mary Shelley about voltage and corpses. (Aldini was the more shocking nephew of Galvani—get it? More shocking?) The quest to explain the Wyrd as paranormal probably had its biggest champion in J. B. Rhine of Duke University (in academia) and the editor of *Astounding,* John Campbell. The hopeful arc of "Psi powers are science, science is good, we are getting smarter" is one of the most powerful myths of modern America. Its outward manifestations like the UFO phenomenon, Zenner cards to test for ESP, sensory deprivation research, and so forth, are ingrained in our popular culture—and at times positivist occultism has been the only safe harbor for humans whose magical nature has wounded the social parasite.

It should be noted that the "magic is all psychology" school (i.e., LaVey) is not the positivist occult school (i.e., John Lilly), but to people who are hostile to magic, these are seen as one and the same. The contemporary American Left-Hand Path has always had a strong connection to positivist occultism beginning with early Church of Satan member Jacques Vallée, who was also the back door for the large amount of French esotericism Anton added to his synthesis (largely uncredited, of course).

Young Robertt Neilly, who was born with the second *t* in his name—much as Ingo Swann really began as Ingo Swann—was gifted (or cursed) with great sensitivities. He was the creepy kid who saw ghosts, "knew" things that adults didn't want him to know, played with séances (much like your author was cursed by watching *Dark Shadows*), and so on. The host culture could provide unflattering explanations for such things (e.g., "That kid ain't right."), but Robertt had enough self-love and deep curiosity that opened a different door.

On Halloween when he was sixteen, he heard about Toronto Society of Psychical Research and knocked on their door. "Go away kid!" But persistence paid off, and they let him in three years later. As we noted with Runa, the sign of a Vampyre is being able to find the right resources at exactly the right time. The TSPR wasn't your average bunch of ghost busters. Founded by Alan Robert George Owen, a university lecturer in genetics and mathematics (at Cambridge, where you can have four first names), the group took a scientific approach to the paranormal; that is to say, it was a hotbed of positivist occultism. Young Robertt stood out for lacking degrees in math or hard science, but they did let him in because of his ability to produce phenomena. The group was involved with the best-documented creation of a meta-mind, "Phillip," and although Robertt was not directly involved with that conjuring he was—so to speak—brought up there. Let's talk about Phillip and Skuld.

Skuld is (as we have seen) a debit created by actions of conscious, powerful humans. If you create a magical vacuum it will be filled. Using the standard equipment of Spiritualism—darkened room, lightweight table, circle of sitters—the TSPR called up Phillip, who was not your average ghost. You see, Phillip Aylesford was a fiction—a character with a biography full of color from the age of Charles II, including being knighted at an early age, falling in love with Romani (suspected of witchcraft), and dying by his own hand—one of the traditional methods of becoming a vampire. The initial séances produced nothing, but eventually the usual stuff showed up: strange breezes, strange sounds, table rapping, and so on. It was considered 100 percent proof of the meta-mind to believers and 100 percent an example of "childish defense mechanisms" to skeptics. From this experience, Robertt learned the power of connecting minds to make another mind.

In 1979 three vampire films hit the market, the comedy *Love Bites,* Werner Herzog's *Nosferatu,* and *Dracula* with Frank Langella. This splitting of the myth into camp, alien horror, and romance had a powerful effect on Robertt. The first showed that you had to lose self-importance to play with the myth—face it, most adults are too uptight to play. The second showed that at the heart of the myth there is something very alien. The third showed the power of romance. The subtitle *A Love Story,* dealt with the sexy-seductive side of the myth (since we often misspell "sex" as "love") but then hinted at the possibility of love—rather than blood—as being the key to the Vampyre's Remanifestation. Given Robertt's later role with that word, this cannot be overstated. It is also why this film bears the "R" for required in the Recommended Vampyric Curriculum's film list.

In the meantime, Robertt had found the Temple of Set. A central notion of the temple (as in all occult groups) was that magical power and sensitivity were good things—both to be exploited for personal gain and then used for personal refinement, and lastly to (in some way) even help further the notion of consciousness as a thing to be improved, not a static given. This looked a good deal like home. But there's always the problem of knocking on doors; sometimes they are answered. Robertt began to sense that there was something behind Vampyre myths. He looked in vain in the occult literature—if vampires were mentioned at all, it was the bad guys, as attractive to have around as mosquitoes. The novels and the books gave powerful, intriguing images, but occult writing gave a different view. He did come across a review of Hodder's *The Vampire,* in which the leader of a magical order had to use a vampiric talisman to survive. Plot problems arose when good and bad guys tried to get the talisman. Wow, here's a perfect myth: energy is used to maintain a lineage that ultimately serves mankind, and then this idea shows up when the temple is having its own crisis. A door opened and Something came through (but more on that later).

One of Robertt's first interests was re-creating the psychic research of the TSPR that had saved him earlier in his life among the black magicians of the Temple of Set. Many of the experiments were equally inconclusive; in fact, it seemed that self-centered black magicians might be scoring less well. However, there were two results. First, when he was experimenting with meta-mental work, a shadowy figure seemed to be around, showing up in the perceptions of everyone involved. Second, the attempts to both copy the soulful look of vampires in the movies and to engage in telepathy created the Vampyric Gaze, the number one pillar of Vampyric magic. Then Robertt tried a successful formula from the past: the use of a narrative. Instead of calling a fictional ghost he asked one of the participants (me) to write a bare-bones narrative: picture yourself meeting other Vampyres in a castle, while burning Uncle Setnakt's Telepathy Incense. This changed everything—the participants all had very similar visions. They visualized the castle at night (not a big stretch for black magicians). They saw it as a room without a roof. (Okay, that seemed unlikely for all of the participants.) They were surrounding a cauldron (not the biggest stretch). We took each other's hands. We began to levitate and rose into the night sky. Now we seemed to be well beyond the simple group-cueing part.

But on a more personal level Robertt has experiences. He had the classic abducted-by-aliens experience. What to do with this? It doesn't match Setian cosmology. So, he tried to ignore it. But undigested gnosis will break apart your life—stresses will occur in relationships, jobs, health. You can't ignore what you have called up, which is the major reason that humans should avoid Black Magic altogether. The social parasite will fight back hard. Robertt fought back as long as he could and then proceeded to investigate his gnosis. Many even within the temple were resistant. Others view his experiences as meaningful but culturally determined: if he had been Celtic, it would have been an encounter with the Sidhe; Germanic would be dwarves and elves; so for a twenty-first-century Canadian, it was aliens. Such eruptions of Otherness, much sought after by people who aren't wired to have them, have certain consequences. The experiencer can decide to be a victim and opt for Right-Hand Path sainthood, or a ritual specialist and deal with the community that has had similar liminal experiences. The experiencer can integrate himself into the world—have a job, drive a car, have relationships—or he can flee into the woods and be a hermit. The Vampyre chooses the latter in both instances.

He explores the idea of *Synesis,* a term from Aristotle that is usually translated as either "listening carefully" or "comprehension." It has two elements: first, deep communication—wordless sharing—can heal the soul by introducing it bit by bit to conditions beyond cultural and biological life. The usefulness of telepathy is not "Pick up some bananas at the store, dear!" It's "Know my Essence when you need to find me."

It is for your friends, your family, your familiar, and the Great Other. In grammar, synesis is agreement in idea rather than number and gender. For example, by synesis I can say, "Each of my students *are* doing their homework." Instead of "Each of my students *is* doing his or her homework." In a nongrammatical sense it means I can recognize that Set and Tezcatlipoca are the same god. The second aspect of Synesis is that it prepares me to encounter the great Other as part of my Vampyric Initiation. The aspect of "listening carefully" was part of the structure of the Order of the Vampyre in its earliest days; Robertt instructed initiates to explore the Words of "Thelema," "Indulgence" and "Xeper" as the philosophical backbone of learning Vampyric techniques, and, as you can see, my own teaching method evolved from there.

Robertt provided several ideas that are helpful for the Vampyre: deep communication takes work, pay attention to the corner, the channel is not always the thinker, stories are where things flow together, the Vampyric Lover is the final mask, the Vampyric demon is the penultimate mask, polarity is proof, process can drain your energy, some folks won't get you. After this we will look at the vulnerabilities that come with the Word.

Most of the occult world and even more of the pop-psychology world would disagree with Robertt's maxim, "Deep communication takes work." But as soon as humans have their first trauma, the masks start being placed. We don't even know our own set of masks, and opening to Vampyric exchange not only makes you aware of the other's Essence but also your own. And unprocessed gnosis hits you like a ton of bricks (see above).

People who are open to the Great Other, sometimes say smart things because their process might be prophetic. That is to say the channel is not always the thinker—the deep diver has brought back a pearl, such as the Word "Remanifest," but has to release it into the meso-cosmos so that it may be explored. In archaic societies the role of the oracle was understood; in the modern age of false egotism, it is not understood. For the Vampyre this means: YOU ARE NOT AS SMART AS WHAT YOU SAY—a truth that is perhaps tattoo-worthy.

In the world of philosophy, and its bastard child, occultism, ideas are overvalued. If only one could just list the important ideas, and others could read the list. But Robertt discovered that deep communication is not at the written-word level (any more than the visible part of an iceberg is the mass of ice). It is in story, interactive story, that deep communication occurs. In its lesser forms (like watching certain movies) communication can occur if we listen deeply. In more interactive forms—when minds work together as a meta-mind—then it can be sought and managed. The etymology of *synesis* is "flow together," and stories are where things flow together. This truth has been noted as a formula for business success by Napoleon Hill in *Think and Grow Rich* or a method to subvert text by William S. Burroughs and Brion Gysin in *The Third Mind*.

Every religion has a methodology for communication—usually visualization and meditation. The purest form is probably the Tibetan practice of yidam yoga. The monk visualizes himself as any of the "Protective Deities." The flaw with this is that the practitioner is fitting himself into another's mold. The Vampyre should create the perfect lover—including all kinds of love, from the rawest sexual passion to that feeling that comes when momma kisses a skinned knee. Review and know all your loves. First, as an image that teaches you how to be a Vampyre, then as an image of yourself. As always when confronting positive and negative female energies in your psyche, surprises can occur. The committed lesbian may find Santa Claus in her perfect lover archetype, or the straightest man may encounter Jagger. When you find your perfect lover you will discover that you have been feeding it vast amounts of energy all your life, but it is more than willing to return the energy to you in erotic and emotional exchange. In the east this is the secret of Tantra, in the West the myth of the incubus or succubus. The Vampyric Lover is the ultimate mask of the Great Vampyre.

Now, the *other* side of vampires is that they are scary. We banish them all the time. Walking to your car at night, hear that branch snap behind you? Was that a laugh I heard just before I woke up? Why does it bother me to go into the basement by myself—even though I am an adult human? What did we mean when we told a fellow teenager, "My mom will kill me?" Fear is the great energy gateway, and

202   🦇 The Vampyric Initiation

Vampyres enjoy scaring themselves because they built the Demon Vampyre. This archetype will also teach you. The Demon Vampyre is the penultimate mask of the Great Vampyre. Like with the Vampyric Lover, the Vampyre builds up the scariest form he or she can imagine. Stick with what scares you—and remember not to share this with anyone you wouldn't share your PIN code with. It doesn't matter if your final figure looks like Slender Man or Frosty the Snowman. It has been taking your energy for years, but it will willingly give your energy back when you stare it down and realize (with a giggle) that it is your mirror image.

The two extremes above reveal that polarity is proof. Any idea that has risen above intellectual comprehension into a transformative substance presents itself as polar: frightening/benign, good/evil, masculine/famine. Only things that go beyond (but do not contradict) the intellectual can be used by the Vampyre in his or her metamorphosis. Synesis is the process whereby the mind discovers that it is not alone in the psyche but is the rational negotiator of its many parts.

When people begin their quests they encounter a good deal of low-hanging fruit such as "If I eat better, I have more energy." Or "If I examine my superstitions, I may be able to design more streamlined and effective magical practices." Or "My relationship with my mother is screwing up my sex life." Or "I spend too much time on the internet." These early revelations have little cost, provide clear direction, and have almost immediate benefits. The deeper stuff, the material that our psyche needs resolved (rather than the pathologies of social control), is much harder to get to, harder to make into clear directives, and harder to explain to our families and friends. Process can drain your energy. The hard work of finding the deep fetters that you or others placed on your soul is very personal. You won't find a book that addresses your needs, or a support group—and effective fetters are booby-trapped. As you contemplate them you realize that they tap energy in several directions. Here is a simplistic example: Jon and Sue decide to give up smoking. This is a daunting task for anyone, but Jon began smoking when he was fourteen: every night he would smoke with his nonverbal dad and watch Westerns on TV. All of his ideas of masculinity and all of the ties to dad are deeply intertwined with smoking. Giving up smoking is human effort for Sue, a superhuman effort for Jon—and their relationship dynamic is about to be tested.

If your path to the esoteric is well paved and often trodden, there will people who will understand each of your steps. Since the Vampyre has to deal with the energy flows in and out of him or her, the Vampyre has to deal with the personal. Some folks won't get you. If you are following a one-size-fits-all path, you will find people who know the rough spots, or can offer you tips. The Vampyre is always in his or her own territory. They may seem trivial ("You think watching movies is spiritual?") or simplistic ("Yeah, we all like sex; you think about it too much.") or risk filled ("You skydived because you're afraid of flying?") The Vampyre has to lose self-importance. He or she may find or create others of their kind, but being alone or even being mocked is part of the process.

Now we'll look at three vulnerabilities of the path of Synesis: new orthodoxy, fear of other's process, and passivity. New orthodoxy is the bane of all esotericists: as they find a working theory for their experience, they have a new faith. It is important to balance your new thoughts with work in a community (Wyrd) and the need for the unknown (Runa). Fear of other's process is the vulnerability that comes from the personal nature of the Vampyric Path: the Vampyre sees others who were bold where she was timid, or were timid where she was bold. The all-too-human need of validation overcomes them. Here is where the Vampyre must fight the tendrils of the social parasite. Passivity is a tempting state for all oracles: they worked hard to bring back a message. They are tired. Only true Vampyres can deal with the harsh truth that the number one person they brought back their message for is themselves.

OPENING RITE OF SYNESIS

Turn the candles to the North (i.e., away from you). The Graal liquid should be Greek wine. Get a children's Halloween bag (or plastic pumpkin). Place eight nice candies on a platter on your altar.

Say the Vampyric Invocation and then repeat the following Graal Work:

> *I drink the wine of the Greeks and ask my many selves to dialogue. Let each self that can say, "My knowledge is not total, but my Thirst for the truth will last for lifetimes." Come to this symposium. Let false selves who feed on lies to speak more lies, now fly away as smoke from my candles.*

Blow the black candle out. Each time you mention a word, pick up a candy and put it in your bag. When you have all eight, shake your bag until you put it down.

> *I have knocked on Eight doors with my trick-or-treat bag, dressed as a vampire. I received eight candies.*
>
> *From **Try**, I learned that there is much more to the Cosmos than anyone knows, and if I put aside the rules that make me a herd animal, I can directly experiment with these things.*
>
> *From **Thelema**, I learned that there is much more to me than I can rationally know including a part that knows what's Right for me.*
>
> *From **Indulgence**, I learned that I can trust pleasure to awaken myself.*
>
> *From **Runa**, I learned that the difference between mysteries without and mysteries within is an illusion.*
>
> *From **Xeper**, I learned part of me exists outside of time summoning events and thoughts to me in the best order, and that I can dialogue with that part through word and deed.*
>
> *From **Remanifestation**, I learned that my true self does not grow as a line but claims Being as a spiral—sometimes visible, sometimes invisible.*
>
> *From **Arkte**, I learned to care for all living beings including myself.*
>
> *From **Wyrd**, I learned that as I gain Being all aspects of my life are blessed and energized (which sometimes feels strange).*

I am ready to put down my bag as Hotei did and listen to the Master Vampyre. When he tells me to pick up my bag I will be a real Vampyre.

Put down your bag.

Wait until you hear—anything: a car door slam, a creaking board, a dog barking outside. You'll know.

Pick up the bag. Bow deeply three times.

I will meet you in a month, Master Vampyre. I will seal our Pact for all the ages.

Close the rite in your normal fashion. Give out the treats to friends, coworkers, beggars, and so on. By the way, persons eating the candies will show some aspects of the Word for about a week. If you eat them all yourself, you will show aspects of adult diabetes.

LIFE ANALYSIS

1. Have you ever experienced telepathy? What was it like?
2. Do you know the moods of people who share either a blood tie or a love tie with you?
3. What beliefs do you have that others would call pseudoscience? Do these beliefs help you in some way?
4. Have you ever been a channel to another entity—or simply gave an inspiring speech that you felt you did not know where it came from?
5. Have you ever felt an egregore—a spirt of a group or an institution?
6. After the past eight months how has your mind changed about the idea of "Vampyre"?

VAMPYRIC ANALYSIS

1. Ask people about what figure really scared them as kids. Try visualizing yourself as that figure in their presence. What happens? Don't overdo this one.

2. What aspects of your ideal lover are you missing in your current relationships? How are you giving yourself this need?

3. When in your life have you had an experience of telepathy? How did it feel?

4. How have you hidden your intuition from others? (For example, once I had an overwhelming desire to leave work and go home—I don't mean the desire we all get at three o'clock on Friday—so I told my boss I was getting food poisoning. When I got home, the first hour nothing happened, and I felt like an idiot, then a certain phone call came. . . .)

PERCEPTION EXERCISES

1. Seek first to understand and then be understood. This is right out of the *7 Habits* book. Not only will you gain true bonds with people by listening to them first, you will open the way for deeper listening.

2. Gather a few objects—for example, a quartz crystal, an apple, your grandfather's pocket watch. Sit quietly with them; still your mind and your breathing. Limit your gaze to the objects and see if you can sense or feel them. Learn to know things wordlessly.

3. Look at the shadows of humans or animals. Try to suck in the emotional state of the person or animal by "tasting" their shadow.

4. Go to a crowded mall and sit by the fountain. Unobtrusively attempt to know the feelings and missions of folks who surround you.

TECHNIQUES TO TRY

Uncle Setnakt's Telepathy Incense

I had the job of creating a unique incense for a very diverse group—some would have charcoal disks and consecrated incense burners, while others were living in student dorms. They wanted the incense to hold and trigger memories (so it should have its own smell and be cheap enough to make a lot). It also had to be self-lighting. Here's the recipe:

- Six parts of self-lighting Come to Me incense
- One part very fine frankincense
- One part "working" copal (see below)
- Three sprays fine cologne (see below)

The Come To Me incense is a glittery red powder available at botanicas (or even Walmart online). It does not require charcoal. You should buy the highest-quality frankincense you can locate and grind it as finely as possible with a mortar and pestle. Frankincense is mildly psychotropic; go ahead and inhale the dust (don't snort it!). Visualize each of the people you are attempting to contact as you grind the product. If you live in a region with an active curandero tradition, buy locally sourced copal. (If you don't live in such a region buy from a shop that is so located, like Papa Jim's in San Antonio.) You will need to grind it as well—discarding twigs and pieces of rock salt. Blend the ingredients well, stir the mixture three times with a wooden spoon while saying these words:

> *Shezmu, thou redden the night sky with blood of enemies. Shezmu thou brought the magic of memory from Punt to Egypt to all the world. Shezmu bless my incense so that the gods may speak one to the other as it was in the time of the Third Ordering.*

Then take your best cologne—the one you wear on the third date—and spray it on the mixture three times, each time saying another word:

> *Thelema! Indulgence! Xeper!*

If you are creating this incense for a work with other Vampyres, label it carefully when you mail it to them.

The Rite of Humbling and Wonder
As you go to sleep, picture everyone you know well and say, "A wondrous being, I will not be blinded by their mask." See how this changes the atmosphere of your workplace or school.

The Marketplace Oracle
This is an ancient Hermetic practice that can be more useful to the Vampyre than runes or tarot. Find a place where people gather. Find a

quiet spot. Think about some problem you have. Formulate a question. Ask the question out loud: "Should I move in with Margaret? What say you Thrice-Greatest Hermes?" Go into the crowd, listen. The first coherent utterance will be your answer. Go back to your quiet place and write it down. Repeat two more times.

Initiatic Rite of Synesis

Orient the candles as your heart prompts you. Choose a pleasing, non-alcoholic Graal liquid. Choose a spot for the Great Vampyre to appear from; align the strobe light to leave the spot in shadow.

Say the Vampyric Invocation and repeat the following Graal Work:

> *I drink from the memories stored in my DNA. I drink from the memories of my ancestors' ancestors. I drink before humans fled the Ice.*

Turn on the strobe to about seven flashes a second. Speak slowly to the dark place. Imagine the Demon Vampyre.

> *You are not Edward. You are not Lestat. You are not Dracula. Those are masks you have used to stalk me. You are not Upir and Nelapsi. You are not Vampir or Lampir. You are not Striga, nor Alp, nor Gwrach y Rhibyn. Those are masks you've put on to stalk my ancestors' ancestors. I know you. I've ALWAYS known you.*
>
> *You are not Tlahuelpuchi, you are not Kappa, you are not Rakshasa nor Vetla. You want to drink my blood, eat my flesh, and birth a new me.*

Picture the Demon Vampyre until you grow afraid.

> *I know you. You are my lover.*

Picture the Vampyre Lover.

> *You want to heal me, tell me I'm okay, tell me it will be better. You want to lick me, suck me, fuck me. Your love and lust is my ticket to immortality.*
>
> *No. You are beyond that. You stalked me by Love and Fear*

according to the Pact you lay down with humans. You are beyond humans. Beyond the galling laws of time and space. You are the Great Vampyre. You . . .

Advance to the dark spot. Stand (or sit) there and finish the liturgy.

. . . ARE ME!

Close the rite in your usual fashion.

🖛🖛

Now you have both seen your original face and glimpsed the Great Vampyre. For those of you brave enough to have gone through this long tunnel you have come forth by night as a new sort of entity. For those of you not that brave—or just not ready—you and the full Vampyre will begin to have some questions, some needs, and some challenges. We'll consider these in the third section of this book, "Advanced Practices."

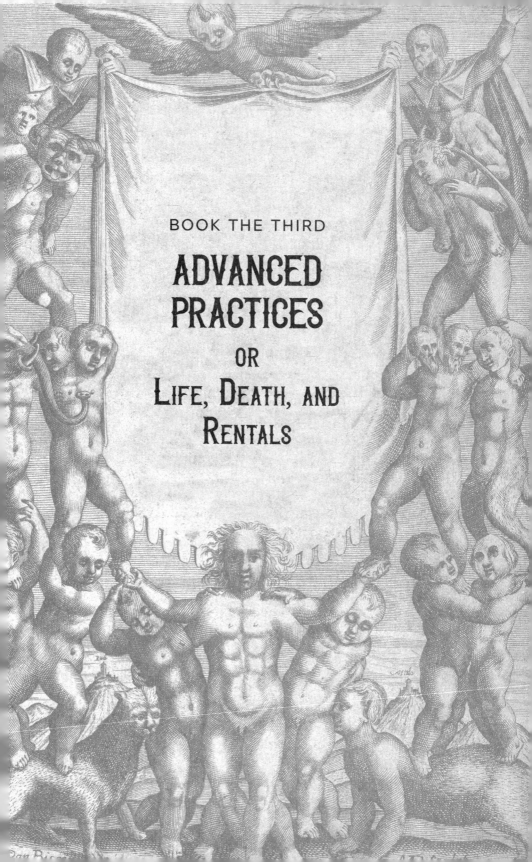

BOOK THE THIRD

ADVANCED PRACTICES

OR

Life, Death, and Rentals

17

ADULTING, OR VELMA THE VAMPYRE

If I were smart, I would not write this part of the book. I'd charge huge fees to money-plump victims, who would feel bad about themselves—but I am (sadly) ethical rather than smart. So here goes.

Part 1 of the book was the basics. Part 2, a method to take the basics into a highly energized state. This part will deal with the tough and secret part that most occultniks hate—and oddly call "real life." The fourth part is a collection of answers for questions that will come later. The occult industry is not a friend to Vampyres—it teaches a dependence on lore: the next book, seminar, podcast will surely have the secret. The Vampyre can be self-guiding once a deep and practiced awareness of energies, a gratitude for results, and a pre-Sleep approach to strategy have been established. Ritual and magic are focusing and training activities.

Now, I will address deep issues for the practitioner, but first I must say that I am not addressing money. The issues for this chapter—home, employment, diet, and exercise—are not about cash. Yes, if only I had vast supplies, I could do anything! But the self-change that the Vampyre must make is not fueled by cash; cash is good and may appear as a by-product of change. The ideas I will talk about can't happen at levels of subsistence and are difficult (but not impossible) at levels of poverty, but oddly become difficult at upper levels of wealth as well. It took me three decades of teaching humans from all walks of life to come to this observation.

The myth of the vampire, driven by the needs of cinema, push four areas into sharp focus: lair, wealth, diet, and activity level. For the latter two we aren't talking about blood and the "forever young" part of the myth but the need for these ideas in creating the seductive and powerful being.

VELMA: A CASE STUDY

Now that you've given up on the notion of Carfax Abbey, where do you live? The Vampyre has three requirements: her home must accumulate energy, her home must radiate mystery or power, her home must be secure on the practical level.

Let's examine these in the case of a practitioner I know who I will call Velma the Vampyre. I'll explain her story. Her human name isn't Velma and her Vampyric name isn't Velma, either, but she has a fetish for dressing as Velma Dinkley from *Scooby Doo* (and this description will piss her off—gently; never piss off a Vampyre non-gently). She was the second of three daughters of a Midwestern family. Mom and Dad belonged to a strict Protestant group that thought college education was a bad thing for girls, and when Velma trustingly came out to them near the end of high school, they thought that public education had done its foulest deed. So Mom and Dad withdrew all support from Velma. Velma's out-and-out Satanic remake did make her queen of the Goth lesbians for a few years. And hard work in night school bought her a B.A. in about a decade. Now Velma lives as an assistant librarian in a Midwestern city. To most eyes Velma would not be seen as a Vampyre.

She works in a library in a disadvantaged neighborhood, and the cost of living puts her in a large and nondescript apartment building. We'll return to her later when discussing employment.

If you drive up to her building you can spot her apartment. It is high on the street side of the building, its tiny balcony brightened by bold clay pots bearing blooming plants in the summer and seasonal decorations in the fall and winter. Nothing about her balcony screams "Goth" or "Vampyre"—except in the weeks leading up to Halloween—but it is referred to by all in the neighborhood: "I live one building over from the building with the flowers." Or "I'm two apartments below." And so on. All perceptual energy that scans the area is drawn to her apartment and by her Will taken and released back to the viewer. The viewer inevitably thinks, "Whoever has that apartment is happy!" or "They must have their shit together!" Or any of a dozen other powerful messages. Literally, all day the apartment is charged.

The second parameter, "It must radiate power," is accomplished by Velma's presence in tenant meetings. When an issue comes up—apartment security, painting the lobby, and so forth—Velma goes in a power suit and always reminds people *which* apartment is hers before she offers a well-thought compromise to matters being discussed. In some matters Velma uses her Vampyric power to rule matters that are important to her, in others she makes sure that the inevitable conclusion is seen as deriving from her sovereignty.

The third matter, practical security, has three aspects. First, Velma has only invested her own money into the building twice, using her powers to otherwise get what she wants. She had her bedroom/ritual chamber soundproofed. She bought a security door—that she had installed despite building regulations that all doors be uniform. Second, Velma has practiced all the security drills that the building has implemented: she knows what to do in case of fire or other more unlikely disasters. Vampyres cultivate a sense of caution that helps them maintain their existence mentally as well as psychically. Third, Velma is a favorite of the guards. She flirts with some, is a "helpless female" with others, bakes a cranberry bread for others. In all mythic ways she is the Lady of the building.

I could've chosen others. I know a treehouse-dwelling Vampyre in Hawaii, an owner of a fourteenth-century farmhouse in France, and one fellow who literally lives above a carnival fright show in Florida—but I'm choosing Velma, who manifests the Vampyre lifestyle in the seemingly least likely Vampyric environment.

The second question, employment, likewise separates the wannabes and the Vampyres. Again, the romantic component could be highlighted—from the gent that is a caretaker at a rather posh cemetery to the college professor who has built her career around Gothic and horror literature—but I'm sticking with Velma on this one. The Vampyre has the same needs as others—good insurance, consistent wages, good coworkers—so I won't address that. I'll add four additional needs: the job must require occasional use of one's powers, the job must give you access to meaningful resources, the job must not occupy all of your mental time, the job must align with your vision of the world. Velma occasionally uses her powers to create a great children's story hour or deal with obnoxious patrons, but the use that most impressed me was seen in a speech to city government a few years ago. The city's fathers had decided to cut back on library hours at "underused"—that is to say, "bad neighborhood"—libraries. Velma, having first gathered her data, gave a short speech on the power of imagination to fight crime and poverty. She defended her library—and drew applause from the assembled. It not only reversed the city's policy but also brought more funding to the library.

For the second criterion—access to meaningful resources—her job provides her with rare books and films though interlibrary loan. There has seldom been a research project that I've engaged in that Velma hasn't offered useful advice and resources. Of course, anyone can use interlibrary loan, but not everyone is paid to sit and go through the catalogues of the world's libraries! The second resource available to her is a rather generous vacation plan that has enabled her to go on a variety of interesting vacations—from attending the International Conclave of the Temple of Set in Hawaii, Porto, Munich, and so on, to rather more personal vacations with a rather attractive traveling companion.

Her job seldom requires overtime and does not use too much of her mental energy. She can legitimately spend some of her working time reading vampire novels or tracking down obscure vampire films. Although her job has occasionally taken her free time—such as the weeks fighting the city council—for the most part it ends when her shift is over and does not start until the next day. Like her housing, her job is an extension of her Vampyric state, not a distraction.

The fourth criterion, that the job must align with her vision of the world, is manifest in four ways. First, she maintains a small but significant Vampyric presence in her library—the novels, the related nonfiction, and so on. But this is the least of her work. She has an ongoing LGBTQ support group for street youth. She makes sure her parents' hatred is ritually destroyed repeatedly by keeping similar forces at bay for younger victims of similar hate. This not only has a healing effect on her own psyche (see the next chapter on Vampyric pathologies) but fights against the forces of ignorance. Third, she encourages the practice of arts and letters in annual Halloween writing contests; she acknowledges the gateways that enabled her own mental escape and has taken her position guarding the same. As part of this work, she aids other practitioners—for example, giving some of us reading or speaking slots at her library. Lastly, in addition to providing a home for her two rescue cats, Shaggy and Scooby, she feeds birds and feral cats at her library (in two separate areas, I might mention).

MAINTAINING THE VAMPYRIC VESSEL

The "diet" remarks will be short. They were given to me by a Westerner, who is a non-reformed Aghori. When I heard these (i.e., in a moment of Synesis), I knew I had to add them to my teaching. I fail at these often as my puffy body shows, but it is the right of all occult teachers to occasionally preach more than they should. The Vampyre is in an odd world. The forces of ignorance would prefer him to eat junk—too much fat, too much food infested with the cruelty of its slaughter, too many chemicals of unexamined effect. On the seeming opposite side of the coin, various dietary cults will prescribe regimens—no meat, no cooked food, no preservatives, less sodium, more vitamins A, C, D, or whatever. The first diet dulls the mind and the senses but empowers the social parasite. The second also empowers the social parasite but may improve health. I say "may" carefully. A couple of decades ago a bottled water firm here in Austin preached against the low quality of our tap water but offered a healthier (if more costly) alternative in their bottled spring water. The New Age crowd rallied under their banner. Sadly, their water source contained a rather nasty parasite that damaged livers—I know people who still have troubles from those halcyon days.

So, what can the Vampyre do? Here are four guidelines: Determine how many calories you need; a nutritionist can help, but good science and careful awareness of any special metabolic conditions is all that is needed. Found the figure? Good! Now eat about 90 percent of that amount every day, always making the healthiest choices you can. Avoid cruelly slaughtered meats, and meat in general if you can. That is step one. Now that you are hungry all the time, which will sharpen your Vampyric senses and actually increase your self-generated energy, think about step two.

For step two, break taboos and eat as sensually as you can for that other 10 percent in self-designed feats of Indulgence. Make these occasions into acts of sensual worship to the living idols of your own body—or chosen companions. Buy the richest chocolates; drink the best craft beers; if you eat meat, eat it bloody and let the juices roll down your chin. Maybe your companions can lick it off. If your taboo food is processed food, your Indulgence food might be Moon Pies. Indulge in local cuisines. Choose feasting locations with Vampyric resonance like haunted hotels or picnic spots at places of wild natural beauty on warm moonlit nights.

Now—these two steps being done—you are ready for step three: the worship of your body as a living representative of the life force and the taboo-breaking worship of your body as a living temple to the Powers of Darkness. Look to good science again. What are you missing? Ask your doctor. For most humans in the modern world, vitamin D is in short supply. Find out, get a good supply, and take it. Don't do this because you read about it here, do this based on a real physical from a competent doctor.

And now for the fourth step, the hardest of all: keep your mouth shut about the first three steps. The social parasite demands that we talk about food to the rest of the human herd. This is a control factor—it keeps your survival methods subordinate to the species. Listen to other people's advice if it is advantageous for you to do so, trade recipes if you enjoy cooking as a pastime, but fight the urge to allow others knowledge of your watering holes. For more guidance read about the 5-M rite in better books on Tantric practice (see "Recommended Vampyric Curriculum," chapter 27). One size fits all seldom fits Vampyres.

Now, for the e-word—*exercise*. Almost every human has an opinion on this. The unexercised body can't feel or direct energy. Most Westerners sadly confuse their actual feelings of blood flow, oxygen level, hormones, and adequate nutrition with Chinese peasant superstitions. "My chi is really flowing after today's run!" Exercise brings four benefits to the Vampyre: increased capacity for pleasure, increased longevity, increased awareness of bodily energy, and great training and practice in discipline. Without exercise, the social parasite gains control of your energy levels. Exercise should meet certain requirements: it should be mildly challenging (again, this is determined with the help of professionals outside your body); it should provide aerobic training and increase core strength (again, professionals outside of you—not internet knowledge); it should provide enough physical pleasure so that the Vampyre can keep doing it; and last, it should require focus. For most Vampyres a martial art discipline is beneficial. The chosen art should be resonant with your personal Vampyric aesthetic (for example, if you wish to minimize mysticism you might chose Systema, or if you like the sneaky aspect, Ninja training). There are three major things to watch out for: First, and most importantly, what do the graduates/practitioners LOOK LIKE? If your dojo is run by three overweight white guys, I don't care if they claim direct lineage with a centuries-old Chinese school. Second, does it require you to believe nonsense? Good: "You hit people they fall down!" Bad: "You hit people and balls of chi fly out of your hand, enter their body, and they fall down!" Third, if it is assumed that your skills will never, ever be useful in a street fight, then avoid the school. No reputable school will teach or train you for street fighting, but all should recognize that it could happen.

The Vampyre and the occultniks may begin their journey in the same place but will move apart. The occultnik will buy into each new fashion in the occult industry, have great daydreams to escape their day job (or worse still, the smell of Mom's basement), and eat garbage. The Vampyre will make her life an expression of who she is. The Vampyre can be easy to spot or invisible, as desired; the occultniks will be unnoticeable in the larger world.

Velma hasn't felt the need to create eternal companions, nor her wolf-mate, but many find they need a Lover without to complete them—a tricky business.

18
TURNING

A basic part of the vampire myth is that being a Vampyre means creating eternal companions through a romantic and demonic initiation. This is dark and dangerous. If you are new to the path, "dark and dangerous" sounds fun. Believe me, driving 70 miles an hour on a dark and stormy night is fun UNTIL you hit a telephone pole. I will explain the three things you must know, and the two absolutes you must not cross (unless you want to hit the telephone pole at 100 miles an hour).

The First Absolute. Never consider turning someone under legal age. The social parasite comes into being as hormones hit the biological system; hence, all adolescents begin looking for a role model outside of their biological families. This is an evolutionary move to ensure that humans fit in with their tribe/village instead of just their immediate clan. This results in the peculiar language spoken by middle schoolers, the seemingly random taste in unsophisticated music, or their adoption of strange totems. Sadly, this trend has been well exploited by marketeers for more than a century. If you express your Will upon these vulnerable individuals you will not awaken young Vampyres but simply injure their social parasite. If you need a well-documented study, google "Rod Ferrell" or "Kentucky Vampire Murders."

The Second Absolute. Do not try to turn someone against his or her will. Perhaps you are in a committed relationship with someone who finds the whole notion of "darkness" intolerable—or perhaps will not consider that all humans live off each other's energy. Do not think that in your power or wisdom you can make this decision for another. You will not only lose a friend or lover, but you will also gain a deeply empowered enemy who knows your weaknesses and vulnerabilities and whose very existence will be a source of regret and pain for some years, if indeed not for the rest of your life.

The first question is: How do I spot potential Vampyres? They must have seven qualities. The first (and most important) is that you are enchanted with their Essence and not their persona. When you draw their energy by means of the Vampyric Gaze, you must swoon with delight. Personas change—their politics, their appearance, their hobbies, their sense of humor will change with time—and if you help them partially escape the social matrix by becoming a Vampyre, these things will change rapidly. On the other hand, if you find that the person's energy signature resonates with your own, you are in the presence of one who can make the infinite journey a delight.

Second, do they get other people to do things for them without asking? This is a sign of Vampyric skill. Here is a great example. I was speaking on a panel recently with two much more famous writers and one drop-dead-gorgeous newer writer. It was a warm room. Two folks from the audience got up and brought me ice water—then as an afterthought asked the other panelists. If your target attracts that kind of care from everyday folk, she could be a Vampyre.

Third, are they attracted to the genuinely dark? I'm not asking if they like scary movies (although that's no doubt a plus), I am asking whether dark and desolate places attract them. Find out where they seek solace.

Fourth, do they have a personality that shows signs of self-sufficiency? For example, when facing a crisis do they always reach out to friends, or do they seek their own energy? The person who visits a museum to soothe him- or herself after a death in the family has an energetic makeup different from the person who has a beer and pizza party.

Fifth, do they practice magic? I don't mean that they are knowledgeable practitioners; rather, do they use magical means as part of their lives? For example, they have a "good luck" figure in their car or a ritual for wishing ill luck on someone. If so, they are somewhat aware of magic both as a means of change in the world and a desirable truth process.

Sixth, do they react to you differently when you have a dream about them? If so, they are sensitive to your energy signature. This is a mirror image of the first quality.

Seventh, have they expressed the thought "There is something different about you and I like it"?

If you can check off all the boxes above and you have known them for a while, you must consider what will happen if they are repulsed by your offer. They may find it silly, scary, or tinged with madness. All of these are primary defense mechanisms of the social parasite. Could you stand it if you encountered these? If so—and seriously consider these possibilities—you may move to the process of turning.

THE METHOD

To turn a human into a Vampyre requires seven steps. As you pass through them you will think the following: "This must be the hardest step. I can see why this is THE most important step." If you are not having these thoughts, you are not doing it well.

The first step does not require the other human directly. Beginning with the night before a new moon and ending with the night of a full moon, you must do the following: Instead of your standard Vampyric practice you should do the following ritual twice a night, once just before your normal sleeping time and once about ninety minutes before your target wakes up in the morning. Close your eyes and visualize your target. Say the Vampyric Invocation aloud while visualizing your target. Then see yourself and your target at a Vampyric stead of power that you can visit safely at night. The two of you are meeting a cowled figure. Imagine a dialogue. You tell the dark figure that it is your Will that your target become a Vampyre. The figure will ask your target if it is her Will. She affirms this. The cowled figure tells you that you may give of your Essence to your target, but this is dangerous, for what is given is given. You begin to feed your target honey-dripping bliss energy from your heart to her mouth or heart. During this phase of the operation do not seek confirmation from your target. If she tells you she had a strange dream about you, merely note this. If the target resists the operation, stop and try again in three months; if it fails then leave it.

The second step is a seduction. Buy gifts, plan meals, and above all take your target to Vampyric steads of power. Talk about dark things. Admit that you have learned energy techniques for healing, harming, or exchanging with people. If the target is interested, tell her that you can teach her sometime. When the stars are right. The target must be seduced and anxious. Do not rush this process.

The third step is a lesson. Take your target to the Vampyric stead of power you visualized in step one. Teach her the Vampyric Gaze. Take her energy; give freely of yours. You want to give more than you take. The target must feel drunk with power. Tell the target that you are a Vampyre—make it clear that you are not a bloodsucking ghoul from the movies. Ask if she would like entrance into the art. If the answer is yes, tell her to keep a two-week journal of her daily energy exchanges. Tell her journaling is hard if she has never done it before, but ask her to try her best.

The fourth step is an examination. Read her journal. Ask the questions. Ask if she would like an initiation sometime. The next steps are based on her desire.

The fifth step is to allow things to lie fallow for a while. When she asks you, you are ready.

The sixth step is an initiation. Take her, along with with cakes and wine, to the Vampyric stead of power you had visualized in the beginning. There (at night of course) share an intimate meal. Say the Vampyric Invocation. Practice the Gaze upon one another.

The seventh step is called "kill the guru." Do not fall for the temptation of setting yourself up as the target's teacher. Older men particularly have this fantasy—one of the more insidious ploys of the social parasite. It will fill you with self-importance and your target with false unworthiness. Give your target a copy of this book and offer to explore it together.

The effect this will have on you is threefold. Each will strengthen your growth as a Vampyre. First, the act of sharing your deepest self is very hard. It makes you more vulnerable than any of your victims have ever been. The social parasite will hit you with fear and even physical sickness. The deep traumas of your life will warn you. You will learn about all of your best parts because you projected them on your target. You will learn about all of your worst parts because you will have (despite yourself) projected them onto your target as well. Like dealing with your personal demons, you will have mastered the art of using the dark side of your being as your teacher.

The second effect is a cosmic awareness. By doing the initial part of the rite you will again encounter the Vampyric archetype outside yourself. Humans have a very hard time dealing with the divine when they discover that it is real, that it has its own purpose, and that it does not seek worship. Discovering the Vampyric principle or form awakens some of the latent Otherness within you. Whereas you thought you were merely reaching out to another human who reflected what was precious in you, you discover that any such movement in the soul produces a reaching out toward a cosmic principle as well. You have the joy and the burden that you did not find this covered in stained glass and offering plates being passed to you. You also have the great mystery that you and this Other have business together. It knew you. It knew your target. It assented and witnessed your actions, yet it did not answer a prayer. It did not change your target's mind. Most puzzlingly, this formless, wordless presence is connected to place, person, and time—just as you are. Because you and it share this connectivity of one pole being timeless and infinite and one pole being very much bound in a place, a time, and a reason, you and it can exchange essence in exactly the same manner as your Vampyre-to-be. This is the basis of religion but cannot be explained to a follower of the socializing religions.

The third effect both links you to tradition and isolates you from it at the same time. On the one hand you understand—deeply, viscerally understand—the story of the witches' sabbat and their persecution. You are absolutely an heir to this contra-social tradition. You could be persecuted for your deeds, yet you also know that your deeds were holy, harmless, and loving. But on the other hand, you are isolated. You will never know—at least not in the day-to-day way humans know things—if anyone else has ever felt such love or known such risk. You will be forever separated from the daylight world if your love crosses this boundary.

If you make this journey, you risk everything, and if you succeed, you lose everything. Go for it!

Remember, O neophyte, that GOODNESS alone is POWER. SILENCE is STRENGTH, WILL REIGNS Omnipotent, and LOVE lieth at the FOUNDATION.

PASCHAL BEVERLY RANDOLPH

19

VAMPIRE PATHOLOGIES AND VAMPYRIC ETHICS

Franz Hartman seems to be the first person to have discussed psychic vampires. The notion was then popularized in England by Dion Fortune and in America by Anton LaVey. We've all met psychic vampires, and as we learn to practice the daily inventory of our energetic interactions, we can spot them with ease. Tougher is spotting this behavior when it comes from ourselves. It is as harmful coming from the inside as the outside, as we shall see. Let's begin with how to spot them and then discuss what they are doing. Lastly, we will discuss their uses and defenses against them. Throughout this chapter I will use true stories, but as my cousin Jack Webb liked to say, "the names have been changed to protect the innocent."

PSYCHIC VAMPIRES

You can spot psychic vampires in three ways. First (and most importantly), these creatures feed on the emotional force (or if you prefer occultic terms, the Will) of others. People around them feel listless, sickly, guilty, or sad. Second, they are unaware of their feeding, and indeed most of it goes to waste. Third, they back up their feeding by use of social constraint—they are not only allied with the social parasite, they feed it. Let's look at Mark R.

Many people will tell you that Mark is a pillar of his community. He listens to down-and-out folks and gets them jobs. What could be better? Yet he never fails to remind them of his charity and never allows them to think of themselves as in any way worthy of the benison he has provided. In fact if his victims complain of him (or gossip says they did so), he can threaten them with having their jobs go away. He gets tons of Christmas gifts each year; folks volunteer to mow his lawn and wash his car. Of course some people do betray him by not providing enough praise. He has them fired and shamed. If you talk with him, you'll discover that he is totally unaware of his stalking methods. If you don't let him do something nice for you, he becomes irate. "Such a nice man, how sad all three of his wives died early."

Let's look at two more examples. Susan P. runs a music venue. Many male and some female musicians share Susan's bed. She is the mistress of devastating after-talk. Nobody pleases her like (insert name of rival musician). She almost always gets the performers to take a cut in pay or do a free show. Their shame is so great they don't out her. Indeed, most of them walk away believing her critiques.

Lastly, Miriam D. who is the widow of a wealthy banker. She has convinced her daughter Linda that (*a*) she is needed to provide medical care and companionship to her 24/7, and (*b*) her daughter is too unattractive and unintelligent to find a man—if men were attracted to her it was because mom's wealth brought them in. Miriam has been so successful at removing her Linda's Will that folks inevitably comment that they look like sisters. Linda always seems proud and happy at this remark, even when its clear that the speaker sees both women as being in their thirties, not she in her twenties and her mom in her fifties.

So, what makes these folks psychic vampires and not Vampyres? First, they 100 percent believe in the myths they tell others. Mark R. sees himself as a "practical philanthropist." Susan P. describes herself as a "fun-loving, hopeless romantic." Miriam D. thinks she gives her daughter's life "meaning and purpose." Second, their energy-drain is supported by social structures. People who question Mark's motives soon feel they are unworthy. Susan's conquests decide they are bad lovers and probably second-rate musicians. Linda thanks God for a wealthy mother because she assumes she can't fend for herself in what her mom has told her is a "cruel, cruel world." None of their victims receive anything because the path to victimhood is not arranged by seduction and wonder but by strengthening the parts of their being already opposed to freedom. Finally, these three psychic vampires use the energy they receive to build up their self-importance rather than themselves.

So why should the Vampyre be on the lookout for these behaviors in their own self-inventories? Imagine this scenario: You are a poor but hardworking human who needs some cash—but your roommate, who lives in your house rent free, is stealing lots of money that he pisses away. In fact he even steals from you—since every bit of the psychic vampire's booty is given to the social parasite.

So how do you deal with these creatures? First, ask yourself the question: Do I have to interact with him or her? Is it because of job, family, location (or something else)? Then, if the answer is yes, ask yourself that again—but after visualizing a large leech sucking blood from your face. The answer may still be yes—but it will help you move toward the Great Doubt (see chapter 21). If you are the one practicing the behavior, stop. You'll see it by your nightly energy inventory: "I can see that Sam loses energy around me, but my social parasite seems stronger." If you are exposed to a psychic vampire, minimize your exposure and feel no guilt in exploiting them. However, note that you can't steal back the energy they've stolen, for it is tainted with social-parasite purpose; you've seen this—some group takes on a social evil and winds up becoming the same evil.

Following is a (by no means exhaustive) list of psychic vampires with associated uses and cautions.

The Clock Keeper. Every business or institution needs efficiency and timeliness. But you've seen these creatures who are obsessed with others' hours. They write up the single mom who misses a few minutes every couple of weeks getting her kids to school but is way more productive than some others on the payroll. I encountered one of these who would dock fifteen minutes of pay if a soul was four minutes late. And her time system was off by three minutes to boot!

Uses: Make them work under you—be the granter of mercy to the deserving and the mean boss as needed. Otherwise treat them as a dangerous animal.

Caution: Debate and logic are not effective here; this creature feeds on being debated. Encouraging him or her to be a social media troll for a cause you believe in can be a temporary fix.

The Jolly Peasant. Seemingly the opposite of the above, this creature serves the social parasite by encouraging routine disobedience to the social order. They drink on company time, gossip about the boss, have lewd or tasteless knickknacks. They make fun of anyone who wants to do work. If you have been a Vampyre for a while you must have found/created a job that has meaning. These people feed on getting others involved in their pointless rebellions.

Uses: Jolly peasants can be a great source of information—"I'll show you how to bypass the security lock on the Xerox machine." They can work as spies. They can be agitators for minor causes—"We should get to leave ten minutes early on Friday to beat traffic."

Caution: These folk are in no way actually antinomian. They are disrespectful, slovenly, or crude because their social parasite has assigned them that role. Don't waste your energy trying to awaken them.

The Wounded Mother. Miriam D. is a great example. She rules her offspring (or young people she captures) by mixing the veil of vulnerability with the myth of insufficiency. I am not speaking about older women (or men) who deserve our help. The "veil of vulnerability" consists of "I can't" statements: "I can't ride in an Uber!" "I can't program my furnace." If these "can't"s vanish when there's no one around, they aren't "can't"s. These are counterbalanced with statements that belittle/disempower their caretakers: "You are too dumb to live on your own." "If you don't live with me you'll start drinking again."

Uses: The wounded mother is a tough creature since she has the weight of social pressure on her side; however, she can be defeated by exchange—"Sure, Mom, I can come over to help you with your furnace, but can you take some stuff to the dry cleaners for me?" The long-term fix is either finding her a peer group to feed her emotional needs or removing her from your life.

Caution: Do not underestimate the primate programming that binds you to her.

The Sick Human. I have known many brave humans who lost

their fight against illness. Some are the best humans I have known. However, there is a subtype of psychic vampire who lives on the pity they arouse in others (and themselves). They have no communication except for their latest struggles. If invited to a meal they will complain of the foods that others at the table are "allowed" to eat. Despite their dire condition they outlive their peers.

Uses: The sick human has little use except as a cautionary tale. The Vampyre is reminded that human life is fragile, but the condition of the body can always be an aide to joy, power, and knowledge. As Hakuin said, "The body is the buddha."

Caution: The best action is to curse sick humans with clarity. If they survive the shock they will become masters at finding joy in anything, and you have made them your teacher. If the shock kills them, your magic will have brought relief.

The Evangelical Materialist. The Vampyre should use science in understanding such aspects of the objective universe that are best dealt with by science. She should always use skepticism coupled with a wariness of mysticism when dealing with an objective phenomenon. However, the Vampyre is destined to find/clash with the human who has chosen science as his only truth process, and the science is often coupled with evangelical atheism and billionaire empowerment (i.e., belief in a nonexistent world where money is the only value and human worth is derived from this standard). These beliefs are a matter of personal choice and obviously detrimental to Vampyric practice—but the evangelical materialist is seriously/obsessively concerned with you having these beliefs.

Uses: These guys are great letter writers, protestors, and petition signers.

Caution: Their fundamental belief in their correctness makes them very dangerous to your practice when you are involved in the Great Doubt.

The Right Man. Science-fiction writer A. E. van Vogt identified a type of psychic vampire as the "Right Man." He (and rarely she) is NEVER wrong. About anything. He will fight you in an argument about the price of gum in 1976. He is explosively jealous of his spouse. He will remind you of every correct prediction he made (or has convinced himself he made). He may even claim that he came up with an idea ("I invented computers in the 1950s."). The occult world has scores of these types—their self-belief can produce limited miracles, and they need others to buy into their cults of power. These very toxic individuals are very close to being Vampyres in that they will exchange energy. One can become pumped up from their rallies full of highly focused energy. They take the Will of others, shape it into their own, and return it. Manson, Hitler, and Jim Jones are great examples. They differ from Vampyres in that their goal is stasis: every bit of energy they take in is to promote an unchanging self-image. They have perfectly merged the social parasite and the Vampyre.

Uses: These guys often have great energy techniques. They want their followers to be empowered but still unquestioning followers. If you can learn their technology safely, go for it.

Caution: Since their Will-to-Stasis is probably stronger than your Will-to-Growth, it is very easy to become a follower. Watch your energy inventory: Do you ever spend energy defending one of these tyrants? If so, they have stolen your Will-to-Pleasure and made it their own. Question everyone. Except me. Send me money. I am your Savior. Even small bills . . .

The Sadist. The sadist, not the Sadean who is interested in pleasurable exchange, is to be avoided. If sadists are turned on by causing hurt, but NOT turned on by the masochist enjoying the hurt, run. These humans have abstracted an aspect of the human personality that Freud called the death drive—the part that anticipates and even identifies with one's own demise—and have projected it outward. They want to hate and hurt. Their power does not come from their victims but through the actions of a tribal egregore. It does not matter if the egregore is awakened by a burning cross or punching the old lady when she starts getting uppity.

Uses: These guys can create great distractions. Likewise, pitting such groups against each other can create a lot of free energy in humans that is easy to harvest.

Caution: However tempting it may be, do not get these guys to fight for you. If they'll do it for you, they'll do it to you.

The False Tribalist. There is power and beauty in authentic tradition—in fact in many ways the Vampyre is a traditionalist: refusing to separate signifier from signified, looking for keys to her psyche in the traditions of her ancestors, using traditional practices to fight the conventions of the social parasite. False tribalists, however, take on the identity of a group with which they have no organic connection. Certain liberal groups in the United States and certain New Age groups are filled with these. I observed a video recently of a white woman using the white sage (of some California Indian groups) and feathers (looked Lakota to me) at the site of the Temple of Set in Ombos while getting tourists to chant "Om." This was presented as a sign of New Age oneness. In fact, this mindless eclecticism was merely an excuse to put paying clients into a light trance and feed off them. Whereas this could have been a Vampyric working with the Vampyre and her victims walking away with stronger Wills, it was merely a rather exotic form of sleep.

Uses: These humans can sell you nifty toys and will buy your books.

Caution: The initiatory path is lonely; it is easy to think these folk are allies or, worse still, possible wolf-mates.

The "Tantric." Real Tantra is hard work, but since sexual practices do exist in some lineages, many Western books have been written portraying Tantra as a sort of "nookie nirvana." The Vampyre is all about the use of sexual energy, and these self-styled masters would seem to know what they're doing. Be wary. Having sacred sex with someone who has less energy than you will transfer your energy to them. If you wish to do this (see chapter 18, "Turning"), go for it. Otherwise you'll have much better results with a nonspiritual partner (or partners) that just really, really like sex.

Uses: These people buy and sell interesting things and are great for letter writing, petitions, and so on.

Caution: When this type is also a "Right Man," run like hell.

How does the Vampyre defend himself against psychic vampires? Awareness, beginning with the daily energy inventory, is the major defense. Learning what their game is and refusing to play by their rules is the second. Ask the suppoosed Tantric what his lineage is. Tell the sadist that exquisite torture turns you on, but mindless evil is for orcs. Ask the sick human about her health and then recommend better therapies. And so forth. The third line of defense is simple visualization: imagine yourself in the form of one of the demons described in the next chapter. The ultimate line of defense is conjuring a wall around the psychic vampire that no energy may enter and (to the extent you can convey your truth) telling others about the psychic vampire. Be careful in this because his victims have internalized his methods of feeding and have become his servants as much as your servants serve you.

Speaking of service, it's time to bring up the G-word . . .

20

RELIGION AND HEATHENRY

Vampyres do not draw upon or serve a god. In the course of their practice they will sense the Great Vampyre, the force that created the three great principles:

1. In time of need, energy may be drawn in.
2. To evolve, one must refine energy.
3. Giving back refined energy will create a better world for you.

These principles lead to the great change in the Vampyre. He may start as an arrogant asshole with crushing insecurity and dime-store aesthetic and by the simple process of being aware of energy within and beyond him, and taking, exchanging, and giving that energy, will become a longer-lived (and eventually Immortal) Essence that improves the world around him. In this he changes from a creature of simple greed into a dark bodhisattva. Thus he participates in the same purpose as the Great Vampyre.

The Vampyre understands two things. For the average human there must be a figure seemingly outside him or her that does these things. These figures are called gods. The existence of gods hides the Vampyric from the average human. The social parasite is soothed by the idea that it need not consider each moment, nor be baffled when supernatural powers work and when they don't. The social parasite is happy that these nonconscious magical workings keep the species functioning— and keep a fairly stable social matrix. Since the social parasite has made peace with gods, the Vampyre can use this peace to her own advantage in two ways. First, by using gods when needed, and second, by using hidden traditions to explore her own blind spots. We will examine these two paths, calling the first one religion and the second heathenry.

When do we need gods? We need gods when we don't know the way out of a problem. If we know the way out, we can work to get out of things—even if the work is very difficult. If the problem is poverty, we can work our way out of it by discovering that access to needs can be provided by several things, including money, and that magic innovation and hard work can help. It can be hard, but we don't need Zeus to do the magic for us. If we are in an abusive relationship, we know the way out—it can be very hard, but we still know what the target looks like. We need gods when our desire and Great Doubt are one. Then we need to bypass that power of the social parasite so that we can both see and open the way to our path. We must attract the god; that is to say, we are looking into the patterns, the Wyrd of the world for a pattern to add life to. The pattern matches one inside us—it feels right. We activate the pattern, merge with it, and in our heightened state use its abilities. But we must understand that the pattern is still us.

If you want a cheap but accurate metaphor try this: I recall when I had my first phone that also had GPS/map capacity. One day I was to give a talk for a local OTO oasis. I had many errands that day and in the middle of them realized I had left my information at home. I wasn't able to call up their address. I had no idea where it was. I tried calling folks. No one was home. But I noticed a Maps icon on my new phone. How did it work? Within a few minutes I had a disembodied voice giving me details upon each step I needed to take, using information outside of my conscious brain and based on accurate observations of where I was in time and space. I had surrendered my actions to an unseen entity that I could access in a precise manner. Yet when I was done, I didn't owe the entity anything because I was using something I already owned.

To invoke a god or goddess, the Vampyre has three specific criteria. First, the choice has to be aesthetically pleasing—invoking a god who kills Vampyres won't do. Second, there must be effort involved—otherwise you can't bypass the social parasite. Third, the entity involved should have a stake in the outcome. I'll give you a quick list of some suitable deities and then teach you a method derived from Crowley. Of course, this is only a partial list created for the purposes of inspiration.

GODS AND GODDESSES FOR THE VAMPYRE

Brigit—the Celtic goddess of war and poetry who teaches witchcraft and strategy. She is the great teacher for gaining inspiration when doing something dangerous—or for the art of giving inspiration to others.

Chinamasa—one of the Tantric goddesses. She feeds her children/servant with blood—she gives energy to both the strictly celibate and the most flagrant sex worshipper. She can enable one to escape seeming but unexpected fate.

Coyote—a trickster god in many American Indian traditions who can be genius or idiot but always works for the cosmic good (even against his surface Will). He can teach you the way to heal from mental illness or profound states of guilt. He can also teach you how to (temporarily) paralyze the social parasites of others.

Ereshkigal/Irkalla—the Sumerian queen of the underworld controls who can descend to the deepest levels of the Dark and gives perfect advice about when to wage war and when to wage politics. She can help the practitioner leave behind pop-culture fuzzy-bunny ideas of Darkness.

Hecate—originally a goddess of boundaries, she was transformed first by poets and then by witches into the goddess of witchcraft. She can help the practitioner when major life choices are thrust upon them.

Hermes—half god/half Titan who is equally at home with thieves, merchants, and magicians. He can teach the secret rite of how to blend mass manipulation (like putting on a play or an ad campaign) with personal rituals for illumination.

Mami Wata—the mermaid goddess of western, central, and southern Africa who can appear as a prostitute on the street. She entrances her followers with sex, then with lust for material things, then with lust for knowledge, finally with lust for spiritual things. She teaches how to heighten and refine desire and is a perfect teacher of Vampyric knowledge.

Manat—the oldest of the goddesses worshipped in Arabia, her idol was one of the many at the Kaaba. Her name means "she who deals out fate." Her priests would redden wooden statues of her and shave their heads. She teaches how to steal luck from the unworthy. Women who shave their heads or radically cut their hair when getting out of a bad relationship have perfect resonance with this archetype.

Nephthys—wife of Set who creates the future, a very dark, terrifying, necessary time. Her title, Nephthys, means "Lady of the Temple"— think of her as either the sexiest woman you met in the shadows OR the fierce grandmother who teaches magic (Professor Minerva McGonagall). Her real name is the real name of your soul. Her birthday is August 31 (like Lechuza Mundo). She teaches that the future is the Dark Side of the Force.

Odhinn—god who reconciles dark magic and mystery with taking care of family and kingdom. He teaches how to use self-sacrifice and the pursuit of mystery for aims both bright and dark.

Persephone—the Greek goddess of the netherworld, wife of Hades. Unlike his brother Zeus, the good guy who rapes every boy and girl he takes a fancy to, Hades seduces Persephone (albeit brutally). She punishes or blesses the dead. She can help you remember your purpose in the toughest of times or make your enemies forget theirs.

Set—the Egyptian god who gives power (Opens the Mouth) over all other gods and who can kill death (Osiris) and painful indecision (Apep). He can teach you decisiveness and the long game.

Tezcatlipoca—a dark Aztec god who is the patron of the prince and the slave, of fear and ecstasy, of the power to destroy others by revealing their true selves to them. He can teach what to do if you have suddenly become prince (from slavehood) or a slave (from princehood).

Yanlou—the ruler and enforcer of the Chinese Buddhist hell who sends death, disease, and misfortune to miscreants such as people who post PDFs of this book online. He is great to Become when you are sorting out a situation where you have fucked up, but people who are hurting you have fucked up more. He will send you misfortune that will teach you your true self if you overcome it, while destroying your enemies by causing them pain.

VAMPYRIC INVOCATION OF A DEITY

Now I will teach a method of invocation. There are eleven steps to the process. It is surefire. So be careful. You must put your regular practice aside. You must pour as much emotion into each phase as possible. The first nine steps should be on separate nights. If you feel more time or energy needs to be spent on them, make it so.

1. Decide if you need to invoke someone. Are you in a blind alley? Are you willing to take a risk? Are you going to understand that the answer may not look like an answer until hindsight shows it as one?

2. Decide whom to invoke. Read, research. Pick according to a blend of emotion (this feels right) and scholarship (hard facts and good research indicate this is the one).

3. Set up a temple. Fill it with images of the deity. Look up foods and smells associated with it. Add to this. Then on your altar write and conceal your reasoning. "I am invoking X because of . . ." and be very specific. Light an appropriate incense each night you do this work.

4. Compose a plea as of slave to master. Read at your altar on your knees. Brace for the whip. See the god on a massive throne above you, very strict. As you fall asleep chant to yourself: "I serve X."

5. Compose a plea of a child to parent. Place any items from your childhood around your altar—kid pics, stuffed toys, and so on. See the god on a throne above you looking at you with fatherly/motherly love. As you fall asleep chant to yourself: "X loves me."

6. Compose a prayer to the deity. Use (and correctly pronounce) cult titles. Dress for church. If you prayed on your knees, do so. If you didn't, don't. If you didn't go church, do what you imagined your

friends doing. Picture the god enthroned hearing your prayers. As you fall asleep chant to yourself: "X is great. X is good."

7. Write a letter to the diety as a friend. Talk about the project you are going to do together. Sit comfortably as you read it. Strive for the mood of writing to someone whom you used to know quite well that's coming to see you after a long absence. Picture the god in your chamber, glad to see you. As you fall asleep imagine that you are sending postcards of your favorite places to the god. Be sure to include your home, your place of business, and tourist stuff in your town.

8. Compose a love letter to the deity. Describe erotic favors. Dress for date night. Read your letter disrobed. With the strongest possible imagination visualize your sex with the deity. Bring yourself to climax, offering your pleasure to the deity. Repeat the procedure as you fall asleep; cry out the name of the god at the appropriate moment.

9. Compose a magical summons in this form: three repeated third-person sentences, three repeated second-person sentences, three repeated first-person sentences. For example: "Odhinn is the Mighty Father of Magic. Odhinn is the Mighty Father of Magic. Odhinn is the Mighty Father of Magic. Welcome art Thou who found the runes and took them up. Welcome art Thou who found the runes and took them up. Welcome art Thou who found the runes and took them up. I am Odhinn, master of Galdr and Seidhr. I am Odhinn, master of Galdr and Seidhr. I am Odhinn, master of Galdr and Seidhr." As you speak the summons, visualize the god standing before you. When you finish the ninth sentence, step into his or her place. Feel that visualization surrounding you. Feel it becoming you. When you feel at one with the deity, speak to command the universe to make the way open for that which you desire. Speak with authority. When it is done shower and go to bed. Take down your temple the next day. Return to your normal Vampyric practice. Tell no one of your Work.

10. If in the fullness of time, if you feel that you have received your answer—and I find if I don't get an answer in six months, I'm not getting one—reassemble your temple, light your incense, and in your own words thank the deity. Do no other Work that night.

11. The next night go to your temple. Do not light the incense of the

god, but you may use your own. Take a glass of a favorite nonalcoholic beverage. Say the Vampyric Invocation. Then say, "I am the Vampyre [VN], and I thank my energy for empowering the Wyrd of X. The making of gods is a great gift to mankind and a great skill to have used. I bless those that made the pattern of X, and I bless and thank myself for the use of that pattern to gain wisdom, power, and pleasure." Add other words about what you learned or achieved. Do no other Work that night.

THE BENEFITS OF RELIGION

The results of this invocation are always surprising. By using this external pattern you will have brought aspects of yourself into the world that you may see and enjoy or else be tested by—or both. This is a difficult process: doing the invocation is hard, recognizing the results is hard, taking the time to be humble and give thanks to the god is hard (because your life will have become hectic when this occurs), and lastly, thanking yourself is hard (because the social parasite will reason with you—"If you were that powerful why do you still have to earn a living, have diabetes, have holes in your socks, etc.?").

Those are the easy-to-see benefits of religion. Heathenry is the re-creation of a magical or religious system in a more open-ended way. The methodology was created by Stephen Flowers. It involves discovering something that appeals to you in the past and making it live again. There are two reasons for doing this. First, it is a pleasurable and artistic act. Second (and most importantly for the Vampyre), it will reveal blind spots in your own being—secrets your social parasite will have hidden from you. The first reason is that heathenry is a pleasant revolt against the here and now. If you find the anxiety of gift giving, party going, and eggnog drinking to be a drain each year in December (and if you are doing your energy inventory you will know), imagine what fun you will have telling your friends that you celebrate Saturnalia. And you should do so with true grace and style so it becomes art and not just a joke.

However, the second part is more mysterious. If you find a magical/religious system that calls to you, answer the call by re-creating it. First the call must be mysterious—you don't know why. It should be a small system—one that fought against the religions of social control such as Christianity, Islam, mainstream Buddhism, and so on. Something about it resonates with something in you. The difference between mysteries without and mysteries within is an illusion.

First, read the best scholarly sources you can find—do not just search the internet for a few minutes or buy a book from the New Age section of the store. What did the practitioners do? Why did they do it? Here you will find your first mystery: that action/belief that you can't figure out is an exact correlation to a part of yourself you can't fathom. Say you're drawn to the mysteries of Orpheus. You find in his poems that he says Zeus raped Persephone and that she bore him Dionysus, the god of ecstasy. Then Hades hooked up with her and she had the Furies—you can tell that of lot mainstream Greek thought raged against this alternate tradition—but you can't figure it out. This is just like the Great Doubt. One day after a profound depression you visit a graveyard, a stead of power for you. Suddenly out of nowhere you feel bliss. You experience a a wordless flash that connects the lady of the underworld with bliss: the myth you have studied has allowed you to access secret parts of yourself.

The next step, once you have studied the data, is to create a subjective synthesis. How could you re-create the beliefs and practices in your modern life? Maybe you can't visit the ancient cult sites. What would be your local equivalent? Or let's say you are Anishinaabe Nation (Ojibwa, Chippewa, Ottawa) and you hear about Mock Sa We, the shape-shifting vampire/shaman, and you want to re-create part of your heritage: How would you create an initiation? Once you have created a subjective synthesis, ask yourself: Is this beautiful? Is it useful? Once you can answer yes to both questions, you can proceed to the third stage—enactment. Do the deed and get the results.

With this process you will have found your own door, and by going through it found your own hidden truths. The gods didn't do this for you—you did it for the gods. You are a creator of gods, and by that process you lifted your own energy beyond the divine level.

So, if you can create gods what do you have to worry about? We'll see in the next chapter.

21

THE GREAT DOUBT, THE GREAT DEATH, THE GREAT JOY

There are said to be three steps in the Chan/Zen tradition called the Great Doubt, the Great Death, and the Great Joy. The Vampyre likewise has and values these things, but, again, these are so against the grain of both the occult industry and popular belief, I avoided talking about them. I will reveal these things now, and if you have been practicing for a while, you may understand them. Before I get to the three gates, I'm going to teach you an old technique from Tibetan Tantra for self-improvement. In the eleventh century a Tibetan nun named Machik Lapdrön mixed some old-school Tibetan shamanism with Dzogchen teachings and developed Chöd, a method of killing the social parasite. One of the methods—meditating in graveyards and desolate places—was introduced to you early in this book. Here comes another: the Vampyric demon sacrifice. Cool name, huh? Less easy to do. A modification of Chöd was created by an emanation of Machik Lapdrön named Tsultrim Allione. She received the blessing of the Dalai Lama to teach a version in the West. I have adopted her method, called "Feeding Your Demons," for our practice.

Most spiritual practices tell you it's not your fault. The devil made me do it! Then you've got to call on someone to help you out. White Magic. This teaches the soul that it is not powerful, exactly the message the social parasite wants to send. All humans who are awakened sense they need to work on themselves, since the social parasite fears its death—as unlike you, it is not an immortal being. The social parasite works to change the methods that bring you to power and awareness into methods that bring it (fleetingly) into power and awareness. The Dzogchen school thought to outright kill the social parasite—a seemingly wise idea, but limited, as we shall see. However, some of its tools are precious gems. Old-school Tibetan shamanism is a relic from the central Asian enlightenment that Lechuza Mondo was touched by.

As we become Vampyres we discover that our human baggage doesn't all fall away. We may give up the Sunday school superstitions of our youth, the beliefs that advertisers and politicians have schooled us in—but the really heavy bags and over-packed trunks we still cling to. These are bags like PTSD, anger issues, addictions, and disempowering prejudices that are so dear to the social parasite that we will leave behind magic, loved ones, enjoyable and profitable jobs to bear them. Most religious movements fail because they insist on us dropping these bags—which of course merely means that you will pick up an additional bag labeled GUILT. At the beginning of Vampyric practice we discover that so much more energy is available to us that these bags seem lessened: an athlete has less trouble carrying an eighty-pound pack than an average human, but the athlete would rather not do so.

VAMPYRIC DEMON SACRIFICE

The Vampyric demon sacrifice is a fivefold process for eliminating the big bags. We'll examine the steps using the Vampyre Suzan as an example.

First, identify what you think is the problem. Suzan always picks abusive men. Despite warning bells, she lets them into her life. Suzan thinks it was because her dad was a jerk.

Second, conjure up the demon. Suzan knows she always has twenty minutes free on Saturday afternoons. She darkens her house. She sits in one chair opposite another. She half closes her eyes and imagines the fiercest demon she can. At first she comes up with comic images. Nope. Eventually she finds one that really scares her—half the doll from *Trilogy of Terror* and half her aunt Edna on life support the week before she died. She waits until she can keep the image steady in her mind. This took two sessions.

Third, confront the demon. Suzan asks the demon why it always makes sure she has loser men. The demon says, "Because your dad hit your mom." "Nope. That's what I think; what do you think? Answer me truthfully and I will reward you." "Because your mom told you that you were worthless." "That feels closer, but it's not scary. I dealt with mom issues a long time ago. Why do you bring me abusive men?" "You think you deserve it. You feel non-abusive men will stay around until they see how fucking awful you are, and then they'll abuse you, and you can't even tell yourself you deserve better." Suzan's body violently twitches. *This* is it. "What do you get out of this?" "Your fear and suffering and above all your disappointment feed me." "I see. What if I fed you bliss every week instead, would you stop torturing me?" "Sure, but you won't. You're weak. You are nothing." "But I will." Suzan directs a stream of honey-tasting energy at the demon, feeding it until it is content. Then she opens her eyes and lights up her apartment. She busies herself with other tasks.

Fourth, feed the demon. If Suzan's nightly energy inventory tells her that no abusive men came into her life, she conjures up the demon and feeds it bliss energy. If her inventory reveals an abuser, she must conjure the demon and with true sadness tell it: "This week I cannot give you the best of foods, for you have failed in our pact." The demon will whine and writhe but must not be fed.

Fifth, release the demon. After a year of no abusive men, she conjures up the demon. "Demon, we have kept troth. I have fed you for a year. Now I must remind you of two things. First, I made you from my mind stuff." "Yes, you did." "Second, you have taught me that I made up the notion of my awfulness and you—O blessed guru—have allowed me to dissolve this burden in bliss." "Yes." "Now I am going to dissolve you in bliss and reabsorb you. As my teacher you will remain in honor forever." Suzan lets the golden honey-dripping light pour over the demon, eliminating his form. She then breathes the bliss back into her. There is nothing but Suzan.

The method takes time—just as creating the big bags took time. It requires vigilance—you must feed or starve the demon daily. There are three great cautions with this method. First, you must keep the practice secret. Suzan can tell her therapist that she is working on her relationships but must not speak about the demon. Second, you can only deal with one problem at a time, dealing with several can lead the demons into ganging up on you. Third, if you have not developed sufficient skill to control the demon (who is after all you), you must abandon the practice.

THE GREAT DOUBT

Dealing with the big bags of your life is amazing, but it will not save you from the Great Doubt. In Zen practice seekers become aware of their own minds, which is a very different affair from becoming aware of your own thoughts. This is done by several methods, one of which is the koan, a puzzle that removes certainty. Haukin's famous koan is "What is the sound of one hand clapping?" This koan points to the unspeakable truth of "not one, not two." The question is not nonsense—clearly there is a clapping sound. Nor is it sense—clearly there is not a meaningful answer. The mind gnawing on the question enters a state of Great Doubt, not just on the semantics, but other concerns as well: "Why do I practice Zen?" "Do these guys really know anything, or is this an emperor's new clothes thing?" "Are other people really getting this?" "If I come up with a dramatic answer will my master like me?" "Did I enter a monastery and give up social prestige just to get a master's approval?" The doubts spin into each other until an outside stimulus—a falling leaf, the sound of a pot clanging in the kitchen, the meow of cat—opens the self to the wordless, nameless self, which is not the creature with gender, race, social obligations. It is much the same way as the Buddha himself was Awakened, when, after six days of meditation, he glimpsed a shooting star. The novice may believe that the moment of Awakening is of supreme importance, but greater still is the period of *tagi*—the Great Doubt, the moment from hearing the koan to transcending the social parasite. This troubled time, this seething Darkness, is the womb of experience.

The Vampyre does not have the luxury of working with a teacher in a monastery. He or she works and lives in the day-to-day world of his or her host culture. No one will present the Vampyre with a koan. But day-to-day experience does present one again and again. It can come in several forms.

Here is one: "If I am so powerful why is life so hard?" For example, I can easily create minor miracles. I can concentrate for a few minutes and friends from around the globe will call me. I discover I need a certain book, and driving past a used bookstore, I feel I should stop—and the rare volume is sitting on the shelf with a very affordable price tag. Yet tiny events—this week, for example, needing to get a simple piece of paperwork done—can require ridiculously hard efforts. Lesser humans around me get praise. A bird flies out of its way to shit on my windshield. Have I just been lucky? Is my sense of magic a delusion? Thoughts spin outward: Why aren't I rich? Why do I feel the need to waste my time answering email from would-be disciples? Why am I not as happy as my dumb neighbor? Then suddenly—a moment. I feel the urge to drop in at a certain bookstore. Standing outside is an old friend I had not seen in five years. All of the hard aspects of his and my life fall away. We visit for half an hour. I am healed. He is healed. I walk in the store and get a copy of a book on Greek religion that I had been looking for for five years. But more importantly I have a moment of seeing me. Not the Ipsissimus or the writer or the guy from a little town in Texas. Just an opening. The Doubt is gone.

Here is a second: "If I have powers of foresight why didn't I see this coming?" As one's Vampyric skills grow, the power to anticipate the future grows. The Vampyre, being a stalker first of others and then herself, must gain a future sense. Every event seems to go well. Suddenly a massive betrayal. A person loved and trusted knifes me in the back. Where was my power then? Have I grown equally powerful at denial? If I were living a normal life I wouldn't have even met this person who attacked me. I'm just an idiot who has learned to hypnotize myself. Should I seek vengeance? Should I walk away because I am a "better man"? Do I lament this on Facebook? Do I hide this since some of my income comes from being a wise sage? Should I confess this? Should I blame myself? I ruminate over the time spent with my now enemy. I look for faults in my actions, signs of upcoming treachery in his. I neglect my wolf-mate, my initiation, I am careless at my job, I attribute my ill luck to my enemy's sorcery. Then my cat leaps in my lap unexpectedly. Suddenly my Great Doubt is gone. Suddenly I see beyond the moment and into Eternity. I am restored. I am happy.

Many Vampyres are defeated by the Great Doubt. They give up their practice. They seek to use beer or speed or TV or Facebook to distract themselves. They do not surrender themselves to the torture that leads to bliss. They do not become victims to their own Vampyric selves. Thus, they do not self-initiate. One of my brightest students walked away from practice when she was betrayed by a lover. She sought refuge in the old orthodoxy from which she had come. Of course, the things that magic had brought her left her. But more importantly she did not Sleep in a blissful new myth. Now she sees her suffering as the result of "evil" and hopes that her guilt will convince Christ to reward her in another life. She became a great lesson to me because of the levels of joy and power she had obtained—she taught me the importance of practice regardless of years of initiation.

THE GREAT DEATH

Beyond the Great Doubt is the Great Death. I alluded to it in the story above, but I will make it plainer now. The Vampyre knows the Great Secret that Undead = Unconstrained. But Great Secrets are easy to forget. Indeed, the social parasite can make you forget Great Secrets because it knows what you know. As we begin our practice we take refuge in things other than our Vampyric self. This is inevitable and necessary. Yet it leads to the Great Death, and only after the Vampyre survives the Great Death can she consider herself a Vampyre. Everything else is training for that moment. I will give you three examples of the Great Death. The sad truth is that no one knows when it may occur—and it will take a form that is not obvious.

Our first example is the Vampyre Selena. Selena was hot. Smoking hot. Get-paid-big-bucks-to-pose-naked hot. Get-a-job-as-a-weather-girl hot. When she was young she was mistreated by crude men seeking her energy. Then she found some relief in a sex-magic group that told her her beauty was power. She excelled in Vampyric arts—nature had given her much, and cosmetics and style gave more still. She could create vast sexual attention both outside herself and even simply looking in a mirror. Of course, she gained attention even among other Vampyres. Like most of us she aged slowly and her reign as a Vampyric queen seemed as certain as gravity. She learned very little about other ways of generating energy and neglected her energy inventory and statements of gratitude. Time coarsened her features. She was still beautiful but not the center of attention by simply stepping into a room. Instead of learning new arts she became bitter toward other attractive people and slowly withdrew from the world. She had taken refuge in the very thing that had caused her trauma and grief in her early years and resorted to nostalgia and artificial stimulants to feed her Vampyric hunger. Eventually she viewed her life as an inevitable failure. She became Selena—not the Vampyre Selena—surrounded by pictures of a former self, and subject to the beliefs of the very people who tried to harm her.

Our second example is the Vampyre Adolophus. He took refuge in his self-observation. His magical progress was slow but constant, and he weathered severe setbacks by being a great self-observer. He bragged about small tricks—such as never needing an alarm clock or being excellent at remembering his dreams. He equated his self-awareness with power. He did not take the cues his body offered him: "Where does your awareness go when you fall asleep?" or "Why did you trip on the socks you left on the floor?" His amazing memory—or more precisely what he imagined his better-than-average memory to be—was proof of his Vampyric being. The fact that Vampyres are said to sleep in coffins—sometimes for decades—did not inform him. He didn't think what the myth might be telling him. A severe medical condition in his forties left him on pain drugs for some months. Suddenly he didn't want awareness—and also discovered that his memory was faulty. The truth that memory is our best fiction (as Wyrd teaches us) had never penetrated him. He left practice behind as he became less sharp. He never found those moments that show he exists beyond his body or his awareness. He had used his focused mind to avoid the Great Doubt—so the Great Death took him. He rejected what he had learned and took cold comfort in the works of Ayn Rand.

Our third example is the Vampyre Jeremiah. Born on third base, as the saying goes, he was the heir to a vast family fortune. In addition to buying him great style, it afforded him amazing trips. He visited sites in Central America, Egypt, Cambodia; bought appearances in indie horror films; arranged amazing expenses. His collection of arcane books, magical artifacts, and macabre art was amazing. He donated to a few occult societies and had speakers of renown visit him. He learned little about finance, or frankly *how* his family had accumulated its great wealth. He attributed his inherited wealth to some hidden power or virtue in his psyche—listening to the social parasite's common lie of reincarnation. Suddenly a scandal broke, TV reporters swarmed over his great house, and his dad's dishonest dealings were brought to light. Jeremiah saw his house of cards blown away. He sold off his collection with little thought and wound up working at a menial job. He did not try to use either his powers or his common sense. He did not rise from his coffin.

Why do I tell you these grim tales? To confront you with the deep reason you chose the vampire myth. The Vampyre is someone who rises from misfortune. However, the social parasite has given you the lie that magic will make you invulnerable. When that lie is exposed, the social parasite will gladly take up the room in your psyche that you have filled with your refuge. The social parasite will tell you that you are unworthy, or that you lacked power, or that there is no such thing as magic. The social parasite will tell you that your grief and shock are a final state. It may tell you that your grief and shock are due to a certain group—the Jews, the immigrants, the bankers, and so forth—because hatred is a solid drain on energy.

The Great Death is inevitable. You are not the things you have summoned for learning or pleasure. Losing some aspect of your world is never losing yourself, and the grief you feel is as real and important as the joy you felt. You were not wrong to enjoy it. You are not being punished. Ultimately the one thing you can take refuge in is your Vampyric self that you have glimpsed through passing beyond the Great Doubt.

THE GREAT JOY

The remaining gate is the Great Joy. Again, its coming is hard to predict. Humans are hardwired to receive this at the moment of their biological death, when the pineal gland releases metatonin (not melatonin) into the body as it did when you were born. This chemical (equivalent to DMT) pacifies the social parasite and allows the same moment of enlightenment that comes when you pass beyond the Great Doubt. You suddenly understand everything—even the social parasite. This supreme Joy exists to give you entrance into immortality. This is every human's right, but it has been stolen from them by the god religions.

The Vampyre does not wait for this moment. She always seeks the Great Joy. If she persists in her practice, such moments are inevitable. It is called satori in Zen, "cosmic consciousness" in New Age parlance, and several other things. Vampyres perceive this as being perfectly unified with energy. The energy that they seek with endless desire, the energy they acknowledge in statements of gratitude, the energy they monitor at all times—IS who they are. They do not dissolve into the energy and vanish like the demons they conjured in the Vampyric demon sacrifice; instead they are absorbed into their now greater self. This experience that ordinary humans may have once or twice in their lives is the right and privilege of the Vampyre.

But the Vampyre knows—it will fade. She understands that this, too, is a distraction from practice. She is prepared to Sleep again and Rise again. This is the secret of the spiral force. Ultimately it becomes the state that carries the Vampyre beyond this world. The Vampyre does not need to face these things alone.

22

GROUP WORK

A group of Vampyres is called a velvet. Groups are rare and mainly celebrate their existence by energy exchange. There is a great deal of exploration to be done with the possible dynamics. However, I will focus on two interesting techniques: the Velvet Sending and the Dream Round.

THE VELVET SENDING

The Velvet Sending may be used to heal, destroy, or influence a human. The goals must be agreed upon by the participants. If you don't agree, do not participate. True Vampyres will accept your decision as they do not want to use peer pressure and thus empower their social parasites. Once the goal is obtained, you must create a group egregore for the purpose.

Take the first letter of each Vampyre name—for example, B, L, S, J, O. Create a name by adding vowels between the consonants, creating a magical-sounding name: Lajoseb. Then, writing the letters in block form—LAJOSEB—make them into a sigil using Austin O. Spare's methods. If you are unfamiliar with these, there are hundreds of Chaos Magic sites on the internet to instruct you. Obtain a photo of your target. On the back, write the sigil in the appropriate color: red to destroy, green to heal, purple or orange to influence. Set this aside until the sending.

Next, create the burning solution. This is a dangerous procedure: you'll need a well-lit area with good ventilation and a fire extinguisher nearby. You will need a stoppered container. Pound frankincense to a fine powder—you will need one teaspoon. Mix this thoroughly with one tablespoon of charcoal starter and half a teaspoon of food coloring

250

of the appropriate shade. Pour into the container. Store it as you would any volatile chemical. You will want to play with the formula so as to know the size and heat of the flame before the ritual.

Discuss the rite's dynamics with your velvet. They should be able to come to the site of your working dressed to go out afterward—not as Gothic weirdos (unless that is their normal mode). They will arrive silently. The Vampyres should sit around a table. On the table is a burning bowl, the burning solution, the photograph, and any other links to the target, if possible, such as hair or nail clippings. And such magical tools as you use in your practice. Lighting should be low—and if candles are used, they should be placed far from the burning solution. Also, since open fire will be briefly used, smoke alarms should be disabled.

The Vampyres should sit silently for some minutes. Then the master of ceremonies proclaims the Vampyric Invocation. Afterward the master says a variation of this:

> We have decided to [destroy/heal/influence] one [Name of target] for reasons we all know well. Are all here still in agreement?

The photo is passed around counterclockwise; each Vampyre Gazes at it and indicates affirmation with the goal.

The master proceeds.

> Let each close his or her eyes and begin the Work.

All close their eyes and imagine as vividly as possible their interaction with the target—draining him vampirically, healing him, or hypnotizing him. When they are done they open their eyes.

When all are done, the master says:

> Very well, we have changed his life. Let us now affirm our Deed.

The Vampyres hold hands in a circle. Another Vampyre speaks:

> At our convoked Will we summon into being (Name of egregore). It lives for one purpose. It is as powerful as our convoked Wills. It achieves its goal and dissolves into bliss merging with the Great Vampyre.

The Vampyres chant the name of the egregore nine times and release their hands.

The master places the photo into the burning bowl. All Vampyres raise a hand and point at it. The master says:

> *We send our Wills and (Name of egregore) to (Name of target) to heal/destroy/enchant him.*

He shakes the burning solution then pours it on the photo. He lights the mixture, saying:

> *I send our Wills into the Hidden Realm, and we await our Wills' return to the visible spectrum.*

The Vampyres continue pointing at the bowl until the flames are gone.

The master leaves the circle to secure the site for group departure. When all is secure—candles blown out, cats safely inside, etc.—the master will say, "Let's go!"

Everyone leaves, preferably either to a group event (movie, bowling, coffee) or to their homes. The rite is not to be discussed until the result occurs. Note that the result may appear very differently—the cursed human reforms or leaves the area because of a new job. The sick individual passes suddenly without pain. The enchanted individual chooses a new path that still affects things in a beneficial way for the velvet. In any positive case give thanks in a gratitude working. If no positive case results, adapt.

THE DREAM ROUND

Guiniviere Webb invented the dream round. The dream round is a way to explore the deeper realms of the psyches of the velvet to achieve healing from trauma, increase health or prosperity, or simply for fun. It has a few ironclad rules—let's look at those first.

1. Do not interpret the dreams of yourself or others in conversations, emails, and so on. Try not to interpret them in your own head

anymore than you would interpret seeing a dog in a parking lot.

2. Do not lie about the content of your dreams.
3. Report everything each day without reading the reports of others first. "Hits" are not the goal, rather a sign of the process working.

Vampyres always dream but may have trouble remembering their dreams. Dreams are always precise and unfathomable; for example, if you wish to dream of fixing the problems in your relationship and you dream of apple picking—this is a precise answer from your psyche. Your psyche has given you a clear image. Manifest it symbolically or literally. Your job is not to interpret it but simply to bring it up from the depths. Think of it as hiring a power witch to cast a spell for you. You don't intercept her cauldron, her hat, her weird mutterings—you merely enjoy the results.

Here is the method. The nightly results must be written down and sent to an email list upon awakening. Reading the reports of others must occur each night before the mirror and water ritual. You should label your reports thus:

Name
Night
Dream (for a full dream)
Fragment (for just a scene)

The dream round should last five nights. Preferably, it will run Thursday to Monday nights, as the changes in your sleep cycle will increase your dreaming. The most powerful and coherent dreams will come just before waking. When reporting your dreams you may use phrases like "Then I had intense sex with another Vampyre." For actual dream content, "I had oral sex with Susan, hope that doesn't make her feel awkward."

A purpose should be agreed upon by the velvet—note that this style of working can go across huge distances. Your first round should probably be "Being a more powerful Vampyre." Let's see how that would look.

First Night

Just before bed, look at yourself in a large mirror. Address yourself: "I am the Vampyre [VN], and I welcome my velvet so that we may dream this night." Raise a large goblet of pure cold water and drink it while watching yourself. Go to bed quickly. Sleep aids should avoided, if possible. An exception would be melatonin, which promotes dreaming. If someone in the velvet has compounded Uncle Setnakt's Metamind incense, you may cense the chamber with this.

Upon waking, send off your dreams; if you cannot recall your dreams report this as well. You may remember your dreams afterward during the day—add these to your report. If an unusual coincidence occurs such as "I dreamed of three red Mercedes-Benzes parked next to each other, and at lunch I went to a new restaurant and parked next to three red Mercedes-Benzes." You will repeat this process daily during the round.

Second Night

Take the time to carefully read the reports of others before doing the mirror and water ritual. Then spend a few minutes in total darkness thinking about the topic "When in my past have I been a more powerful Vampyre? Or when did I learn an important lesson about being a more powerful Vampyre?" Then turn to your mirror with your goblet. Tonight you say, "I am the Vampyre [VN], and I draw from the Well of Urdhr, where all Wyrd is kept the memories of being a more powerful Vampyre in the past. I welcome my velvet to share in this unholy communion." As you fall asleep, try to visualize things that either came up in your meditation or that struck you in reading the dreams of yourself and others.

Third Night

Do the same as above, except you read the material from the first two nights. Your in-darkness meditation should be "How can I be a more powerful Vampyre now?" Your invocation should be "I am the Vampyre [VN], and this night I draw from the Well of Verdhadi, the Well called the present by the Unawakened, where all things are now becoming manifest. I will dream of how to be a more powerful Vampyre in the here and now. In the name of Hecate, I welcome the rest of my velvet to join in this unholy communion." As you fall asleep try to visualize things that either came up in your meditation or that struck you in reading the dreams of yourself and others.

Fourth Night

Do the same as above, except you read the material from the second and third nights. Your in-darkness meditation should be "How can I become a better Vampyre in the future?" Your invocation should be "I am the Vampyre [VN], and this night I draw from the Well of Skuld, which holds all things that should come into being. I will dream of how I can be a more powerful Vampyre in the Yet-To-Be. In the name of Kali, I welcome the rest of my velvet to join in this unholy communion." As you fall asleep try to visualize things that either came up in your meditation or that struck you in reading the dreams of yourself and others.

Fifth Night

Do the same as above, except you read the fourth-night materials and anything else that struck you during the round. You may skip the in-darkness meditation. Your mirror and water invocation should be "I am the Vampyre [VN], and tonight I exchange deep secrets and true celebrations of the Vampyric Essence. May my velvet grow in power and wisdom, wealth and vitality." As you fall asleep try to visualize things that either came up in your meditation or that struck you in reading the dreams of yourself and others.

After the last set of reporting, let things lie fallow for a week. Often people will have an especially intense dream a day or two afterward. At that point one of the velvet should write a report of dream "hits." For instance, "On the first night L, J, and S dreamed of big black dogs, B dreamed of driving in a convertible (which she had never done), and then her boyfriend showed up with a convertible and his black Labrador. On night two, O and L dreamed of a Chinese restaurant." Everyone should read and amend the report as needed.

The effect of dream rounds is extraordinary: most people have a good time, and folks often receive beneficial chaos afterward (like romance or job offers). This leads to the immediate thought of "Let's do this again!" or worse, "Let's do this all the time!" Several years of experience has shown that overuse of the process removes the sense of wonder and magical effectiveness of the procedure. Never have less than three months between rounds, and once or twice a year seems optimal. There are a few more caveats. First, if you share a bed with someone, that person will tend to have intense and related dreams regardless of his or her spiritual practice or beliefs. This may lead to beneficial or difficult conversations. Second, if a group practices often, there will be certain aspects of the dreamscape that will appear again and again—a gazebo, a castle, a river, and so forth. Neither ignore nor obsess over these details. Third, this is a deeply bonding experience; if your velvet loses a member, or personal tensions arise between members, this is a source of great sadness.

I have engaged in this practice for fifteen years. At first I was focused on the dream hits—"Hey, we all dreamed of going down a waterslide." I was devasted if I couldn't remember my dreams on nights when everyone else was having fun. Then I recognized the not-so-subtle face of the social parasite in these feelings. I didn't struggle against the feelings, which always feeds the social parasite, but I chuckled at it. Letting these feelings go increased the effect of the dream rounds. Oddly, the number of dream hits lessened, but when they occured they were overwhelming—"We all dreamed of having breakfast at Brennan's in New Orleans. It was Christmas Eve. Setnakt was wearing a red sweater."

Dreaming with others helps one face the final mysteries.

23

LIFE, DEATH, AND LIFE-IN-DEATH

The big draw of the vampire is eternal life as a pretty human. The Vampyre must deal with disease, aging, and the problems of being pretty. This chapter will help the established Vampyre with these problems as well the relationship of the Vampyre to death and the afterlife. I'll offer you some methods for the struggle that have proved successful.

The first question seems trivial: Is the Vampyre required to be beautiful? The answer is in most cases yes, but all in cases the Vampyre must be fascinating. This does mean the gym and good diet, but also an understanding of a deeper truth. In so-called primitive societies shamans put on masks to influence, beckon, or scare away spirits. The same is true for you every time you step out of your lair.

Illness

Now let's talk about disease. For the Vampyre the first question is short-term, long-term, or chronic? For short-term diseases stop all daily work except for statements of gratitude. Add the following—on a nightly basis tell yourself that the fevers, aches, coughs, and so forth are signs of your transition from X to Y, where Y is a desired state (say, living within your means) and X is a current state (in this case, let's say overspending). Treat the disease as a magical trance, your resolution as a magical wish, and in your recovery practice an activity that receives the fulfillment of the wish (for example, spending time setting up a coupon folder while watching a free rerun).

For a long-term illness—assuming you have received a good diagnosis and treatment—continue your magical work, but add the following wish every night: "I dedicate a fourth of my energy to my recovery, when I will Z." Z is a reward activity for recovering; taking a pilgrimage to a spot of Vampyric power such Point Pleasant, West Virginia, might be one such reward.

For the chronic disease—such as diabetes—that you will have for the rest of your incarnation, do the following: Occasionally (I recommend you check by throwing two six-sided dice and doing this when you roll 1 and 1), make your evening wish the following: "I, the Vampyre [VN], remind myself that I am not my body, but I treasure my body. I call soothing and strengthening energies from the outer edge of Infinity to aid my body, I summon the latest research to me to make wiser decisions for my body, and I call upon the Powers of Darkness to inspire me to wise and safe pleasures for body, mind, and soul!" You may weep at your new state, but you must not wallow in depression—use your Vampyric practice (and if need be, medicine) to fight depression or low energy. All human bodies die; you must love yours and treat it with the same care you use for your animal companion.

If you wish to heal another human—whether or not they are a Vampyre—you have three or four major methods. The first and most reliable is to make believe they are adhering to the following advice themselves and then make your sending to match this. It matters not if they are atheist or Christian—merely assume their body is wiser than their social parasite. The second method is simply visualizing them in good health and willing some of your daily bounty of energy to them. The third and fourth methods are darker. If they are having trouble accepting a chronic state, take a personal possession or another item with a magical link such as hair and nails. Curse the ill person with clarity using the same sort of imagery and methodology that you would use to curse someone to die because you are seeking to kill false perceptions and delusions. The fourth rite for healing is about pain removal and storage. For the Vampyre, a receptacle should be found. I prefer a scary-looking wooden tiki, as this secret comes from Hawaiian shamanic practice, although it was oddly popularized by the sitcom *The Brady Bunch*. Imagine and quantify your pain: Let's say you have a headache. Is it big? Small? What color is it? Hmm, bright red and the size of a shot glass? Empty it into your pain battery. Treat it like water. If others are open to you touching them, lead them through the same visualization while stroking the pain along. This practice is called *Aka-Aka*, or "Shadow-Shadow," in both the Hawaiian and Maori languages. You can send energy from your battery by bringing it near your target and willing transference to happen or by giving the tiki to your target. I keep mine in my home safe as a little something extra if someone robs me.

Wait a minute? Did you say, "Curse someone to death"? Do you really mean that? Yes, in the same sense I keep weapons in my home. I don't advocate death curses any more than I go around shooting annoying neighbors.

Aging

Well, since this is a right and happy chapter, let's move on to aging. The Vampyre has a strong tendency to vanity. This is partially good, as it is rooted in the Will to Power, and partially bad, as it is also rooted in the youth culture of the social parasite. There are three issues with aging: the usefulness of ending bad conditioning, the usefulness of refining, and the true problem of focus. Let's deal with each.

By far the best part of aging is learning to disidentify with a particular vision of yourself. The social parasite wants us to fit in—and the easiest way to do this is to have a very fixed picture of ourselves. Thus, we do not grow or change, but when confronted with the decline of body or mind, we respond exactly the same way we do with guilt. We leak energy like a sieve. The mental work of accepting aging has many components, but four are very important for the Vampyre: spend time with other humans whom you exchange energy with daily: visit places that enshrine Truth or Beauty, like museums and gardens; volunteer for some cause that furthers life worship; and last, work on accepting loss of your friends (we'll come back to this).

The physical parts should be easy by now—using good information and good self-discipline to take care of yourself. The fresh exchange of energy revitalizes the mind. The visiting of gardens and museums cultivates transpersonal memory. This means that a very old, very thick sort of energy becomes available to you. The volunteering (look back at the Arkte section) means you will grow new neural pathways as you are transferring your self from being focused on just your body to a justice cause. Lastly, learning to accept losses of humans prepares you for your own transition: it will teach you just what your animal companions have taught you.

The second major area is the usefulness of refining. Your brain will lose its capacity for detail, the right brain (so repressed in our culture) will become dominant. This is great—if you remind yourself often that you are moving into the big picture as preparation for leaving the small picture. It is also difficult work. Once upon a time, I could go shopping for twenty things without a list; now if I'm getting more than four, a list must be made. My ninety-seven-year-old mother can remember who loves her and whom she loves but would be hard-pressed to recall her address. In the left-brain world she has faded, but in the right-brain world she is well prepared for the best step of her being. The best spiritual activity will become the writing of a memoir—a Vampyric gift of the record of your relationships with the world—either for your biological family or for Vampyres you have sired. Perhaps both. This material not only blesses the recipient with the same kind of slow, thick energy you can receive from a museum but also enables you to have a foothold in this world for further Work you might need to do.

The last part of aging, the problem of focus, is the great test. You have gone though great challenges in the Great Doubt and the Great Death, but this is the last challenge. You will lose the effectiveness of mind, senses, and body. The other state of being may slowly emerge—as it does in all humans—but you must resolve to tell yourself as often as you can that the Fire of Time is for making gold. The fire is real—even your Will cannot hold it back forever. Your brain may not recall why you came in the room, but processes you started long before that stage will continue to work on you as you change.

Death

Death is an important transition; you've been mitigating its effect for your entire Vampyric career. From choosing graveyards and battlefields as steads of Vampyric power to choosing movies where your hero sleeps in a coffin, you have prepared to die and go beyond physical death. Here are some concerns: your exit, your tomb, and your legacy. Each of these is as important as your lair and yet another reason to be associated with a school such as the Temple of Set. Humans have to consider their demise in a world of life-extending but not life-enhancing technology. One of my students, JCK, was handed a diagnosis of uncurable pancreatic cancer. He spent his last year writing thank-you letters and entertaining guests at his home. He knew how long pain medications would make a difference. He Skyped a last ceremony with Vampyre friends on Halloween Day, then took life-ending drugs in the presence of his long-term girlfriend and some local friends. After he passed, he was cremated, then in the thaw of Canadian spring had a mock Viking longboat second cremation among local artists in Whitehorse. He chose his exit and left surrounded by loving energies. His tomb is a small lake in Canada known to family and his friends both esoteric and common. A gifted artist and jeweler, he made magical artifacts for a chosen few, and his last days are recorded in the documentary film *The Left Hand Path*.

So for the living what's our relationship to the dead? The Vampyre is aware of their presence and observant of the state between life and death. Anyone who has worked in a hospital or old-age home has stories of the strange visons and odd powers the dying often have. The Vampyre cultivates these powers long before her own passage. First, she collects such stories from her own family and friends. Second, she visits places associated with such transitions. Third, she communicates with the dead—not with a Ouija board and a circle of folks around a table. The dead are made to feel welcome in her presence. She cherishes mementos of her friends, she speaks well of them, she visualizes them during meditations. She does not make demands of them, nor does she seek to make them her servants. She simply lets it be known that she is aware of them, respects them, and can transfer information about this world to them. Finally, she—on very rare occasions—might take the twofold oath of working for a cause that her dead friend also worked for and promising to report to that friend on the state of the cause each Halloween and upon dying.

Beyond Death

The afterlife is not a dream state, a great darkness, a rebirth into this world. It is more radically different from anything you know, but you have been prepared for it by all of your life experiences. Here is a simple meditation. Picture yourself at age seven. What were your interests? What did you want to be when you grew up? How much of the world did you know? What were your abilities? What were your constraints? Now, contrast that state with your life now. What powers, constraints, experiences do you have? When I was seven, I went to bed at 8:30. I could watch black-and-white TV with my parents—any of three channels. I had been to Houston, to the beach, to a cabin in the Rocky Mountains. I had a crush on my second-grade teacher. Compare that life to now. The change from that to this is a microscopic change compared to the change to a post-mortem state. Most human essences seem to spread out thinly and vanish. The Vampyre chooses to learn adaptability, curiosity, and exchange—as well as have a sense of pleasure and daring. That ultimate state must be incarnate in your present state now. That unknown but inevitable reality is the source of your power and obligations, as the next chapter will show.

24
Debt and Gifts

The Vampyre is the recipient of a gift and the giver of a gift. The Vampyre also takes and has a complex interrelationship between her current and future selves. The Vampyre must unlearn the social parasite's model of credit and debit and learn the more archaic model of gifting. The best study for this is Marcel Mauss's 1925 essay, *The Gift: Forms and Functions of Exchange in Archaic Societies.* Archaic times (as we noted in chapter 7, "Brainy Stuff") were the times when Vampyres ruled, and the Vampyre is free to pick any method that maximizes wisdom and joy.

Mauss argued that giving and receiving is a complex act having a spiritual as well as a material basis that creates bonds of an ineffable nature: "In this system of ideas one clearly and logically realizes that one must give back to another person what is really part and parcel of his nature and substance, because to accept something from somebody is to accept some part of his spiritual essence, of his soul."*

Let's examine this act of giving in four areas: self to future self, future self to self, self to other, and the bond with the Great Vampyre. I'll start with a simple example of the first sort. Every year I pack up the Halloween decorations quickly—I throw them in a plastic tub and stick them on a high shelf in the garage. Doing so prevents vandalism. When I unpack the stuff, I disentangle the lights, pull straw out of the ban-ner, and so forth. Last year, however—and even though I was tired— I packed the stuff away carefully. So this year I had an extra hour to

---

*Marcel Mauss, *The Gift: Forms and Functions of Exchange in Archaic Societies,* trans. Ian Cunnison (London: Cohen and West, 1967), Norton Library.

play or work. My past self had gifted me. Now, for non-Vampyres this is a simple tale of overcoming bad emotional self-regulation (otherwise known as procrastination), but the Vampyre understands that making and *consciously* receiving such gifts is a form of energy exchange that integrates the self and makes it easier to receive gifts in the other direction.

Vampyres can receive gifts from their future selves, but it takes practice to recognize them. Giving gratitude to past selves is a good way to practice. Let's look at a gift from a future self. The Vampyre Justin had been on a two-day combined business and pleasure trip to the Big Apple. Right after breakfast on Tuesday he had checked out of his hotel. That hadn't been the original plan—he was going to check out at noon. Why had he done this? He suspected it was a future gift. He took his suitcase with him and bought coffee and a book at a nearby bookstore, trying to get his magical bearings. Before he had ordered a second coffee, sirens filled the street. A fire had broken out in the lobby of his hotel. He had gifted himself a chance to miss the chaos and perhaps even injury. He had a second cup of coffee and then left for the airport early. Sometimes the gifts are large—like meeting one's wolf-mate by chance—and sometimes small; but, in addition to the material element, the subtle essence is deeply beneficial to the Vampyre. It needn't be recognized at the time; most recognitions of such gifts occur later.

The exchanges between self and other can occur in two ways. Let's start with other to self. In a simple way this can be that sense of obligation that you have because you get something. A coworker buys you an herbal tea sampler (even though you don't drink herbal tea), so you get her some candy. It simply makes for better energy flow. On the other hand, if a psychic vampire gives you something to create a sense of obligation, you should refuse the gift. It sends the bad intention back. It may be socially awkward (i.e., causes pain to your social parasite), but it is magically correct. But perhaps someone buys you something insightful: for example, an employee of yours buys a used library book for you that shows deep insight into your soul. The price tag may have been small, but the sheer correctness of the gift shows two things. First, the person is under your Vampyric power, probably because of her sensitivity if you have not sought to influence her directly. Second, you should respond with a gift consciously wishing to exchange with her or deepen your influence upon her. In the end, you will discover that it is a human that has gifted you. You may notice it in your nightly energy inventory—"Every time I interact with Rob, I feel better!" Or you may notice it in some moment of introspection—"My old Latin teacher in high school really helped me become the Vampyre I chose to become." In both instances the Vampyre is under an obligation to seek to gift this human if possible. Exchange is always more powerful than taking.

Before we go on to the question of the Vampyric gift, let's tackle the question of life introspection. We've talked about Wyrd, the power of stories we tell ourselves. Thinking about your past life under the aware-ness of your new life is a basic Vampyric urge. It grows out of the nightly energy inventory. The Vampyre must estrange herself from the linear processes of time—she seeks to be more than a product of causes and conditions and become more and more her self-creation (Xeper).

If you discover a great gift as you look over your years, you should seek to exchange with the giver. If you discover a theft (even if the thief had talked you into it) you must call your energy back. The good news is that if you have been practicing the techniques in this book, you have no need to be close to your target physically. It does help to know where they are and have a current picture, but this is not 100 percent neces-sary. I am not talking about revenge—revenge is usually bad emotional self-regulation. If you are so bound up in the thief that he or she still makes you angry, your social parasite will foul up your attempts to get your energy back. This does not mean don't be angry—think of it this way: A bank teller really embarrassed you over a math error. You dis-cover that the bank owes you $20, but you decide to drink a soda and calm down before you complain. You'll still feel anger, but your Will will be stronger. Here's a general guideline: if you try three times (wait-ing half a year between attempts) and are still too unfocused to call your energy back, you've been had.

Now we get to a great question: What is the gift you owe the Great Vampyre? If you have practiced the art long enough you will perceive the Great Vampyre, not as a space being that talks to you—we hope—

but as a principle as real in the magical universe as gravity is in the observable universe. Conventional religions have no trouble with this—the god wants sacrifices, gold, followers, gold, megachurches, gold—you get the drift. The Great Vampyre does not desire this, It/He/She doesn't even want more Vampyres—that may or may not be something you want. What It desires is the enhancement of Its perception. By now you will have come to understand that perception is how sentience sustains itself. Let this sink into you, and let that seed a tree become!

You may still have some questions; the Vampyre Setnakt has a few answers!

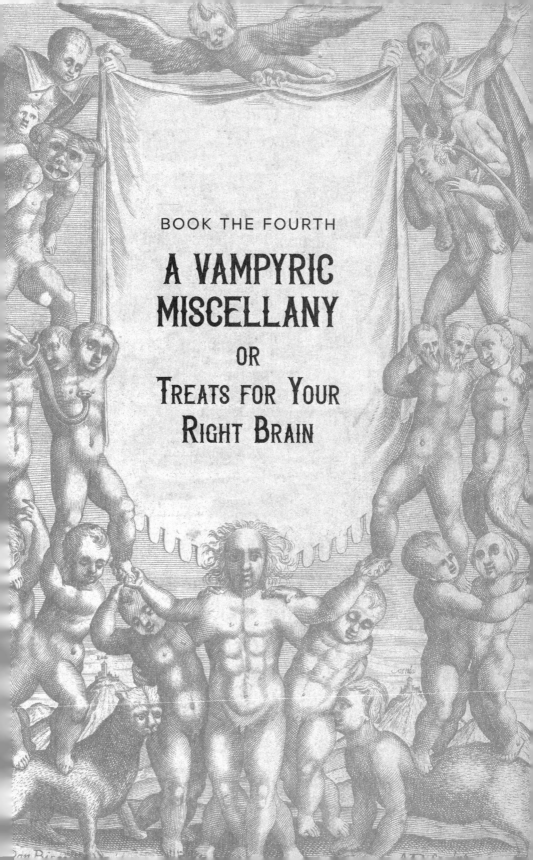

BOOK THE FOURTH

A VAMPYRIC MISCELLANY

OR

TREATS FOR YOUR RIGHT BRAIN

25

FAQs

Some questions arise again and again, here are some answers.

Q. It's really about blood, right? You say, "No blood." It's because of cops, right? But it's about blood!

A. Nope. Blood is symbolic—a juicy red protein. It does not carry energy; it does not give the Vampyre power. It is not a secret teaching. It points to the visceral nature of practice but is not the key to practice.

Q. It's really about sex, right?

A. Sexual energy and desire are key components in raising/taking/exchanging energy. But sexual desire and practice are personal choices. You can be a celibate, a partner in a monogamous relationship, a gay bathhouse legend, a porn star, and anything in between. Vampyres must be aware of the energy of sex within and beyond them at all times—and must challenge (at least on a subjective level) what the social parasite tells them their sexuality is. If you can subjectively raise desire for someone who is really not your type, you will have mastered desire.

Q. So what about drugs? You even admit to drug use at the beginning of your practice.

A. My drug use flunked me out of school, ate several IQ points, and convinced me for years that someday an old Yaqui shaman would spot me. But let's talk about you. Let's say you need some advice. Magic *without* drugs is like working hard to get the phone number of an expert in the field you need advice in. You discover a good time to call her. You have already paid for her advice, and of course triple-checked her references. You call. You get the advice, thank her, and arrange for another call after you have tried out the advice. You think calmly about the advice and make your decisions carefully. Here is what drugs *plus* magic is like. You've got a phone in your pocket, right? Dial some numbers randomly until you get an answer. Ask that person on the other end for life advice. Then do whatever it is you understand them to say. Since you're a Vampyre you've got a lot more energy than the average person to put behind your actions. Let's see how well that works.

Q. I like some of the practices described in the Vampyric Initiation section of this book, but I don't want to make the commitment to do the whole ceremony. Can I just do what I want?

A. I got a membership at the local gym. I would have better fitness if I used all the machines, the pool, and the indoor track. But I don't. I think it's better that I use what I use—even though I'm paying for all of it.

Q. You're just hoping people who buy this book will join the Temple of Set.

A. Gods no. Just the smarter, more dedicated ones. Hopefully most people will decide that it's too hard—or at least try the basic practices. That will hook some.

Q. I am a member of a local vampire group. Our leader is a five-hundred-year-old vampire, and he says all that's needed is for us to give him sex/blood/money/attention—he doesn't teach *any* of *this* stuff. Why should I do this?

A. By all means follow him! He's clearly more advanced than me! Except for investment strategy—I mean, after five hundred years he should have a nicer trailer . . .

Q. You give very precise verbal formulas in your incantations, but I'm more free-form, is that okay?

A. I give precise formulas to give you things to think about. If you can't understand why I say a certain phrase or do things in a certain order, you are probably not grasping the operation. I recommend the cookbook approach. The first time you do it, follow the recipe exactly, and as you gain in skill, customize it. The use of a single, repeated invocation is very helpful in making your brain quiet down and focus. It will connect you with the work of other practitioners.

Q. Your book is too male-centric, and you focus too much on male teachers.

A. Correct. It is my hope that women will master these techniques and cast their books on the world.

Q. Your book is too white-centric, and you focus too much on white teachers.

A. Correct. Didn't you just read the last question? I hope that Vampyres of Color (VOC) will create their own books without certain filters I no doubt have (and hopefully will include my name as Uncle Setnakt, "pretty fly for a white guy").

Q. You didn't tell me where I could get a dentist to make me fangs or where to buy a coffin.

A. Nope, sure didn't.

Q. I like the shamanistic thread but not the watch vampire movies thread—it's really just shamanism isn't it?

A. Shamanism plus a modern crowd-sourced myth. The modern myth empowers the dark parts of yourself and tears up the conventionality of your social parasite.

Q. Did you really do all this because you watched *Dark Shadows* when you were in elementary school?

A. In the nature of initiation, the Vampyre discovers that the Great Vampyre will have knocked on his or her door more than once. Since the Vampyre is a shape-shifter, it will look differently. For me it looked like *Dark Shadows,* then seventies neo-shamanism, then it showed up in a Geraldo Rivera show, then meeting Stephen Flowers, then reading Mircea Eliade, then the Temple of Set, finally the Order of the Vampire. Initiation does not come along once in the life of an initiate; that being said, once it is fully perceived the battle between Vampyre and social parasite begins—and it is a life-and-death struggle in many ways.

Q. What are the dangers of the Vampyre Path?

A. First, ego-inflation. If you think you're a predator in a world of prey, of course your ego will be inflated. Only when you realize that there are much bigger predators than you that can bring about your ruin will you self-correct. Picture an unwashed man (or woman) in a faded Goth T-shirt holding a hand-lettered cardboard sign by the side of the road. It reads "I will Vampyre you for food." Picture him every day, you feel cocky.

 Second, as emphasized in chapter 24, "Debt and Gifts," Vampyres are great procrastinators—in fact, passing through and beyond your procrastinator phase a few times is part of Initiation.

 Third, the practice looks stupid. Its power is in its affront to your sense of social responsibility and normality. Deviance alerts and enrages the social parasites of others. Those with whom you share either DNA or a household are particularly triggered. They will attack you out of "love" and "concern." Don't be angry with them, but make sure you don't have to fear them.

Q. Are there vampire hunters?

A. Yes. Oddly enough there are nutjobs who will check you out with mirrors, spray you with holy water, or scream Bible verses at you. This is not a major danger—anymore than being accosted in the street by any nutjob in the city. If you are private about your practice this won't happen. But if you are more playful about your practice—say in your jewelry or Halloween jokes—it can. As long as you can play with these people, this can be a huge rush of energy. But keep in mind, although a Vampyre's lair should draw energy to it, it should also be safe and warded by security forces—not just your sigils!

Q. Are there Vampyre politics?

A. Of course there are, but for the most part you'll discover them by practicing your daily energy inventory. Are there things that increase your energy? Vote for them! Are their causes that increase your energy? Volunteer for them. Be wary of people who tell you that the Vampyre is a creature of the Right, the Left, or is apolitical. Why are they concerned about how you develop, safeguard, or spend your energy? Vampyres must always know that they are not fixed in their beliefs because they are unconstrained. Beliefs will change. You may have started as an Ayn Rand–quoting objectivist and have become a tree-hugging liberal. The initial phase might have given you freedom from your Democrat family, the latter gave you energy when you saved owls by being chained to a tree overnight. Trust two things: what your energy levels tell you, AND when the last time was you REALLY challenged yourself.

Q. Should I be making more Vampyres?

A. Turning others is an act of love and deep vulnerability. Imagine you were sharing a house with everybody you've had a crush on since middle school. That should answer the question.

Q. Why is a school important?

A. A school gives you real-life examples of practice. The occult world is full of so-called masters with really great stories, or books about the amazing powers you gain, or the ease of practice. If it were that easy imagine what the world would be like. In a school you can meet practitioners who have survived the Great Death and who still grow in wisdom and power. You can see millionaires and folks on food stamps, white and black folks, people of different ages, politics, cultures—all of whom strive for the same goals you do. You can exchange energy with these folks, which will greatly speed your evolution. You can be remembered.

Q. I've got more questions.

A. Write Inner Traditions and tell them I should write another book. But let's see if we can summarize what you've learned in the first three books.

26

VAMPYRIC PRECEPTS

    I. Start now, don't wait for another book, another teacher, an omen.

   II. Always be aware of energy within you and around you.

  III. It is better to exchange energy than merely to take it.

  IV. The Vampyre is a gift from a part of yourself you don't know yet.

   V. The people who deliver the gift to you deserve thanks.

  VI. Aligning yourself with giving is the first step to a meaningful immortality.

 VII. Visible waves on the sea of pop-culture show leviathans beneath.

VIII. Mastery is the ability to invoke beginner's mind, journeyman's strength, and elder's power at any desired instance.

  IX. In time this myth will fade, but the Essence will choose another one.

   X. Nightly work—the review, the gratitude, the wish, setting up to dream—is everything.

  XI. In the beginning your practice looks like everyone else's, in the middle it looks only like yours, in the end no one but a fellow Vampyre can see it.

 XII. Respect what comes to you.

XIII. It doesn't matter what people say about you, it matters what they feel about you in the dark.

XIV. You will get what you need (but you may not know this) when you get what you want as well; reread precept IV.

27

RECOMMENDED VAMPYRIC CURRICULUM

The Vampyre is self-initiating in her early steps. The information gained by using the Gaze, the energy inventory, and the statement of gratitude is more valuable than the exercise of imagination and intellect. However, as these skills begin to work on the soul-body complex both imagination and information become useful tools in your self-alchemy. This chapter deals with films, books, and television.

THE MOVIES

The Vampyre is the only crowd-sourced myth. Arriving with industrialization, it succeeded with middle-class folk who were interested in improving their lot but who were also dealing with depersonalization and alienation. It took a blend of Dacian and Saxon folklore, a "vampire scare" from folks' grandfathers' times, and it began circulating among novels and then films, comics, and TV. It created imagery based on what people found scary and/or seductive, and as such was a perfect vehicle for the Left-Hand Path. The modern Vampyre can choose from any of these sources, but certain ones are a quicker route to power. We'll deal with film first. The classics will tell you where certain myths came from; the epics will deal with immersive experience; the thoughtful ones may suggest certain avenues for you to pursue; the Vampyre as outcast will allow you to get beyond cultural attachments; and the Vampyre films without vampires will allow you to explore certain aspects of the archetype. Do not fret if your favorite films aren't on this list—they are excellent for you because they're your favorites!

The Classics

A Fool There Was (1915). Theda Bara was the "vamp," a woman whose sexual charisma destroyed men. This rarely seen silent epic cemented the idea of glamour and sexuality as the vampire's powers. No blood, no biting, no coffins—pure Vampyric magic.

Nosferatu (1922). Albin Grau, a magician of the Left-Hand Path group Fraternitas Saturni, created the decidedly Jewish (in the sense of contemporary derogatory stereotypes) Count Orlof based on Dracula. This ugly creature is outsmarted by a loving woman and disappears into smoke when sunlight hits him—a first in cinema. The film was vastly overadvertised and lost money. When Bram Stoker's widow, Florence, saw the "Dracula" name in the advertisements, she sued Prana Films (note the name!) and won the right to destroy every print she could find. The court case and resulting burning of several prints (but not all) created a big interest in the novel *Dracula,* which led to the London and New York plays and the subsequent film.

Dracula (1931). This is the seed from which the current myth grows. The screenplay is based on the 1924 stage play *Dracula* by Hamilton Deane (London) and John L. Balderston (New York). Balderston had hired Bela Lugosi, an unknown Romanian actor, for the role. Lugosi excelled in the role, despite his relatively minor roles in Hungary. He *became* Dracula. He quested for getting a movie, even representing Florence Stoker in the negotiations with Universal. Universal wanted the picture—it would be great for Lon Chaney Sr.! Lugosi was crushed. Then Lon's bronchial cancer was exacerbated by fake snow (special effects), and he died. Lugosi knocked on Universal's door again. Again, they said no—they didn't want a foreigner with "Communist leanings." But Lugosi offered the low-ball price of five thousand a week. After seven weeks of filming, *Dracula* was born. Every single role that Lugosi played afterward was tied to this role, even his sad appearance in *Plan 9 from Outer Space.*

The Epics

Taste the Blood of Dracula (1970). All of the Hammer vampire films have mythic merit. This was Christopher Lee's fourth time playing the count—he wanted to stop playing the role. He was to be replaced by a Crowley-esque figure Lord Courtley. But the fans' vampiric pull brought Lee back. It connects the lore of the Vampyre with ceremonial magic and Graal Work.

Blood and Roses (1960). Roger Vadim's re-creation of LeFanu's *Carmilla,* one of the roots of the current myth dripping with lesbian lust and innocence is better understood by its French title, *Et mourir de plaisir,* literally, "And die with pleasure."

Dracula: A Love Story (1979). Frank Langella plays the count as a seeker of love, the perfect lover who will understand his need. The last scene suggests that despite a solar death, the love of his chosen one will restore him.

The Thoughtful Ones

Lifeforce (1985). This film is—for better or for worse—an attempt to turn Colin Wilson's *The Space Vampires* into film. These entities reveal the power of energy as the source of civilization and suggest that entities have evolved elsewhere that use energy in manners inconceivable to our Eros-denying civilization. The energy the space vampires feed upon is tied to vitality, eroticism, and paranormal powers.

The Hunger (1983). A film that connects the vampire mythos with ancient Egypt, this stylish film addresses the question of need. Would you live forever if the cost were cruelty and addiction?

Interview with a Vampire (1994). This one deals with the implications of others partaking in the Vampyric life. Set in modern-day San Francisco, the story wanders through history, revealing in the co-vampiric bond of theater and audience, or the meaning of life-in-death.

The Vampire as Outcast

Blacula (1972). In 1780, Prince Manuwalde seeks Count Dracula's help in ending the slave trade. Dracula mocks him, makes jokes about enslaving his wife, and then changes him into a vampire. A gay couple buying his coffin as a conversation piece soon release him. The prince—alternately more sophisticated and charming than twentieth-century whites or a horrible beast—shows how the host culture needs and fears, lusts after and despises its marginalized, and how this creates a magical/psychological space for the Vampyre to work in.

A Girl Walks Home Alone at Night (2014). The first (and no doubt only) Iranian vampire Western deals with ethics and estrangement in the Iranian underworld. The girl is a full-on vampire with fangs and blood-lust, but she is also a force for social good and compassion. This movie has a strong effect on Westerners who want to see all Iranians as either bad or oppressed. As such this film confronts and transcends social norms.

Martin (1978). A film by George Romero. Martin is an insane youth who uses vampire myth—blood and sex—as a way of understanding an insane world. He is both supported by and constrained by his family, who share some aspects of his delusions. An important film for the Vampyre as it will help confront family issues.

Vampyre Films without Vampires

Silence of the Lambs (1991). A film about vampiric personalities, in this case Jame Gumb, whose desire for a different life leads him to kill and skin women. His desire kills his social parasite, but no ethical force has grown in its place, ending any possibility of his evolution. Hannibal Lecter, the extremely bright and insightful cannibal who maximizes energy flow in every situation, feeds off Clarice Starling's trauma. Jack Crawford, Starling's trainer at the FBI, is the typical psychic vampire of the older male mentor type who feeds off a younger woman's energy. And finally, the Vampyre Clarice, who, having dealt with the vampiric energy of these three men, transforms herself into a hunter with ethical and almost superhuman powers.

Beachbum (2019). The poet/beach bum/addict/womanizer will be among the least likable pictures of human excess that you have ever seen. After his drunkenness kills his beloved ex-wife, he does not stop his conventional evils but instead *uses* them as a means of transcending his simple social parasite role of "I'm a bad boy!" into becoming both a great artist and even a giver of wealth and magic to the many.

Fight Club (1999). A nameless narrator seeks connection by attending support groups for diseases he does not have. A romantic encounter awakens him to the possibility of happiness; shortly thereafter his apartment explodes, and he meets Tyler Durden, who introduces him to stealing human fat to make soap, sexual license, violence as entertainment, and destroying the corporate world. Tyler is the free opposite of his enslaved self, yet he discovers that Tyler is actually a dissociative personality of his. In many ways this is a film about the Vampyric personality versus the social parasite.

THE READING LIST

The reading list is divided into three ranks and five modes. The first rank is probably best for the first couple of years of practice, the second and third for later practice. In general, the first rank can provide answers to the first questions that will occur to you, the second and third ranks deal with more subtle questions. The modes are "Vampires," "Big Thinks," "Esoteric Wisdom," "Fighting Dirty," and "Self- Defense." I'll give a sentence or two about each.

First Rank

Vampires

The Annotated Dracula (1975). Leonard Wolf explains the religious, historical, and sexual themes of Bram Stoker's classic with notes, photos, and drawings.

The Vampire Film (2012). Jeffrey Weinstock studies the themes in vampiric cinema, from lack of sexual boundaries to ambivalence of the undead to social codes. As such this is an essential study of the modern myth.

Unholy Hungers: Encountering the Psychic Vampires in Ourselves & Others (1996) by Barbara E. Holt. The only good book on vampire pathologies—a warning for the practitioner and a self-defense guide.

Big Thinks

Mindstar (2015) by Michael Aquino. A philosophical study in the nature (and perils) of having an immortal soul.

Consciousness: An Introduction (2018) by Susan Blackmore. One of the best introductions to consciousness studies. Explains the origin of the social parasite, which she describes as socially created and includes useful information on altered states and secular spirituality. Works by this author are generally recommended.

Is There Life after Death? The Extraordinary Science of What Happens after We Die (2006). Anthony Peake examines the possibilities not only of survival after death but also reasons for extraordinary perceptions (nonlocal) that humans occasionally have access to.

Esoteric Wisdom

Carnal Alchemy: Sado-Magical Techniques for Pleasure, Pain and Self-Transformation (2013) by Stephen Flowers, Ph.D., and Crystal Flowers. This book provides the magical basis for taking energy, giving energy, pleasure, and pain. The Vampyre need not use the external props of BDSM—no whips and chains—but will find this book to be the best esoteric guide to energy work.

The Magical Shield: Protection Magic to Ward Off Negative Forces (2016). Frater U. D. writes perhaps the only sane book on dealing with avoiding adverse forces. Unlike most books in this vein, this book invites—even requires—investigation by the user. One of the best books for energy workers.

Uncle Setnakt's Essential Guide to the Left Hand Path (2011). Don Webb's guide to Left-Hand Practice is the only book in the field whose writer I often agree with.

Fighting Dirty

The Satanic Witch (various editions). Anton Szandor LaVey gives us a misogynistic text on stealing power from others (especially theft of power by women from men). The book is limited by LaVey's use of the pimp principle (see the "Indulgence" chapter in Book the Second) and presenting his fetishes as male universals. Not recommended to folks on a sodium-free diet as it must be read with several grains of salt.

Winning Through Intimidation (various editions). Robert Ringer's funny book on being a real-estate broker offers useful tips on reading people, use of body language, and use of legal contracts to solidify gains over the psyches of others.

How to Be a Jewish Mother: A Very Lovely Training Manual (1964). Dan Greenberg's very funny book will teach you how to use guilt (the biggest button on the healthy social parasite) to gain power over others.

Self-Defense

The Gentle Art of Verbal Self Defense (1974) by Suzette H. Elgin will teach how not to be caught in the web of words and even how to use the words of those who seek to harm or manipulate you to your advantage.

Second Rank

Vampires

The Delicate Dependency: A Novel of the Vampire Life (1982). Michael Talbot deals with compassion and thoughtfulness in the vampire. In *Encyclopedia of the Vampire,* my friend (and often editor) Darrell Schweitzer called the novel "one of the most impressive explorations of a vampire mind ever written."

Vampire God: The Allure of the Undead in Western Culture (2009). Mary Halab gives us a study of the vampire as modern, crowd-sourced myth illuminating the work of Anne Rice, Stephanie Meyers, Bram Stoker, and Montague Summers—and dealing with this myth as a reaction against social/sexual/political norms. In many ways, this is an etic study of the same material as is found in this book.

The Vampire, His Kith and Kin: A Critical Edition (2011). Montague Summers's seminal work on vampires clarified and updated by John Edgar Browning. The Reverend Summers read Greek, Latin, French, and German and thought you should, too, so in addition to providing useful translations, Browning also gives us an interesting biography of the quirky reverend and his attack on modernity and rationality.

Big Thinks

Philosophy as a Way of Life: Spiritual Exercises from Socrates to Foucault (1995). Pierre Hardot reminds the reader that philosophy was never meant to be an academic subject but rather a means to discovering the world through thought and deed. This great scholar of classical philosophy will be a great aide to the Vampyre as she frees herself from the social matrix.

Passing Through the Gateless Barrier: Koan Practice for Real Life (2016). Guo Gu gives us an insightful translation and commentary in the forty-eight koans of the *Gateless Barrier* collected in the thirteenth century by Chan master Wumen Huikai. These contemplations and paradoxes can make the Vampyre aware of simply living in the now without the social parasite's filtering. A good book to work through.

Aghor Medicine (2008). Dr. Barrett's study of the medicinal practice and philosophy of modern day Aghoris in India illumines not only the Left-Hand Path use of the disgusting and forbidden but also the role of such folk (like Vampyres) in the greater good.

Esoteric Wisdom

Kali Kalua: A Manual of Tantric Magic (2010). Jan Fries provides a REAL book about Tantra—not another "Tantra as nookie nirvana" text. He deals with lust, disgust, fear, and death. This is a useful book for the established Vampyre.

Setting the Table, Laying Down Tricks: Hoodoo Recipes (2015–2016). Grace Mabon's three-volume set explores magical cooking in the HooDoo tradition from meals for wealth and wisdom to meals that allow the Vampyre to dominate her victim. The Vampyre works in the sensual realm, and this tradition almost comes premade for us.

Uncle Setnakt's Nightbook (2016). Don Webb provides certain esoteric information and energies that will deepen the practice of an established Vampyre.

Fighting Dirty

The Command to Look: A Master Photographer's Method for Controlling the Human Gaze (2014). William Mortensen wrote what is perhaps the best book for the visual aspect of the Vampyre's art. It had a massive effect on the theories of Anton LaVey. This edition from Feral House has supplemental essays on LaVey's thought and is a great manual for the established Vampyre.

The Full Facts of Cold Reading: The Definitive Guide to How Cold Reading Is Used in the Psychic Industry (2019). Ian Rowland shows all of the dirty tricks that "psychics" use to give accurate readings to complete strangers. I don't recommend this book to new Vampyres, as they will overuse its techniques and freak out their acquaintances. This is an informational text; the author has how-to texts both for psychic and business uses.

What Every Body Is Saying: An Ex-FBI Agent's Guide to Speed-Reading People (2008). Joe Navarro teaches how to read people AND also how to send signals. This book illustrates which nonverbal clues telegraph untrustworthiness and deception and which radiate sincerity and compassion. The author is a former FBI agent who commonly used these techniques to help crack cases. The book cautions about jumping to conclusions and encourages using clusters of nonverbal patterns to help discover whether a person is lying or just under stress.

Self-Defense

Waking the Tiger: Healing Trauma (1997). Peter A. Levine begins with the observation that animals face life-and-death drama every day but are seldom traumatized. What is it about humans that keeps us from being this way? He shows how to bypass the social parasite and heal ourselves.

Third Rank

Vampires

A Velvet of Vampyres (2013). Don Webb's Vampyre fiction, some of which is included in this volume.

Inkarna (2012). Nerine Dorman's young adult novel deals with life, death, and gender. Using Egyptian afterlife concepts, it touches on the link between the body and the soul and the arbitrariness of social constructs.

Blood Gift (2016). Amy Lee Burgess writes about Vampyres in an Awakened way, unlike most of the novels on the topic. Worth tracking down.

Big Thinks

The Labyrinth of Time: The Illusion of Past, Present and Future (2012). Anthony Peake explores the relationship between consciousness and time. He surveys both esoteric theories and contemporary psychology and physics. Books by this author are generally recommended.

The Master and His Emissary: The Divided Brain and the Making of the Western World (expanded edition, 2019). Ian McGilchrist gives an extensive study of right- and left-brain thinking and its effect on history. A tough but rewarding 616 pages.

Creative Evolution (various editions). Henri Bergson gives us useful thoughts on the order of nature and the form of intelligence, including the geometrical tendency of the intellect, and examines mechanisms of thought and illusion. He opens the way for the consideration of an evolutionary view of the nature of consciousness, thus setting the stage for later thinkers like Gebser and Lachman. Works by this author are generally useful.

Esoteric Wisdom

Getting Castaneda: Understanding Carlos Castaneda (2017). Peter Luce offers us a summary of the fictional magical system developed by Carlos Castaneda from the sociology of Garfield, fifties pop American occultism, nineteenth-century nagualism, and the magic-realist novel *Pedro Páramo*. This is a great modern myth for energy workers, but be forewarned: Luce is not a skeptical reader of Castaneda.

High Magic: Theory and Practice (2005). Frater U. D.'s two-volume set shows how most of Western magic works with some philosophical and historical context. I would have recommended this book for beginning Vampyres but worry it might distract from Vampyric practice at first.

Infernal Geometry and the Left-Hand Path (2019). Toby Chappell introduces a much-guarded secret magical system that has its roots with the Temple of Set and the Church of Satan.

Fighting Dirty

Think and Grow Rich (1937). Napoleon Hill gives the esoteric secrets of business (or anything) success. This is a practical manual of weaponized mindfulness.

The Art of Seduction: An Indispensable Primer on the Ultimate Form of Power (2001). Robert Green's book is not about power, it's about manipulating the desire for pleasure, and feeding off the joy of manipulation.

The Persuasion Handbook: Developments in Theory and Practice (2002). James P. Dillard presents a comprehensive survey of techniques and theories of persuasion. It outlines methods of control—both inner and outer—for the established Vampyre.

Self-Defense

After the Ecstasy, the Laundry: How the Heart Grows Wise on the Spiritual Path (2001). Jack Kornfield shows how experiences of self-insight (satori) or spiritual bliss (samadhi) can be integrated into day-to-day life. If one wounds the social parasite, one must also heal it, train it, and entertain it. An essential book for those deep in the path.

TELEVISION

Dark Shadows. A Gothic soap opera that aired from 1966 to 1971. The recurrent character of the Vampyre Barnabas Collins deals with the struggle of passion and compassion, Vampyric power, and human facility.

Forever Knight. A police thriller with a vampire detective that ran from 1992 to 1996. The series deals with good and evil, conscious desire and senseless lust, and the relationships of someone free from the social matrix who nevertheless cares about humans.

Dead Like Me. A comedy series running from 2003 to 2004. The show revolves around "reapers"—humans who have died but not gone to their final(?) state and are obliged to help other humans pass on, while being stuck as ageless beings in a workaday world. Very helpful for the Vampyre trying to figure out her day job.

Working through this material will give the Vampyre the equivalence of a bachelor's degree, but I doubt we'll be seeing any formal B.V.A. (Bachelor of Vampyric Arts) soon.

28

"Transylvanian Superstitions"

BY E. GERARD

This is the original text that was the seed crystal for Bram Stoker. Emily Gerard's essay "Transylvanian Superstitions" appeared in volume 18 of the British periodical called the Nineteenth Century *(1885). Here Stoker took his raw desire to write a bestseller, his unresolved love and hate of his boss, and a growing popular myth and created the seed, whose fruits we are harvesting. The Vampyre begins work at once, and then seeks the beginning of the idea with which he is working, as well as designing its end. There is more here than meets the eye.*

Transylvania might well be termed the land of superstition, for nowhere else does this curious crooked plant of delusion flourish as persistently and in such bewildering variety. It would almost seem as though the whole species of demons, pixies, witches, and hobgoblins, driven from the rest of Europe by the wand of science, had taken refuge within this mountain rampart, well aware that here they would find secure lurking-places, whence they might defy their persecutors yet awhile.

There are many reasons why these fabulous beings should retain an abnormally firm hold on the soil of these parts; and looking at the matter closely we find here no less than three separate sources of superstition.

First, there is what may be called the indigenous superstition of the country, the scenery of which is peculiarly adapted to serve as background to all sorts of supernatural beings and monsters. There are innumerable caverns, whose mysterious depths seem made to harbour whole legions of evil spirits: forest glades fit only for fairy folk on moonlit nights, solitary lakes which instinctively call up visions of water sprites; golden treasures lying hidden in mountain chasms, all of which have gradually insinuated themselves into the minds of the oldest inhabitants, the Roumenians, and influenced their way of thinking, so that these people, by nature imaginative and poetically inclined, have built up for themselves out of the surrounding materials a whole code of fanciful superstition, to which they adhere as closely as to their religion itself.

Secondly, there is here the imported superstition; that is to say, the old German customs and beliefs brought hither seven hundred years ago by the Saxon colonists from their native land, and like many other things, preserved here in greater perfection than in the original country.

Thirdly, there is the wandering superstition of the gypsy tribes, themselves a race of fortune-tellers and witches, whose ambulating caravans cover the country as with a network, and whose less vagrant members fill up the suburbs of towns and villages.

Of course all these various sorts of superstition have twined and intermingled, acted and reacted upon each other, until in many cases it is a difficult matter to determine the exact parentage of some particular belief or custom; but in a general way the three sources I have named may be admitted as a rough sort of classification in dealing with the principal superstitions afloat in Transylvania.

There is on this subject no truer saying than that of Grimm, to the effect that "superstition in all its manifold varieties constitutes a sort of religion, applicable to the common household necessities of daily life," and as such, particular forms of superstition may very well serve as guide to the characters and habits of the particular nation in which they are prevalent.

The spirit of evil (or, not to put too fine a point upon it, the devil) plays a conspicuous part in the Roumenian code of superstition, and such designations as the Gregyna Drakuluj (devil's garden), the Gaura Drakuluj (devil's mountain), Yadu Drakuluj (devil's hell or abyss), &c. &c., which we frequently find attached to rocks, caverns, or heights, attest the fact that these people believe themselves to be surrounded on all sides by a whole legion of evil spirits.

The devils are furthermore assisted by witches and dragons, and to all of these dangerous beings are ascribed peculiar powers on particular days and at certain places. Many and curious are therefore the means by which the Roumenians endeavour to counteract these baleful influences, and a whole complicated study, about as laborious as the mastering of any unknown language, is required in order to teach an unfortunate peasant to steer clear of the dangers by which he considers himself to be beset on all sides. The bringing up of a common domestic cow is apparently as difficult a task as the rearing of any dear gazelle, and even the well-doing of a simple turnip or potato about as precarious as that of the most tender exotic plant.

Of the seven days of the week, Wednesday (Miercuri) and Friday (Vinere) are considered suspicious days, on which it is not allowed to use needle or scissors, or to bake bread; neither is it wise to sow flax on these days. Venus (called here Paraschiva), to whom the Friday is sacred, punishes all infractions of this rule by causing fires or other misfortunes.

Tuesday, however (Marți, named from Mars, the bloody god of war), is a decidedly unlucky day, on which spinning is totally prohibited, and even such seemingly harmless pursuits as washing the hands or combing the hair are not unattended by danger. On Tuesday evening about sunset, the evil spirit of that day is in its fullest force, and in many districts the people refrain from leaving their huts between sunset and midnight. "May the *mar sara* (spirit of Tuesday evening) carry you off" is here equivalent to saying, "May the devil take you!"

It must not, however, be supposed that Monday, Thursday, and Saturday are unconditionally lucky days, on which the Roumenian is at liberty to do as he pleases. Thus every well-educated Roumenian matron knows that she may wash on Thursdays and spin on Saturdays, but that it would be a fatal mistake to reverse the order of these proceedings; and though Thursday is a lucky day for marriage, and is on that account mostly chosen for weddings, it is proportionately unfavourable to agriculture. In many parishes it is considered dangerous to work in the fields on all Thursdays between Easter and Pentecost, and it is believed that if these days are not set aside as days of rest, ravaging hailstorms will be the inevitable punishment of the impiety. Many of the more enlightened Roumenian pastors have preached in vain against this belief, and some years ago the members of a parish presented an official complaint to the bishop, requesting the removal of their *curé,* on the ground that not only he gave bad example by working on the prohibited days, but had actually caused them serious material damage, by the hailstorms his sinful behaviour had provoked.

This respect of the Thursday seems to be the remains of a deeply ingrained, though now unconscious, worship of Jupiter (Zoi), who gives his name to the day.

To different hours of the day are likewise ascribed different influences, favourable or the reverse. Thus it is always considered unlucky to look at oneself in the glass after sunset; also it is not wise to sweep the dust over the threshold in the evening, or to give back a sieve or a whip which has been borrowed of a neighbour.

The exact hour of noon is precarious on account of the evil spirit *Pripolniza,* and so is midnight because of the *miase nópte* (night spirit), and it is safer to remain within doors at these hours. If, however, some misguided peasant does happen to leave his home at midnight, and espies (as very likely he may) a flaming dragon in the sky, he need not necessarily give himself up as lost, for if he have the presence of mind to stick a fork into the ground alongside of him, the fiery monster will thereby be prevented from carrying him off.

The finger which ventures to point at a rainbow will be straightway seized by a gnawing disease, and a rainbow appearing in December is always considered to bode misfortune.

The Greek Church, to which the Roumenians exclusively belong, has an abnormal number of feast-days, to almost each of which peculiar customs and superstitious are attached. I will here only attempt to mention a few of the principal ones.

On New Year's Day it is customary for the Roumenian to interrogate his fate, by placing a leaf of evergreen on the freshly swept and heated hearthstone. If the leaf takes a gyratory movement he will be lucky, but if it shrivels up where it lies, then he may expect misfortune during the coming year. To ensure the welfare of the cattle it is advisable to place a gold or silver piece in the water-trough, out of which they drink for the first time on New Year's morning.

The feast of the Epiphany, or Three Kings (*Tre crai*) is one of the oldest festivals, and was solemnised by the Oriental Church as early as the second century, fully 200 years before it was adopted by the Latins. On this day, which popular belief regards as the coldest in the winter, the blessing of the waters, known as the feast of the Jordan, or *bobetasu* (baptism) feast, takes place. The priests, attired in their richest vestments, proceed to the shore of the nearest river or lake, and bless the waters, which have been unclosed by cutting a Greek cross some six or eight feet long in the surface of the ice. Every pious Roumenian is careful to fill a bottle with the consecrated water before the surface freezes over, and preserves it, tightly corked and sealed up, as an infallible remedy in case of illness.

Particularly lucky is considered whoever dies on that day, for he will be sure to go straight to heaven, the door of which is supposed to stand open all day, in memory of the descent of the Holy Ghost at the baptism of Christ.

The feast of St. Theodore, 11th of January (corresponding to our 23rd of January), is a day of rest for the girls, and whichever of them transgresses the rule is liable to be carried off by the saint, who sometimes appears in the shape of a beautiful youth, sometimes as a terrible monster.*

The Wednesday in Holy Week is very important. The Easter cakes

---

*Romania did not adopt the modern Gregorian calendar until 1919 and at the time of Gerard's writing was using the Julian calendar. Though this passage may refer to Saint Theodosius, whose feast day is January 11 by the Eastern Orthodox liturgical calendar, this could instead be an error. In her later, expanded book on Romania, *The Land Beyond the Forest*, Gerard provides a footnote to this passage: "The Serbs have also a corresponding day, called the Theodor Saturday (*Todoroma Sumbota*)," and refer to their terrorizing monster as a "*sintotere*," or centaur. *The Land Beyond the Forest: Facts, Figures and Fancies from Transylvania* by Gerard (New York: Harper & Brothers, 1888), 192. Theodor Saturday is a Serbian spring holiday preceding Easter that venerates Saint Todor, an occasionally demonic figure who rides horseback to spread fecundity and performs feats of dragon-slaying along the lines of Saint George.

and breads are baked on this day, and some crumbs are mixed up with the cow's fodder; woe to the woman who indulges in a nap to-day, for the whole year she will not be able to shake off her drowsiness. In the evening the young men in each home bind as many wreaths as there are members of the family: each of these is marked with the name of an individual and thrown up upon the roof. The wreaths which fall down to the ground indicate those who will die that year.

Skin diseases are cured by taking a bath on Good Friday, in a stream or river which flows towards the east.

In the night preceding Easter Sunday witches and demons are abroad, and hidden treasures are said to betray their site by a glowing flame. No God-fearing peasant will, however, allow himself to be tempted by the hopes of such riches, which he cannot on that day appropriate without sin. On no account should he presume to absent himself from the midnight church service, and his devotion will be rewarded by the mystic qualities attached to the wax candle he has carried in his hand, and which when lighted hereafter during a thunderstorm will infallibly keep the lightning from striking his house.

The greatest luck which can befall a mortal is to be born on Easter Sunday while the bells are ringing, but it is not lucky to die on that day. The spoon with which the Easter eggs have been removed from the boiling pot is carefully treasured up, and worn in the belt by the shepherd; it gives him the power to distinguish the witches who seek to molest his flock.

Perhaps the most important day in the year is St. George's, the 23rd of April (corresponds to our 5th of May), the eve of which is still frequently kept by occult meetings taking place at night in lonely caverns or within ruined walls, and where all the ceremonies usual to the celebration of a witches' Sabbath are put into practice.

The feast itself is the great day to beware of witches, to counteract whose influence square-cut blocks of green turf are placed in front of each door and window. This is supposed effectually to bar their entrance to the house or stables, but for still greater safety it is usual here for the peasants to keep watch all night by the sleeping cattle.

This same night is the best for finding treasures, and many people spend it in wandering about the hills trying to probe the earth for the gold it contains. Vain and futile as such researches usually are, yet they have in this country a somewhat greater semblance of reason than in most other parts, for perhaps nowhere else have so many successive nations been forced to secrete their riches in flying from an enemy, to say nothing of the numerous veins of undiscovered gold and silver which must be seaming the country in all directions. Not a year passes without bringing to light some earthern jar containing old Dacian coins, or golden ornaments of Roman origin, and all such discoveries serve to feed and keep up the national superstition.

In the night of St. George's Day (so say the legends) all these treasures begin to burn, or, to speak in mystic language, to "bloom" in the bosom of the earth, and the light they give forth, described as a bluish flame resembling the colour of lighted spirits of wine, serves to guide favoured mortals to their place of concealment. The conditions to the successful raising of such a treasure are manifold, and difficult of accomplishment. In the first place, it is by no means easy for a common mortal who has not been born on a Sunday nor at midday when the bells are ringing, to hit upon a treasure at all. If he does, however, catch sight of a flame such as I have described, he must quickly stick a knife through the swaddling rags of his right foot, and then throw the knife in the direction of the flame he has seen. If two people are together during this discovery they must not on any account break silence till the treasure is removed, neither is it allowed to fill up the hole from which anything has been taken, for that would induce a speedy death. Another important feature to be noted is that the lights seen before midnight on St. George's Day, denote treasures kept by benevolent spirits, while those which appear at a later hour are unquestionably of a pernicious nature.

For the comfort of less-favoured mortals, who happen neither to have been born on a Sunday, nor during bell-ringing, I must here mention that these deficiencies may be to some extent condoned and the mental vision sharpened by the consumption of mouldy bread; so that whoever has during the preceding year been careful to feed upon decayed loaves only, may (if he survives this trying *régime*) be likewise the fortunate discoverer of hidden treasures.

Sometimes the power of discovering a particular treasure is supposed to be possessed only by members of some particular family. A curious instance of this was lately recorded in Roumenia relating to an old ruined convent, where, according to a popular legend, a large sum of gold is concealed. A deputation of peasants, at considerable trouble and expense, found out the last surviving member of the family supposed to possess the mystic power, and offered him, unconditionally, a very handsome sum merely for his assistance in the search. The gentleman in question, being old, and probably skeptical, declined the offer, to the great disappointment of the peasant deputation.

The feast of St. George, being the day when flocks are first driven out to pasture, is in a special manner the feast of all shepherds and cowherds, and on this day only it is allowed to count the flocks and assure oneself of the exact number of sheep. In general, these numbers are but approximately guessed at, and vaguely designated. Thus the Roumenian shepherd, interrogated as to the number of his master's sheep, will probably inform you that they are as numerous as the stars of heaven, or as the daisies which dot the meadows.

The throwing up of wreaths on to the roofs, described above, is in some districts practised on the feast of St. John the Baptist, the 24th of June (July 6th), instead of on the Wednesday in Holy Week. Fires lighted on the mountains this same night are supposed to protect the flocks from evil spirits.

The feast of St. Elias, the 20th of July (August 1), is a very unlucky day, on which the lightning may be expected to strike.

If a house struck by lightning begins to burn, it is not allowed to put out the flames, because God has lit the fire and it would be presumption if man were to dare to meddle. In some places it is believed that a fire lit by lightning can only be put out with milk.

An approved method for averting the danger of the dwelling being struck by lightning is to form a top by sticking a knife through a piece of bread, and spin it on the floor of the loft during the whole time the storm lasts. The ringing of bells is likewise very efficacious, provided, however, that the bell in question has been cast under a perfectly cloudless sky.

As I am on the subject of thunderstorms, I may as well here mention the *Scholomance,* or school supposed to exist somewhere in the heart of the mountains, and where all the secrets of nature, the language of animals, and all imaginable magic spells and charms are taught by the devil in person. Only ten scholars are admitted at a time, and when the course of learning has expired and nine of them are released to return to their homes, the tenth scholar is detained by the devil as payment, and mounted upon an *Ismeju* (dragon) he becomes henceforward the devil's aide-de-camp, and assists him in "making the weather"; that is to say, preparing the thunderbolts.

A small lake, immeasurably deep, lying high up among the mountains to the south of Hermanstadt, is supposed to be the cauldron where is brewed the thunder, and in fair weather the dragon sleeps beneath the waters. Roumenian peasants anxiously warn the traveller to beware of throwing a stone into this lake lest it should wake the dragon and provoke a thunderstorm. It is, however, no mere superstition that in summer there occur almost daily thunderstorms at this spot, about the hour of midday, and numerous cairns of stones round the shores attest the fact that many people have here found their death by lightning. On this account the place is shunned, and no Roumenians will venture to rest here at the hour of noon.

Whoever turns three somersaults the first time he hears the thunder will be free from pains in the back during a twelvemonth, and the man who wishes to be ensured against headache has only to rub it against a stone or knock it with a piece of iron.

The Polish harvest custom of decking out a girl with a wreath of corn ears, and leading her in procession to the house of the landed proprietor, is likewise practised here, with the difference that instead of the songs customary in Poland, the girl is here followed with loud cries of "Prihu! Prihu!" or else "Priku!" and that whoever meets her on the way is bound to sprinkle the wreath with water. If this detail be neglected the next year's crops will assuredly fail. It is also customary to keep the wreaths till next sowing time, when the corn is shaken out, and mingled with the grain to be sowed will ensure a rich harvest.

The feast of St. Spiridion, the 12th of December (corresponding to our 24th), is an ominous day, especially for housewives, and the saint often destroys those who desecrate his feast by manual labour.

That the cattle are endowed with speech during the Christmas night is a general belief, but it is not considered wise to pry upon them and try to overhear what they say, or the listener will rarely overhear any good.

This night is likewise favourable to the discovery of hidden treasures, and the man who has courage to conjure up the evil spirit will be sure to see him if he call upon him at midnight. Three burning coals placed upon the threshold will prevent the devil from carrying him off.

Christmas carols and dramas are also usual among the Roumenians, under the name of Kolinda, supposed to be derived from Kolinda or Lada, goddess of peace. Amongst the parts enacted in these games, are those of Judas, who stands at the door and receives the money collected, and that of the bull, called Turka or Tur, a sort of vague monster fantastically dressed up, half bull, half bear, with a clattering wooden bill, and a dash of Herod about his character, in so far as he is supposed to devour little children, and requires to be propitiated by a copper coin thrust into his bill. In many districts the personating of these characters is supposed to entail a certain amount of odium upon the actors, who are regarded as unclean or bewitched by the devil during a period of six weeks, and may not enter a church nor approach a sacrament till this time has elapsed.

A leaf of evergreen laid into a plate of water on the last day of the year when the bells are ringing will denote health, sickness, or death, during the coming year, according as it is found to be green, spotted, or black on the following morning.

The girl whose thoughts are turned towards love and matrimony has many approved methods of testing her fate on this night.

First of all she may, by cracking the joints of her fingers, accurately ascertain the number of her admirers, also a freshly laid egg broken into a glass of water will give much clue to the events in store for her by the shape it adopts. To form a conjecture as to the shape and build of her future husband, she is recommended to throw an armful of firewood as far as she can from her; the piece which has gone furthest will be the image of her intended, according as the stick happens to be tall or short, broad or slender, straight or crooked. If these general indications do not suffice, and she wishes to see the reflection of his face in the water, she has only to step naked at midnight into the nearest lake or river. Very efficacious is it likewise to stand at midnight on the dunghill with a piece of Christmas cake in her mouth, and listen for the first sound of a dog's barking which reaches her ear. From whichever side it proceeds will also come the expected suitor.

Of the household animals, the sheep is the most highly prized by the Roumenian, who makes of it his companion, and frequently his counsellor, and by its bearing it is supposed often to give warning when danger is near.

The swallow is here, as elsewhere, a luck-bringing bird, and goes by the name of *galinele lui Dieu* (fowls of the Lord). There is always a treasure to be found near the place where the first swallow has been espied.

The crow, on the contrary, is a bird of evil omen, and is particularly ominous when it flies straight over the head of any man.

The magpie perched upon a roof gives notice of the approach of guests, but a shrieking magpie meeting or accompanying a traveller denotes death.

The cuckoo is an oracle to be consulted in manifold contingencies. This bird plays a great part in Roumenian poetry, and is frequently supposed to be the spirit of an unfortunate lover.

It is never permissible to kill a spider, as that would entail misfortune.

A toad taking up its residence in a cow-byre is assuredly in the service of a witch, and has been sent there to purloin the milk. It should therefore be stoned to death; but the same liberty must not be taken with the equally pernicious weasel, and if these animals be found to inhabit a barn or stable, the peasant must endeavour to render them harmless by diverting their thoughts into a safer channel. To this end a tiny threshing-flail must be prepared for the male weasel, and a distaff for his female partner, and laid at a place the animals are known to frequent.

The skull of a horse placed over the gate of the courtyard, or the bones of fallen animals, buried under the doorstep, are preservatives against ghosts.

The place where a horse has rolled on the ground is unwholesome, and the man who steps upon it will be speedily attacked by eruptions, boils, or other skin diseases.

Black fowls are always viewed with suspicion, as possibly standing in the service of a witch, and the Brahmaputra fowl is curiously enough considered to be the offspring of the devil with a Jewish girl.

If a cow has gone astray it will assuredly be eaten by the wolf, unless the owner remembers to stick a pair of scissors in the centre rafter of the dwelling-room.

As a matter of course, such places as churchyards, gallow-trees, and cross-roads are to be avoided, but even the left bank of a river may under circumstances become equally dangerous.

A whirlwind always denotes that the devil is dancing with a witch, and whoever approaches too near to this dangerous circle may be carried off bodily, or at the very least will lose his head-covering.

But the Roumenian does not always endeavour to keep the evil one at arm's length; sometimes, on the contrary, he invokes the devil's assistance, and enters into a regular compact with him.

Supposing, for instance, that he wishes to ensure a flock, garden or field against thieves, wild beasts, or bad weather, the matter is very simple. He has only to repair to a cross-road, at the junction of which he takes up his stand, in the centre of a circle he has traced on the ground. Here, after depositing a copper coin as payment, he summons the demon with the following words:—

"Satan, I give thee over my flock (garden or field) to keep till—— (such and such a term), that thou mayest defend and protect it for me, and be my servant till this time has expired——."

He must, however, be careful to keep within the circle he has traced, until the devil, who may very likely have chosen to appear in the shape of a goat, crow, toad, or serpent, has completely disappeared, otherwise the unfortunate wretch is irretrievably lost. He is equally sure to lose his soul if he die before the time of the contract has elapsed.

An apothecary of this town (Hermanstadt) told me that he was frequently applied to for a magic potion called *spiridusch,* which is said to have the property of disclosing hidden treasures to its lucky possessor. Only a few weeks ago he received the following letter, published in one of the local papers, and which I have here translated as literally as possible.

Worthy Sir,—I wish to ask you of something I have been told by others—that is, that you have got for sale a thing they call spiridusch, *but which, to speak more plainly, is the devil himself. And if this be true, I beg you to tell me if it be really true, and how much it costs; for my poverty is so great and has brought me so far that I must ask the devil to help me. Those who told me this were weak, silly fellows, and were afraid, but I have no fear and have seen many things in my life before; therefore I beg you to write me this, and to take the greeting of an unknown man.—N. N.*

Here, as elsewhere, thirteen is an ominous number.

It is unfortunate to meet an old woman or a Roumenian pope; the meeting of a Protestant or Catholic clergyman is indifferent, and brings neither good nor evil.

It is bad luck if your path be traversed by a hare, but a fox or wolf crossing your road is a good omen.

Likewise, it is lucky to meet a woman with a jug full of water, while an empty jug is unlucky; therefore, the Roumenian maiden who meets you on the way back from the well will, smiling, display her brimming pitcher as she passes, with a pleased consciousness of bringing good luck; while the girl whose pitcher is empty will slink past shamefacedly, as though she had a crime to conceal.

Every orthodox Roumenian woman is careful to do homage to the water-spirit, the *wodna zena or zona,* which resides in each spring, by spilling a few drops on the ground, after she has emptied her jug. She will never venture to draw the water against the current, for that would strike the spirit home and provoke her anger.

The Roumenian in general avoids the neighbourhood of deep pools of water, especially whirlpools, for here resides the dreadful *balaur,* or the *wodna muz,* the cruel waterman who lies in wait for human victims.

Each forest has likewise its own particular spirit, its *mama padura,* or forest mother. This fairy is in general supposed to be good-natured, especially towards children who have lost their way in the wood. Less to be trusted is *Panusch* (surely a corruption of the Greek god Pan?), who haunts the forest glades and lies in wait for helpless maidens.

Ravaging diseases, like the pest, cholera, &c., are attributed to a spirit called the *dschuma,* to whom is sometimes given the shape of a fierce virgin, sometimes that of a toothless old hag. This spectre can only be driven away if a red shirt, which must be spun, woven, and sewed all in one night by seven old women, is hung out at the entrance of the afflicted village.

The body of a drowned man can only be found again by sticking a lighted candle into a hollowed-out loaf of bread and setting it afloat at night on the river or lake. There where the light comes to a standstill will the corpse be found. Until this has been done the water will continue to rise and the rain to fall.

At the birth of a child each one present takes a stone, and throws it behind him, saying, "This into the jaws of the Strigoi," which custom would also seem to suggest Saturn and the swaddled-up stones. As long as the child is unbaptised, it must be carefully watched over, for fear of being changed or otherwise harmed by witch. A piece of iron or a broom laid under its pillow will keep evil charms away.

Even the Roumenian's wedding day is darkened by the shade of superstition. He can never be quite sure of his affection for his bride being a natural, spontaneous feeling, since it may or will have been caused by the evil influence of a witch. Also at church, when the priest offers the blest bread to himself and his new-made wife, he will tremblingly compare the relative sizes of the two pieces, for whoever chances to get the smaller one must inevitably be the first to die.

But nowhere does the inherent superstition of the Roumenian peasant find stronger expression than in his mourning and funeral ceremonies, which are based upon a totally original conception of death.

Among the various omens of approaching death are the ungrounded barking of a dog or the crowing of a black hen. The influence of the latter may, however, be annulled and the catastrophe averted if the bird be put in a sack and carried thrice round the house.

Roots dug up from the churchyard on Good Friday are to be given to people in danger of death. If, however, this and other remedies fail to save the doomed man, then he must have a burning candle put into his hand; for it is considered to be the greatest of all misfortunes if a man die without a candle—a favour the Roumenian durst not refuse to his most deadly enemy.

The corpse must be washed immediately after death, and the dirt, if necessary, scraped off with knives, because the dead man is more likely to find favour with God if he appear before Him in a clean state. Then he is attired in his best clothes, in doing which great care must be taken not to tie anything in a knot, for that would disturb his rest; likewise, he must not be allowed to carry away any particle of iron about his dress (such as buttons, boot nails, &c.), for this would assuredly prevent him from reaching Paradise, the road to which is long, and is, moreover, divided off by several tolls or ferries. To enable the soul to pass through these a piece of money must be laid in the hand, under the pillow, or beneath the tongue of the corpse. In the neighbourhood of Fogaras, where the ferries or toll-bars are supposed to amount to twenty-five, the hair of the defunct is divided into as many plaits, and a piece of money secured in each. Likewise, a small provision of needles, pins, thread, &c., are put into the coffin to enable the pilgrim to repair any damage his clothes may receive on the way.

The mourning songs, called *Bocete,* usually performed by paid mourners, are directly addressed to the corpse and sung into his ear on either side. This is the last attempt made by the survivors to wake the dead man to life, by reminding him of all he is leaving, and urging him to make a final effort to arouse his dormant faculties—the thought which underlies all these proceedings being, that the dead man hears and sees all that goes on around him, and that it only requires the determined effort of a strong will in order to restore elasticity to the stiffened limbs, and cause the torpid blood to flow again within the veins.

In many places two openings, corresponding to the ears of the deceased, are cut out in the wood of the coffin to enable him to hear the songs of mourning which are sung on either side of him as he is carried to the grave.

This singing into the ears has passed into a proverb, and when the Roumenian says, *i-a-cantat la wechia* (he has sung into his ears), it is tantamount to saying that prayer and admonition have been used in vain.

The *Pomana,* or funeral feast, is invariably held after the funeral, for much of the peace of the defunct depends upon the strict observance of this ceremony. At this banquet all the favourite dishes of the dead man are served, and each guest receives a cake (*colac*) and a jug (*ulcior*), also a wax candle, in his memory. Similar *Pomanas* are repeated after a fortnight, six weeks, and on each anniversary for the next seven years; also, whenever the defunct has appeared in dream to any member of the family, this likewise calls for another *Pomana;* and when these conditions are not exactly complied with, the soul thus neglected is apt to wander complaining about the earth, and cannot find rest. These restless spirits, called *Strigoi,* are not malicious, but their appearance bodes no good, and may be regarded as omens of sickness or misfortune.

More decidedly evil, however, is the vampire, or *nosferatu,* in whom every Roumenian peasant believes as firmly as he does in heaven or hell. There are two sorts of vampires—living and dead. The living vampire is in general the illegitimate offspring of two illegitimate persons, but even a flawless pedigree will not ensure anyone against the intrusion of a vampire into his family vault, since every person killed by a *nosferatu* becomes likewise a vampire after death, and will continue to suck the blood of other innocent people till the spirit has been exorcised, either by opening the grave of the person suspected and driving a stake through the corpse, or firing a pistol shot into the coffin. In very obstinate cases it is further recommended to cut off the head and replace it in the coffin with the mouth filled with garlic, or to extract the heart and burn it, strewing the ashes over the grave.

That such remedies are often resorted to, even in our enlightened days, is a well-attested fact, and there are probably few Roumenian villages where such has not taken place within the memory of the inhabitants.

First cousin to the vampire, the long exploded were-wolf of the Germans is here to be found, lingering yet under the name of the *Prikolitsch*. Sometimes it is a dog instead of a wolf, whose form a man has taken either voluntarily or as penance for his sins. In one of the villages a story is still told (and believed) of such a man, who driving home from church on Sunday with his wife, suddenly felt that the time for his transformation had come. He therefore gave over the reins to her, and stepped aside into the bushes, where, murmuring the mystic formula, he turned three somersaults over a ditch. Soon after this the woman, waiting in vain for her husband, was attacked by a furious dog, which rushed, barking, out of the bushes and succeeded in biting her severely, as well as tearing her dress. When, an hour later, this woman reached home alone she was met by her husband, who advanced smiling to meet her, but between his teeth she caught sight of the shreds of her dress which had been bitten out by the dog, and the horror of the discovery caused her to faint away.

Another man used gravely to assert that for more than five years he had gone about in the form of a wolf, leading on a troop of these animals, until a hunter, in striking off his head, restored him to his natural shape.

A French traveller relates an instance of a harmless botanist who, while collecting herbs on a hillside in a crouching attitude, was observed by some peasants at a distance and taken for a wolf. Before they had time to reach him, however, he had risen to his feet and disclosed himself in the form of a man; but this, in the minds of the Roumenians, who now regarded him as an aggravated case of wolf, was but additional motive for attacking him. They were quite sure that he must be a Prikolitsch, for only such could change his shape in such an unaccountable manner, and in another minute they were all in full cry after the wretched victim of science, who might have fared badly indeed, had he not happened to gain a carriage on the high road before his pursuers came up.

We do not require to go far for the explanation of the extraordinary tenacity of life of the were-wolf legend in a country like Transylvania, where real wolves still abound. Every winter here brings fresh proof of the boldness and cunning of these terrible animals, whose attacks on flocks and farms are often conducted with a skill which would do honour to a human intellect. Sometimes a whole village is kept in trepidation for weeks together by some particularly audacious leader of a flock of wolves, to whom the peasants not unnaturally attribute a more than animal nature, and one may safely prophesy that so long as the real wolf continues to haunt the Transylvanian forests, so long will his spectre brother survive in the minds of the inhabitants.

Many ancient Roumenian legends tell us that every new church or otherwise important building became a human grave, as it was thought indispensable to its stability to wall in a living man or woman, whose spirit henceforward haunts the place. In later times people having become less cruel, or more probably, because murder is now attended with greater inconvenience to the actors, this custom underwent some modifications, and it became usual in place of a living man to wall in his shadow instead. This is done by measuring the shadow of a person with a long piece of cord, or a ribbon made of strips of reed, and interring this measure instead of the person himself, who, unconscious victim of the spell thrown upon him, will pine away and die within forty days. It is an indispensable condition to the success of this proceeding that the chosen victim be ignorant of the part he is playing, therefore careless passers-by near a building place may often hear the warning cry "Beware, lest they take thy shadow!" So deeply engrained is this superstition that not long ago there were still professional shadow-traders, who made it their business to provide architects with the necessary victims for securing their walls. "Of course the man whose shadow is thus interred must die," argues the Roumenian, "but as he is unaware of his doom he does not feel any pain or anxiety, so it is less cruel than walling in a living man."

The superstitions afloat among the Saxon peasantry of Transylvania relate oftenest to household matters, such as the well-being of cattle and poultry and the success of the harvest or vintage. There is more of the quack, and less of the romantic element to be found here, and the invisible spiritual world plays less part in their beliefs.

Some of the most prevalent Saxon superstitions are as follows:

1. Whoever can blow back the flame into a candle which has just been extinguished will become pastor.

2. In going into a new-built house one must throw in a dog or a cat before entering, otherwise one of the family will soon die.

3. If a swallow flies under a cow straightaway the milk will become bloody.

4. Whoever enters a strange house should sit down, were it only for a second, otherwise he will deprive the inhabitants of their sleep.

5. Whoever has been robbed of anything and wants to discover the thief, must select a black hen, and for nine consecutive Fridays must, as well as the hen, abstain from all food. The thief will then either die or bring back the stolen goods. (This is called taking up the black fast against a person.)

6. It is not good to point with the finger at an approaching thunderstorm; likewise, whoever stands over-long gazing at the summer lightning will go mad.

7. A person ill with the fever should be covered up with nine articles of clothing, each of a different colour and material: he will then recover.

8. Another way to get rid of the fever is to go into an inn or public-house, and after having drunk a glass of wine to go out again without speaking or paying, but leaving behind some article of clothing which is of greater value than the wine drunk.

9. Drinking out of seven different wells is likewise good for the fever.

10. Or else go into the garden when no one is looking, shake a young fruit tree and return to the house without looking back; the fever will then have passed into the tree.

11. Any article purposely dropped on the ground when out walking will convey the fever to whoever finds it. This method is, however, to be distrusted (we are told by village authorities), for the finder may avert the illness by thrice spitting on the thing in question. Spitting on all and every occasion is in general very efficacious for averting spells and other evils.

12. A hailstorm may sometimes be stopped by a knife stuck into the ground in front of the house.

13. A new servant must be allowed to eat freely the first day he or she enters service, otherwise their hunger will never be stilled.

14. It is bad luck to rock an empty cradle.

15. When someone has just died the window must be opened to let the soul escape.

16. It is not considered good to count the beehives or the loaves when they are put into the oven.

17. When the master of the house dies, one must go and tell it to the bees, and to the cattle in the stables, otherwise some new misfortune is sure to happen.

18. If the New Year's night be clear the hens will lay many eggs during the year.

19. It is not good to whitewash the house when the moon is decreasing, for that produces bugs.

20. Who eats mouldy bread will be rich and longlived.

21. Rubbing the body with garlic is a preservative against witchcraft and the pest.

22. Licking the platter clean at table will bring fine weather.

23. A funeral at which the bells are not rung brings hail.

24. When foxes and wolves meet in the market-place then prices will rise (naturally, since wolves and foxes could only be so bold during the greatest cold, when prices of eggs, butter, &c., are always at their highest).

25. To keep sparrows off a field or garden it is only necessary to sprinkle earth taken at midnight from the churchyard over the place.

26. A broom put upside down behind the door will keep away the witches.

27. It is bad luck to lay a loaf upside down on the table.

28. In carrying a child to church to be christened it is important to carry it by the broadest streets, and to avoid narrow lanes and byways, else when it is big it will become a thief.

29. If a murderer be confronted with the corpse of his victim the wounds will begin to bleed again.

30. Avoid a toad, as it may be a witch.

31. Little children's nails should be bitten off instead of cut the first time, lest they learn to steal.

32. An approved sort of love charm is to take the two hind legs of a green tree-frog, bury these in an anthill till all the flesh is removed, then tie them up securely in a linen handkerchief, and whosoever touches this linen will be seized at once with love for its owner.

33. To avert many illnesses which may occur to the pigs, it is still customary in some places for the swineherd to dispense with his clothes the first time he drives out his pigs to pasture in spring. A newly elected clergyman, regarding this practice as immoral, tried to forbid it in his parish, but was sternly asked by the village bailiff whether he was prepared to pay for all the pigs which would assuredly die that year in consequence of the omission.

34. The same absence of costume is likewise recommended to women assisting a cow to calve.

The night of St. Thomas (21st of December) is the date consecrated by Saxon superstition to the celebration of the games which elsewhere are usual on All-Halloween. Every girl puts her fate to the test on this evening, and there are various ways of so doing (too lengthy to be here described), with shoes, flowers, onions, &c. For the twelve days following it is not allowed to spin, and the young men who visit the spinning-room of the girls have the right to break and burn all the distaffs they find, so it has become usual for the maidens to appear with a stick dressed up with wool to represent the distaff instead of a real spinning-wheel.

Some of the Saxon customs are peculiarly interesting from being obviously remnants of Paganism, and are a curious proof of the force of verbal tradition, which in this case has not only borne the transplantation from a far distant country, but likewise weathered the storm of two successive changes of religion.

A very strong proof of the tenacity of Pagan habits and train of thought is, I think, the fact, that although at the time these Saxon colonists appeared in Transylvania, towards the second part of the twelfth century, they had already belonged to the Christian Church for more than three hundred years, yet many points of the landscape in their new home baptized by them have received Pagan appellations. Thus we find the *Götzenberg,* or mountain of the gods, and the *wodesch* and the *wolnk* applied to woods and plains, both evidently derived from Wodan.

Many old Pagan ceremonies are still clearly to be distinguished through the flimsy shrouding of a later period, and their origin unmistakable even through the surface-varnish of Christianity which was thought necessary to adapt them to newer circumstances, and like a clumsily remodelled garment the original cut frequently asserts itself, despite the fashionable trimmings which now adorn it. In many popular rhymes and dialogues, for instance, it has been clearly proved that those parts now assigned to the Saviour and St. Peter originally belonged to the old gods Thor and Loki; while the faithless Judas has had the personification of a whole hoard of German demons thrust upon him. It is likewise strongly to be suspected that St. Elias who in some parts of Hungary, as well as in Roumenia, Serbia, and Croatia, is considered the proper person to be invoked in thunderstorms, is verily no other than the old thunder god Thor, under a Christian mask.

One of the most striking of the Christianised dramas just mentioned is the *Todaustragen,* or throwing out the Death, a custom still extant in several of the Transylvanian Saxon villages, and which may likewise be found still existing in some remote parts of Germany. The feast of the Ascension is the day on which this ceremony takes place in a village of this neighbourhood. It is conducted in the following manner:—

After forenoon church on that day, the school-girls of the parish repair to the house of one of their companions, and there proceed to dress up the "Death." This is done by tying up a threshed-out corn-sheaf into the rough semblance of a head and body, while the arms are simulated by a broomstick stuck horizontally. This done, the figure is dressed up in the Sunday clothes of a young village matron, the head adorned with the customary cap and veil fastened by silver pins; two large black beads, or black-headed pins, represent the eyes, and thus equipped the figure is displayed at the open window, in order that all people may see it, on their way to afternoon church. The conclusion of vespers is the signal for the girls to seize the figure and open the procession round the village; two of the eldest girls hold the "Death" between them, and the others follow in regular order two and two, singing a Lutheran Church hymn. The boys are excluded from the procession, and must content themselves with admiring the *Schöner Tod* (handsome Death) from a distance. When all the village streets have been traversed in this manner, the girls repair to another house, whose door is locked against the besieging troop of boys. The figure Death is here stripped of its gaudy attire, and the naked straw bundle thrown out of the window, whereupon it is seized by the boys and carried off in triumph to be thrown into the neighbouring stream or river. This is the first part of the drama, while the second consists in one of the girls being solemnly invested with the clothes and ornaments previously worn by the figure, and like it, led in procession round the village to the singing of the same hymn as before. This is to represent the arrival of summer. The ceremony terminates by a feast given by the parents of the girl who has acted the principal part, from which the boys are again excluded.

According to popular belief it is allowed to eat fruits only after this day, as now the "Death," that is, the unwholesomeness, has been expelled from them. Also the river in which the Death has been drowned may now be considered fit for public bathing.

If this ceremony be ever omitted in the villages where it is customary, this neglect is supposed to entail the death of one of the youths or maidens.

This same ceremony may, as I have said, be found still lingering in many other places, everywhere with slight variations. There are villages where the figure is burnt instead of drowned, and Passion Sunday (often called the Dead Sunday), or else the 25th of March, are the days sometimes chosen for its accomplishment. In some places it was usual for the straw figure to be attired in the shirt of the last person who had died, and with the veil of the most recent bride on its head. Also the figure is occasionally pelted with stones by the youth of both sexes; whoever hits it will not die during the year.

At Nuremberg little girls dressed in white used to go in procession through the town, carrying a small open coffin, in which a doll was laid out in state, or sometimes only a stick dressed up, with an apple to represent the head.

In many of these German places, the rhymes which are sung apply to the advent of summer and the extinction of winter, such as the following:—

> *And now we have chased the death away*
> *And brought in the summer so warm and so gay;*
> *The summer and the month of May*
> *We bring sweet flowers full many a one.*
> *We bring the rays of the golden sun,*
> *For the dreary death at last is gone.*

or else,

> *Come all of you and do not tarry*
> *The evil death away to carry;*
> *Come, spring, once more, with us to dwell,*
> *Welcome, O spring, in wood and dell!*

And there is no doubt that similar rhymes used also to be sung here, until they were replaced by the Lutheran hymns.

Some German archaeologists have attempted to prove that "death" in these games is of more recent introduction, and has replaced the "winter" of former times, so as to give the ceremony a more Christian colouring by the allusion of the triumph of Christ over death, on His resurrection and ascension into heaven. Without presuming to contradict the many well-known authorities who have taken this view of the case, I cannot help thinking that it hardly requires such explanation to account for the presence of death in these dramas. Nowadays, when luxury and civilisation have done so much towards equalising all seasons, so that we can never be deprived of flowers in winter, nor want for ice in summer, we can with difficulty realise the enormous gulf which in olden times separated winter from summer. Not only in winter were all means of communication cut off for a large proportion of people, but their very existence was, so to say, frozen up; and if the granaries were scantily filled, or the inclement season prolonged by some weeks, death was literally standing at the door of thousands of poor wretches. No wonder, then, that winter and death became identical in their minds, and that they hailed the advent of spring with delirious joy, dancing round the first violet, and following about the first cockchafer in solemn procession. It was the feast of Nature which they celebrated then as now—Nature mighty and eternal—which must always remain essentially the same, whether decked out in Pagan or Christian garb.

Another remnant of Paganism is the *Feurix* or *Feuriswolf,* which lingers yet in the mind of these people. According to ancient German mythology the *Feuriswolf* is a monster which, on the last day, is to open his mouth so wide that the top jaw touches the sky, and the lower one the earth; and not long ago a Saxon woman bitterly complained in a court of justice that her husband had cursed her over strongly, in saying, "Der wärlthangd saul dich frieszen"; literally, "May the world-dog swallow thee!"

The gipsies take up a different position as regards superstition from either Roumenian or Saxon, since they may be rather considered to be direct causes and mainsprings of superstition, than victims of credulity themselves. The Tzigane, whose religion is of such an extremely superficial nature that he rarely believes in anything as complicated as the immortality of the soul, can hardly be supposed to lay much weight upon the supernatural; and if he instinctively avoids such places as churchyards, gallow-trees, &c., his feelings are rather those of a child who shirks being reminded of anything so unpleasant as death or burial.

That, however, these people exercise a considerable influence on their Saxon and Roumenian neighbours is undoubted, and it is a paradoxical fact, that the same people who regard the gipsy as an undoubted thief, liar, and cheat, in all the common transactions of daily life, do not hesitate to confide in him blindly for charmed medicines and love-potions, and are ready to attribute to him unerring power in deciphering the mysteries of the future.

The Saxon peasant will, it is true, often drive away the fortune-teller with blows and curses from his door, but his wife, as often as not, will secretly beckon to her to come in again by the back door, in order to be consulted as to the illness of the cows, or to beg from her a remedy against the fever.

Wonderful potions and salves, in which the fat of bears, dogs, snakes and snails, along with the oil of rain-worms, the bodies of spiders and midges rubbed into a paste, and many other similar ingredients, are concocted by these cunning Bohemians, who will sometimes thus make thrice as much money out of the carcass of a dead dog as another from the sale of three healthy pigs.

It has also been averred that both Roumenian and Saxon mothers, whose sickly infants are thought to be suffering from the effects of the evil eye, are frequently in the habit of giving the child to be nursed for a period of nine days to some gipsy woman, who is supposed to be able to undo the spell.

There is not a village which does not boast of one or more fortune-tellers, and living in the suburbs of each town are many old women who make an easy and comfortable livelihood only by imposing on the credulity of their fellow-creatures.

The gipsies, one of whose principal trades is the burning of bricks and tiles, are often accused of occasioning lengthy droughts to suit their own purposes. When this has occurred, and the necessary rains have not been produced by soundly beating the guilty Tziganes, the Roumenians sometimes resort to the *Papaluga,* or Rain-maiden. This is done by stripping a young gipsy girl quite naked, and dressing her up with wreaths of flowers and leaves which entirely cover her up, leaving only the head visible. Thus adorned, the Papaluga is conducted round the villages in procession, to the sound of music and singing, and every-one hastens to water her copiously.

If also the Papaluga fails to bring the desired rain, then the evil must evidently be of a deeper and more serious nature, and is to be attributed to a vampire, who must be sought out and destroyed in the manner described above.

The part of the Papaluga is also sometimes enacted by a Roumenian maiden, when there is no reason to suspect the gipsies of being concerned in the drought. This custom of the Rain-maiden is also to be found in Serbia, and I believe in Croatia.

It would be endless were I to attempt to enumerate all the different sorts of superstition afloat in this country; for besides the three principal definitions here given, the subject comprises innumerable other side branches, and might further be divided into the folk-lore of shepherds, farmers, hunters, miners, fishermen, &c., each of these separate callings having its own peculiar set of signs, customs, charms, and traditions to go by.

Superstition is an evil which every person with a well-balanced mind should wish to die out, yet it cannot be denied that some of these fancies are graceful and suggestive. Nettles and briars, albeit mischievous plants, may yet come in picturesquely in a landscape; and although the stern agriculturist is bound to rejoice at their uprooting, the softer-hearted artist is surely free to give them a passing sigh of regret.

29

WORK AND ITS REWARDS

The Vampyre does not use words without considering them. In Setian culture we call our practice "work" and our rituals "workings." In an essay for the church magazine The Scroll of Set, *I shared some observations on these occult terms.*

WHAT IS WORK?

In Setian culture we toss the word *work* around all the time. We call Initiation "working on ourselves," and in some post-Masonic nomenclature we call rituals "workings." We sound like our host culture of Protestant America. We like the Fourth Way crowd; they always talk about work. We even say that a I° can become II° by working really hard.

That all sounds great and noble. I'm not sitting on my butt; I'm working, see? Except we become a little vague when we are asked what work is.

This essay will address a few topics, such as the relationship of Xeper and work, what kinds of work can give you the most reward for effort, and lastly what those rewards should be. This essay is designed for the new First Degree, but I imagine it is relevant to everybody.

There is a natural order of things and an unnatural order. In the natural order small kids do not steal their older brother's bikes. Yesterday an eight-year-old down the block pinched his brother's bicycle. He pedaled in a rather wobbly way past me and screamed, "I'm doing it! Now what do I do?" I had (undesirably) entered into a Third Degree and First Degree relationship with him. I had to advise him on the fly

313

how to ride and not head out into the much busier streets nearby. I had ridden a bicycle before, and I had a better view of where he was going because of my height and position on the ground. So I began my priestly spiel about balance and leaning into a curve.

WORK IS . . .

Work is altering the interrelationships within your mind-body-soul complex and the elements in your home, school, and place of employment to facilitate Xeper. Work is rather like maintaining a car. If you maintain your vehicle, you can drive to your job every day, or flee a hurricane, drive to your mother's house at Yule, or even drive off to the most amazing vacation ever. Work is not Xeper, anymore than maintaining your car is driving. Some work is pleasant, some hard. Some aspects of work will come easy for you, other types are hard. Work proceeds better in a community where you can see its rewards, and get feedback on your methods. Work done on the self without a community becomes unbalanced. We will do what is easiest for us to do, and shy away from what is hardest.

Work may be hard, but does not tire you out. It gives you access to energy beyond your normal levels. When Setians loose sight of the first two steads of work, their actions become unharmonious and they burn out.

During the First Degree we need the feedback of others to find our blind spots, but we also need the freedom to make our own judgments about what we want to develop. For some people a really good car sound system is a prerequisite for long travel; for others it's all about getting a GPS. Since Xeper is measured by "power to do things" it is often confused with work. For example, going through a college degree is certainly work, but it is not Xeper. Many aspects of Xeper will have manifested in this endeavor: for example, you may have overcome your fear of public speaking, or learned to quiet your emotions the night your boyfriend dumped you before a test—but the college degree itself is a tool that your Xeper will use. Xeper is the mediator between your changeless core and the work you have wrought on those parts of yourself and the world that does change. Xeper grows each time you gain in knowledge and in access to your Greater Self. Xeper likewise grows when you increase your empowerment and abilities in those aspects of the Cosmos you can rationally decide to improve and work upon. Xeper moves through a series of levels as the Essence that is uniquely you is able to express itself more perfectly in a world you have designed. If you focus only on the inner, timeless you, you are a yogin. If you focus only on changing your life space, you are a Satanist. Each of these paths leads to a form of freedom, but each loses half of what you might Become.

There are certain steads of work that can give you quicker access to Xeper. Some of these your priest may advise you upon, others are too personal, but you should understand their existence. Your first piece of work after reading this article is to see what steads of work you have some mastery in and what steads are undeveloped for you. Your second job will be to begin to use the words *work* and *Xeper* more accurately. Your third job will be to make plans to work better. The magic of the community comes into place here—other Setians are making similar plans for themselves, and thus new opportunities will come into being when you need them the most. The Aeon grows from work, and as it grows the Prince of Darkness may affect the world of becoming to reflect His Essence just as we seek to. The synchronicities between Set's Will and our own is the means whereby Set shares his Essence with us. We may pursue our goals with utter selfishness, but the goals themselves harmonize and work together. We Setians benefit from this epiphenomenon, and our enemies suffer from it as well. Thus social change happens at a deep level.

Setians require four attitudes to turn the day-to-day actions they practice into work:

1. Honest self-reporting. The Setian must learn to neither lie by being too self-congratulatory nor be too harsh with herself. She must learn to be honest with herself, her Temple, and her Recognizing clergy.
2. Daring. The Setian must move past her fears (especially the fear of what others may think). The internal fetters of convention and bad self-image bind the coming of Xeper.

3. Willingness to trust the Greater Self. When opportunities arise "out of the blue," take them. Whether it's a chance to go to a powwow, see new art in a museum, talk to the woman of your dreams in a bar, or sign up for a philosophy class—be aware that the immortal part of yourself is always reaching out to you. Don't be afraid to lose rational control and try new things—just as you no longer fear making rationality be in charge of your habits and routines.

4. Willingness to make the super-effort. We shouldn't work hard all the time. We should play, rest, sleep, dream, and spend restorative time with our family, animal companions, and friends. But we must be aware that our Greater Self will occasionally present us with some really hard task. We must learn to discern these and really push ourselves.

THE STEADS OF WORK

1. Knowledge of Desire. The Left-Hand Path begins with the notion that desire is good, and accepts that it brings both pleasures and pains. The seeker uses her desire to fuel all things, understanding that desire is what isolates her from the universe. Seekers also know that their desire has been obscured from them by a society that wants to control their livelihood and money. Isolating and refining desire is the basis of the Left-Hand Path.

2. Practical self-empowerment. The Setian seeks real power in the real world. It does not matter if the empowerment is the work of getting a new IT certification, taking painting classes, or learning to bowl better. Practical empowerment can be buying a new car, or setting up for your retirement. The Setian seeks to be ever more effective in areas where his or her desire lays. This gives a practical base for Xeper to express itself.

3. Work on the body. The Setian seeks to have greater health, sensual pleasure, and strength in his or her body. The body is the greatest teacher of desire, patience, and the need for constant striving. The body is not a "magical tool"—it is magic. The nature of the work depends on the Setian—Setian A may train for marathons, while Setian B is just watching what he eats. The body is not a hindrance for the soul, it is the Temple through which the soul receives offerings.

4. Work on the emotions. Often humans called to initiation have had great pain in their lives, some early trauma made them resort to magic. Setians must first seek to heal themselves of hurt, then seek to feel more deeply, and lastly make their emotions follow them, rather than they follow their emotions. The nature of this work, which can range from finding a therapist to healing a rift in one's family, is up to the individual Setian.

5. Work on the mind. First, the Setian must learn critical thinking and logic, both to replace unexamined beliefs and to become less the plaything of others. Then he or she must become conversant with the *Crystal Tablet*. Lastly, the Setian must become aware of cognition itself, perhaps by perusing Susan Blakemore's *Consciousness: A Very Short Introduction* or Robert Anton Wilson's *Quantum Pscyhology*.

6. Gaining magical skill. Setians should learn first to use the rubric in the *Crystal Tablet,* then to try as many techniques as they like using both self-created and traditional means.

7. Skill in meta-communication. Setians must learn how to express their Will to others through dress, public speaking, Lesser Black Magic, neurolingustic programming and other skills. The Setian's desire will take more than one head to think through, more than one body to build.

8. Skill in reporting. The Setian learns how to report her triumphs and failings. First, to herself, most likely in the form of a diary; second, to a priest for feedback; and third, in her life, so that she attracts the mates, jobs, friends, and opportunities she desires.

9. Conclave. This is a basic magical task. Pulling it off is a sign that all other steads are doing well. If extreme distances keep you from going to Conclave, how can you bring the Temple to you? Can you make a gathering in your home, have Skype chats, and so forth? Because of the work it takes to get to Conclave or other gatherings, great Initation can pass from mouth to ear in a manner that simply reading a book or an email cannot give you.

THE REWARDS OF WORK

1. Self-knowledge. No other pursuit defines and reveals the Self to the self as does discovering, articulating, and amplifying your desire. In this type of self-remembering you will learn you exist, and you will be able to give meaning to all things in your life.

2. Practical power. You will be able to have greater power and pleasure—not based on someone else's model, but on your own. You will understand that the simple human deeds you choose can be as holy and deep as the most far-flung magical endeavors.

3. Greater health and pleasure. You will feel good in your body. Everything that ever took your body away from you—other kids teasing you, illness, drugs, rape—you will give back to yourself. When you leave shock, dullness, and disease for as much vitality as you can self-generate, you will find a great deal more magical power becomes available to you. If you are doing well by your body, you will be able to accept its aging as the prompts of a friend to help you with your Xeper. In the end, your body is your best priest.

4. A happy heart. Setians are deeply passionate beings, but slowly the average mood that comes by working on the emotions is a happy alert calmness.

5. An easier-to-use mind. You will become uncluttered by faulty logic, and will learn to use your mind in ways that only lucky circumstance could have given you.

6. Greater magical power. You will both be able to enjoy magic as an art form, but be able to get better results.

7. Tribe building. Instead of being a follower in another's tribe, you will build a tribe that follows you. Setians are not a tribe—too many chiefs; rather we are a chosen band of tribal leaders engaged in cultural and world change and having a good time while doing it.

8. Honestly, You will come to be able to speak without fear of authority or social ridicule. You will be able to speak or be silent about yourself among people that have earned your trust and respect as you have earned theirs. You will change in that, by this level, what you speak of will simply come into being.

9. You will become a builder of Setian culture and community. By journeying to Conclave, you will meet lifelong friends, maybe even life partners. By honestly sharing your joys and struggles you will become part of a community that is developing new and better forms of magic and philosophy, new and better ways to see the world, new and better ways to act upon the world. Thus your desires can be fulfilled.

30

A Selected Work of Fiction

THIRTEEN LINES

The relationship between the Vampyre and art is deep and complex. I wrote this tale for Blood Muse: Timeless Tales of Vampires in the Arts, *edited by Esther Friesner and Martin H. Greenberg (New York, Dutton Books, 1995).*

Before I encountered the unfinished sonnet of Henry Salt, I would have said that there was nothing in the world that was worth my life. Everything has changed by my reading the thirteen lines. I now know Love and Terror.

My door into the place of damnation was (appropriately enough) the love of money. I work as a research assistant at the Harry Ransom Center at the University of Texas. We've got quite a collection including the fine copy of Bram Stoker's *Dracula;* you should stop by some time. My job is to aid those scholars and seekers after the mysteries that visit our air-conditioned halls. Sometimes the work is both hard and exhilarating; sometimes there is nothing to do. Being the thrifty sort that I am, I use my free time to produce little gems of independent scholarship that I sell for small recompense. My real name does not matter, but perhaps you know my pseudonym of John Kincaid, who writes lots of articles about the paranormal or the just plain weird.

I had an idea for a honey of an article on strange manuscripts and cursed books. I figured I'd cover four or five texts, plus some pictures, and I've got a feature. Maybe if I played my cards right *Omni* or *Playboy* could be tempted. My formula for success in paranormal writing—what the heck, I can give it to you now that I'm leaving the field—was to cover the same old ground for 75 to 80 percent of the article, and then add one truly new item. This would make my article hot and quotable and ensure that I could sell my next article.

Very, very few people are aware that I am John Kincaid. It would probably make most researchers uncomfortable. Would you want your research assistant to be the man who wrote "Was Lincoln's Father Bigfoot?" No, I didn't think so.

My article on mysterious texts covered the magical papyri of Thebes, the Voynich manuscript, and Dr. John Dee's "Enochian" cipher—all well-researched and well-known texts for the occult crowd. I was browsing through the online catalog for occult curiosities when I came across *Blood Loss and Poetry: An Account of the Inanna Sonnet* by Austin O. Emme (London: Dawglish & Son, 1925):

> An account of the so-called vampire sonnet, its translators since the Middle Ages, and the discovery of the original text in Sumerian, with especial emphasis on the life of Henry Salt, Esq. Private edition of 333 copies. LOST.

The last word dashed my hopes as much as all the others had raised them. "LOST" meant that the book had been part of one of the rare book collections, and that most likely it had walked away with some visiting scholar. Our current security system prevents any such thefts, but in a more trusting age—say, thirty years ago—such a stringent system wasn't in place, and the occasional visitor overcome by bibliophilic lust took a book or two. I decided to post queries on a couple of electronic librarian's lists looking for either *Blood Loss and Poetry* or any information on Henry Salt.

Then I went out to lunch.

🖘 🖙

It was a couple of days before I got a response. A couple of postings revealed that Henry Salt had been an undistinguished curator of Egyptian and Mesopotamian antiquities at the Sallust Museum. A third indicated that he had died during a scandal of 1898, and a fourth proved most interesting.

"We too have lost our copy of Austin Emme's book, but one of our grad students in the sixties had begun a study of 'Scarlet Woman Motifs in Ecstatic Poetry' and provides a copy of the vampire sonnet:

> *Look into the heart of wind on storm night*
> *and find a sudden black rainbow.*"

Just as I read the first couplet, I heard a sudden metallic noise, like a huge wreck, and I ran to my window. Below on Guadalupe Street what had been a small Japanese car and a large four-wheeled Jeep were now one. Three or four other vehicles had hit each other or parked cars in an effort not to smash into the central pair. Students, homeless beggars, street entrepreneurs were pointing and yelling. Amidst the crowd stood the oldest and ugliest woman I had ever seen. She was dressed head to toe in black, Iranian somehow. Sirens sounded, and I could hear my coworkers going to their windows.

I went back to my terminal, but the screen was blank. Goddamit! Had I hit the delete key or otherwise screwed up? I spent several minutes trying to retrieve the missing message, and wound up sending a note to the computer center asking if they could help me.

I worked till dusk. I had gone through a painful divorce a couple of years ago, and one of my best defenses against loneliness is overwork.

It was a beautiful, warm Texas night and I didn't want to hurry home. I walked through campus. UT has a beautiful campus, full of Spanish buildings and fountains. I sat on the edge of one of them, where hippocampi sported in the backlit foam. Very pretty, and the white noise filled my ears as spray soaked my tired face.

And I found myself dancing in an old palace all soft stone and candlelight. My partner wore a black veil that shimmered like moonlight on a lake, and we danced by vast windows which looked upon a world in perpetual night where the ground outside was white as snow, but I knew it wasn't covered with snow, then my head plopped back and I woke up.

I had fallen asleep by the fountain. I felt dizzy and confused, and very embarrassed. I'm sure I looked drunk or drugged. I stood up, a little bit staggered by my experience. Someone laughed behind my back.

I didn't feel like driving home, so I decided to return to my office. I was there several minutes before it occurred to me that I might need medical attention. I was frankly hoping to fall asleep again and regain the sweet feeling of the dream.

As my orientation returned, I decided to check my email. Two more messages on Salt. One was from a colleague in Denver; after pleasantries he got to the point:

"We have the Emme book. Henry Salt went from respected 'Orientalist' (as they said in those days) to a kind of street person. He had acquired a clay tablet bearing a hymn to Inanna, which he translated and then discovered that it matched a medieval French poem. At first he published this as a historical finding—evidence of a poetic tradition going back to the Euphrates. Then he went through a period of trying to form a 'Cult of Insubstantiability' which got him fired from the Sallust. Then he had a change of heart and spent all of his money buying every copy of his articles on the hymn. He even snuck into the Sallust and hammered the tablet to bits. He apparently died in front of the museum a few days later, some said of blood loss. To my surprise I discovered that we've never made a microfilm copy of the book. As soon as we have one made up, I'll send it to you. Thanks for the interesting read."

The other was from the Oriental Institute in Chicago. Its message was more to the point:

"Leave the 'Unfinished Hymn to Inanna' SM 10188 alone. It claims a scholar every couple of decades. Stick with something safe like crack cocaine."

🖙 🖙

Needless to say I was more intrigued than ever. All commercial dreams had vanished. I wanted something that I could know—some mystery that was for me and me alone. There is nothing that can be possessed as fully as something within one's mind.

I waited daily for the microfilm from Denver, and I continued to have my little dreams. I remembered little of them, save for the slow lovely dance with the veiled woman and the delicious sense of swooning that accompanied each dance. I wanted to have her, take her, but even more than that I wanted to speak with her to know her thoughts and being.

I don't recall ever being so much in love.

Certainly not in my marriage to Beth, certainly not in college or high school romances. Never in fiction or movies or fantasy.

My boss called me in and asked what was wrong with me.

How did she mean?

She said that I had been getting really sloppy about finishing assignments. The other day I had been speaking with a man from Utah and that I had just wandered away from him in mid-sentence.

I sort of remembered this, but shrugged it off with a bad joke about Mormons.

She also asked about my health, saying that I was looking pale and wan.

I asked if she was worried about expenses for our health plan. It was, all in all, very unpleasant.

I knew that I could stop, but I wanted to let things go on for a little while at least. I needed a better picture of things, and besides, I felt so dreamy.

🦇 🦇

The microfilm arrived. I'll quote from relevant sections.

> Dr. Salt's initial paper on the clay tablet from Persepolis stressed that it was not a fragment—that the poem was actually incomplete. He speculated that this was perhaps the first poem to be written *first,* before being recited—and that the unnamed scribe simply couldn't think of an ending before the clay dried. (p. 14)

> Salt never revealed his sources for discovering the medieval French, ancient Greek, or seventeenth-century English versions of the hymn; although the existence of some (but not all) of these translations has been verified. His published remarks merely say that these were brought to his attention in a "mysterious manner." This probably marks the beginning of his death as a scholar. (p. 23)

Little is known of the Church of the Yellow Light. Salt took in members from all races and classes. When I tracked down members some twenty-five years later, most could recall nothing. A few had vague impressions of meeting in a drafty cheap hall that Salt had rented, and watching some sort of magic lantern projections. Fewer still had been so stirred by their experiences to try their hands at Theosophy or various occult practices—but for the most part their whole involvement with the Church had been a particularly obscure dream in their dreary dreamlike existence. (p. 48)

Salt gave many alternative translations for the Hymn to Inanna. Some alternate opening couplets include:

- She is Thunder, the Perfect Mind
  Adversity and Advantage is her Name.

- Sweeter than my own thoughts is she
  She, who invented thinking for me

- What cost red blood for golden nectar?
  What cost the world for splendor?

- Suddenly a black rainbow in the blue night
  and in that other world living gold.

Clearly these cannot be objective translations from the Sumerian. Salt's own explanation for the variations (he apparently produced 418 of them!) was that the original had been written in "an unknown tongue." (p. 52)

The last meeting of the Church of the Yellow Light occurred on October 16, 1898. Salt had been giving one of his lectures on the insubstantial, when he abruptly seemed to change his views. He began shouting, "No! She's mine! Mine alone!" and chasing people from the hall. The rumor that he later set the hall on fire is unsubstantiated, perhaps this was the work of a disillusioned follower or maybe a random vagrant. (p. 101)

One of the most ingenious theories was that the poem tried to define the undefinable, or as Salt put it, "to make the Unknown Known." Most of the poets or translators had tried to add a word to the poem, some even attempted a whole line. According to Salt, it was the *strain* of extending the poem that caused the blood loss. The Sumerian version was a mere eight lines long. Salt had located an English language version of 1814 consisting of twelve full lines and the beginning of a thirteenth. Salt's final version of the poem was cast in the form of an unfinished sonnet awaiting its fourteenth line. I have published the verse as appendix B to this volume. Although I find the supposed occult or 'vampiric' nature of the sonnet to be utter rubbish, I must admit I find the lines lines a bit too fascinating. This no doubt speaks of the suggestibility of the human mind, and perhaps lends support to the theories of Dr. Freud. (p. 135)

Although Salt's death was rumored to he caused by anemia, no autopsy was performed nor medical report of any kind made. The sheriff attributed the death to exposure. The body was to have been buried in the family vault, but was stolen by person or persons unknown and no doubt performed its last civil service for aspiring medical students. (p. 167)

The microfilm broke before I could read the thirteen lines of Henry Salt. I had to wait and get help to repair the machine, because I didn't want to risk gumming up the works and possibly losing my chance to read the microfilm for several days.

While I was waiting for the technician to come to fix the microfilm, my boss sent for me.

She told me that my clothes were dirty. She told me that I *smelled*. She told me that I needed a shave.

She said my eyes looked sunken. Was I *on* something?

She told me to go home.

"But I'm waiting for some film to be fixed."

"It's five o'clock. You can look at it tomorrow—when you come in clean and shaved. Get some sleep. Take a vitamin pill for Christ's sake."

"But this is a very important project. I've been working on it since the day of the big wreck."

"What wreck?"

I began to understand. I went home. I would have to make the decision whether or not to read the poem, because I began to see what the implications were.

☜☞

The woman came to me in a dream that night.

As I had expected.

I found myself in the vast stone hall whose windows looked upon miles and miles of ground as white as snow. I could see the land clearly now; it was covered in bones. The soft glow inside the hall, which I had attributed to candlelight in all my dreamy dreams of love, had no source. It came from everywhere and cast no shadows. As I pondered this, a voice came from behind me—a voice so sweet that I could feel it make my sleeping body shiver.

"The light is the force of Mind. Ultimately it is the only light we have in this darkling universe. It is my light."

I turned to face her. She had removed her veil. I took her in my arms and we began to waltz to silent music. How can I describe her face, a face that has the beauty of a thousand moonlit nights? Or the eyes of a blue not of your earth, for it is such a blue that can only be imagined? Or her hyacinthine black hair, whose luster suggests another spectrum—an anti-light whose unknown colors could only be spread by a prism whose angles are unknown to man?

All of this and so much more was she.

"None of this is real is it?" I asked.

"No. Not in the way you mean real." She said, "This is imagination alone. This is the insubstantial. Yet alter anything here, and those things in that other world which are symbols of here are altered proportionally."

We waltzed and waltzed, and stone wall and dark windows spun.

"I am the goddess of this place. I am the source and the Form of all dream lovers. I am real as long as I am loved."

"You are Inanna?"

"I have any name you want to give me."

"And how long would you keep that name? How long would you be faithful?"

"I will be faithful as long as you lived, devoted to you absolutely. My love and lust would be as absolute as could be imagined by anyone, anywhere. For I am the Form of the dream lover."

"And when I died?"

"I would spirit your body here, to lie in the endless lands of insubstantiality. Your bones would join the millions, and I would become the old woman wandering the Earth till another was chosen. One that could see me and my illusions."

"Would you remember me, out of your millions of lovers?"

"No," she said, and I could feel my sleeping twitch with agony, but I did not awaken. She continued, "No, but while we loved the rain of inspiration would fall upon your race. While you struggled to add another line to my poem, a thousand poets would be born. While your blood itself boiled away the idea of Love would become more perfect."

I awoke and I thought of her. I pictured myself crazed and bloodless, trying to live one more day so that I could dream one more night.

I could put it aside. I could throw away the microfilm and delete my computer files. I hadn't taken a vacation in a couple of years. I could go to Vegas, blow some of that money I'd socked away since my divorce. I could get drunk and go to a cathouse. I could . . .

I wasn't even fooling myself. Tomorrow I'd shave and bathe, and put on a clean suit. I'd get up early so I could catch breakfast at a restaurant downtown, where I'd have beefsteak and eggs Florentine to build up my blood.

And I would read Henry Salt's unfinished sonnet and start to work on the fourteenth line.

EPILOGUE

I BID YOU FAREWELL

Jonathan Frid, the actor who portrayed Barnabas Collins in *Dark Shadows,* hadn't meant to be a vampire. The ratings on the soap opera were low, and the producer, Dan Curtis, had an idea: Why not throw a vampire into the mix? In 1967, Frid was done with his acting career and living in New York with plans to head for California to become an acting teacher. He was strapped for cash, and so Curtis talked him into a brief role as the vampire. He was impatient to move, but one day a stagehand walked in to his dressing room with a cart full of big bags.

"Where do you want it?"

Frid asked what it was.

Fan mail—*thousands* of pieces. Frid wrote off California. He played the very popular Barnabas—a villain who becomes a hero. He became a pop-culture icon, gaining an invitation to the White House and getting to crown Miss American Vampire. His last film role was a cameo in Tim Burton's film version of *Dark Shadows.*

Like Frid, I was reluctant. Most occult writers gloss over their own doubts, insecurities, and struggles, but the Vampyre knows when to be fierce and when to be vulnerable. Let me tell you about my first conclave of the Temple of Set.

At that time I wore size 50 pants and affected a pose of a successful writer, bragging that I owned neither wristwatch nor tie. To complete my aura of Bohemian indifference, I wore flip-flops only, and often my big gut peeked out from under my shirt. Actually, I was a low-rent remittance man who was an unemployed college dropout. I had two or three professional writing sales.

329

The conclave was going to be in New Orleans. Two or three weeks before the conclave, the hotel began getting death threats against Michael Aquino. The hotel offered to put the temple up but said they wanted us to know. So new plan: the Aquinos weren't coming. We moved to another hotel. No medallions in public. We were to meet at Jackson Square.

I was terrified. I made my own arrangements to be at yet a third hotel so I could bail quickly. I had been very disappointed that Aquino wasn't going to be there. I had joined the temple eight months prior, and the new was wearing off. Some of my friends had warned me that Stephen Flowers was a Nazi, and the temple was a white supremacist organization. I had decided that I would remain a member for the rest of the year. I figured it would look good on the horror writer résumé but had zero percent interest in a lifelong commitment. I thought about my desire to flee as I walked into the conclave hotel.

OMG.

In the lobby was a skinhead wearing a faded black T-shirt, a Thor's hammer, and a red cloisonné swastika sitting cross-legged and audibly chanting, "Om! Om! Om!" Jesus, I'm out of here. This *is* a white supremist organization. I turned and bumped into an African American woman. She had been staring at the chanter as well. I apologized, ready to head back to my hotel. She scrutinized me closely. She said, "Excuse me, sir, are you here to meet an esoteric organization?" I paused. "Yes, Ma'am." "Then we may see each other later."

Okay, that didn't look very white supremacist. Which of these two would I meet in Jackson Square?

At dusk as folks wandered into the square, I saw her again. She was chatting with the Flowerses. She beamed as I walked up. She introduced herself as Adept Patty Hardy. She would later succeed me as High Priest. We went back to the hotel (about thirty of us) and got the schedule of events. The first working was an Ordination Ceremony: Flowers ordained Patty Hardy into the Priesthood of Set. Boy, if he was a Nazi, he was unclear on concept.

At the ceremony, a blind man, clearly in the later stages of AIDS, recited part of the Word of Set. Afterward I met him—Mitchel Wade.

The next two days were a blur of meetings and learning opportunities. I was impressed with the no-nonsense approach but grew even firmer in my resolution to leave. Why? Because I was nearly thirty; these were mainly beautiful folks in their twenties. After each meeting, I would hide at my hotel to avoid socializing. But on the last day, several folks spent the afternoon in the French Quarter. I saw that no one was hanging out with the blind guy, so I did. He talked about want and need. He told that an initiate always has what he needs—that when he feels he does not, he is Asleep. He may or may not have, get, or keep what he wants. At the time I thought if this guy were a real magician he wouldn't be dying right now, dependent on the kindness of strangers. The temple just had a slicker line of bullshit.

Then it was time for the conclave working. It was a working of the Wells of Wyrd. A bell was rung and the invocation was said. A good-size inverse pentagram hung by fishing line from the ceiling. An Adept had cleverly coated the pentagram in a flammable substance. He was going to set it ablaze at a crucial part of the invocation. It was metal, he reasoned, and would not burn. He was correct, but the fishing line did—sending a spinning, burning pentagram to the floor, where another Adept began jumping up and down on it putting it (and the carpet) out.

Great, I thought, that's my omen. They just set their symbol on fire.

At the working we visited three wells, spoke to the Norn guarding each well, and received some fruit juice. We drank some and saved some. We were to blend the past, the present, and the future, and part we were to give to the temple by pouring some of our blend back into a central container. The last well, that of Skuld, was guarded by a tall Setian. I had passed the other two guardians with token answers. The giant boomed at me: "What will you give the temple in the future?"

"Myself."

"Bad answer; yourself is for you. What is your precious skill?"

"My writing."

"Yes, your poesy. Pass."

I hadn't expected that. The last well was darkened; I passed in. Inside a knight in dented, rusty black armor sat. Wow, how had they snuck this guy in here?

"What do you plan to do in the temple?" It was Magister Wade. I didn't want to say quit, so I said, "Make a path for others."

As soon as I said the words, the armor vanished. I was just staring at a dying man in a black robe. Months later when he passed, I discovered that his magical name was Parsifal. I read the story of dented, rusty black armor.

I staggered to the central place, drank my share, poured the temple's share into the container.

I sat and I wept. I got it. I understood the Self and the Cosmos and the Temple. I wept like a baby.

The rite ended. Stephen Flowers came over to me. He was carrying the small pitcher full of the gifts to the temple. "Don, would you do me the honor of drinking this?" He handed me the juice, and I drank.

I took in the energy. Flowers was recognized to the fifth degree the next year—shockingly fast; it had taken him only seven years. An occurrence not to be repeated until I, too, became a fifth degree and High Priest seven years later. Also wrote a few books, lost fifty pounds, and even learned to wear shoes.

No matter where you are, what you think of yourself now, you can find the energy you need to transform. TRY!

I wish to thank my initiator, Stephen Flowers; Michael and Lilith Aquino; Robertt Neilly; William Butch; Patty Hardy; James Carmen Kirby; and all of my teachers and students in the Temple of Set. Especially my wolf-mate, Guiniviere Webb. I want to thank everyone who has inspired Wonder in me, and the great folks at Inner Traditions—Jon and Patricia and Albo and the rest of the good humans and Vampyres at Inner Traditions.

And finally, I must thank you, dear reader, for helping me to fulfill quiet words whispered to a blind man in a darkened chamber long ago.

☇ I BID YOU FAREWELL. ☇

INDEX